"One Country, Two Systems" in Taiwan

NEW EDITION

D0818623

"One Country, Two Systems" in Taiwan

NEW EDITION

A TRUE SOLUTION FOR THE CROSS-STRAIT ENTANGLEMENT

Hsing Chi

Translation by
Sheng-Wei Wang

International Publishing House for China's Culture

"One Country, Two Systems" in Taiwan

ISBN-10: 0-9754247-5-0
ISBN-13: 978-0-9754247-5-9

Library of Congress Control Number: 2006920945

International Publishing House for China's Culture
2421 Pennsylvania Ave, N.W., Washington D.C. 20037-1718
U.S.A.
http://www.iphcc.org

Printed in the United States of America on acid-free paper
First printing: August 2006

10 9 8 7 6 5 4 3 2

To people who love peace in this world

CONTENTS

Part I The Policy of "One Country, Two Systems"

Chapter 1
THE ORIGIN AND DEVELOPMENT OF THE
"ONE COUNTRY, TWO SYSTEMS" POLICY ....

Section 1: The Origin of "One Country, Two Systems"
Section 2: The Development of the "One Country, Two Systems" Policy
Section 3: The Basic Contents of "One Country, Two Systems"

Chapter 2
"ONE COUNTRY, TWO SYSTEMS"
IN HONG KONG AND MACAO ....

Section 1: "One Country, Two Systems" in Hong Kong
Section 2: "One Country, Two Systems" in Macao
Section 3: The Practice of "One Country, Two Systems"
in Hong Kong and Macao as an Example for Taiwan

Chapter 3
THE MAY 17 STATEMENT
AND NEW DEVOLPMENTS IN HONG KONG ....

Section 1: About "Placing Hope in the Taiwanese People"
from the May 17 Statement
Section 2: The Hong Kong Constitutional Reform and
the Implementation of "One Country, Two Systems"

Part II The U.S. Positions on the Cross-Strait Dilemma and "One Country, Two Systems"

Chapter 4
THE U.S. GOVERNMENT'S POSITIONS ON CHINA'S REUNIFICATION ....

Section 1: A Reflection on China-U.S.-Taiwan Relations (1950–1990)
Section 2: U.S. Policies on China's Reunification Issue after 1990
Section 3: Discussion of U.S. Government Policies toward
China's Reunification Issue

Part III Taiwan's Attitude toward Reunification and "One Country, Two Systems"

Part IV "One Country, Two Systems" in Taiwan

PREFACE TO THE ENGLISH EDITION

Many writers dream of having their books translated into other languages so that their written ideas can spread across the world and exert more influence. In late 2004, I was invited by the organization Chinese for Peaceful Unification-Northern California to give a talk on my book *"One Country, Two Systems" in Taiwan*. There I was blessed to meet Dr. Sheng-Wei Wang, a retired physicist and an engaging political writer who showed great enthusiasm for translating this book after listening to my talk. Both of us knew well the difficulties of publishing a translated Taiwanese book in the United States, let alone one on a topic that may not be a main concern of the general American public. Nevertheless, Dr. Wang's diligence and devotion have paid off and I am grateful to be able to write a preface for this English edition.

The original Chinese book was published in December 2003, a few months before the March 20, 2004 presidential election in Taiwan, and the new edition was published in July 2004. In the new edition, I added one chapter at the end of each of the four parts of the original book (Chapters 3, 6, 9 and 14) with updates on the political developments in Taiwan. Most contents of the new Chinese edition have been translated into this edition. Before turning to the main subject of this book, I feel that a brief understanding of Taiwan's recent history would be helpful for the American reader.

In 1895, the Chinese Qing Dynasty was defeated in the humiliating first Sino-Japan War and was forced to sign the Treaty of Shimonoseki to cede Taiwan to Japan. In 1945, World War II ended when Japan surrendered its fight and Taiwan—after 50 years of colonial rule by the Japanese—was returned to China and became a province of the Republic of China (ROC). The ROC was established in 1911 by Dr. Sun Yat-sen. But later the ROC, led by Chiang Kai-shek's Kuomintang (KMT), lost the civil war against the

Communist troops led by Mao Zedong. Chiang fled with the KMT members and the remnants of his government and military forces to Taiwan in 1949 while Mao Zedong simultaneously established the People's Republic of China (PRC) and occupied the mainland of China. (In the later part of this book, every occurence of "mainland China" means "the mainland of China.") For nearly 60 years the two sides have been separated by the narrow Taiwan Strait and have kept different political systems.

During the Japanese occupation, the Taiwanese continued their history of resistance against the Japanese colonization, which imposed a policy of comprehensive "de-Sinicization" and built up infrastructures designed for exploiting Taiwan's economy and resources. When the ROC recovered Taiwan in 1945, the entire island of Taiwan brimmed over with jubilation.

During the immediate postwar period, the KMT administration on Taiwan was generally viewed as inept and corrupt. Social violence flared on February 28, 1947, in reaction to a government inspector's accidental shooting of a woman who sold contraband cigarettes took place. Several weeks after the 2/28 Incident, many Taiwanese rebelled by participating in island-wide protests and taking control of much of the island. The KMT assembled a large military force to quell the disturbance and in the process killed and imprisoned many, including the innocent Taiwanese. Much of the detail of the 2/28 Incident remains highly controversial and is still hotly debated today. But the KMT's mishandlings later provided the pro-independence demagogues with convenient pretexts for inciting ethnic hatred between those who came to Taiwan before versus after 1945, with their demands for voter sympathy.

With the help of the China Aid Act of 1948 and the Chinese-American Joint Commission on Rural Reconstruction, in the 1950s the ROC government implemented a successful land reform program on Taiwan. Many large landowners turned their sale compensations into capital, began commercial and industrial enterprises, and became Taiwan's first industrial capitalists. Together with the businessmen who came from the mainland, they managed Taiwan's transition from an agricultural to a commercial and industrial economy. Taiwan's phenomenal economic development earned it a spot as one of the four East Asian tigers, along with Hong Kong, Singapore, and South Korea.

Taiwan's political system gradually became liberalized. In 1986, the Democratic Progressive Party (DPP) was inaugurated as the first opposition party in the ROC. After the death of President Chiang Ching-kuo (son of Chiang Kai-shek), his successor President Lee Teng-hui (1988–2000) continued to hand over more and more government authority to the native Taiwanese. Under Lee, Taiwan underwent a process of localization and de-Sinicization in which only local culture and history were promoted.

When the ROC government was under the KMT rule, it actively maintained that it was the sole legitimate government of China; in addition, the ROC Constitution Article I.4 also stipulated that "the territory of the ROC is the original territory governed by it; unless authorized by the National Assembly, it cannot be altered." In 1991, Lee Teng-hui claimed that his government would no longer challenge the rule of the PRC on the mainland; he further proposed in 1999 a "two-state theory" that advocates that both the ROC and the PRC are separate states with a special diplomatic, cultural, and historic relationship.

The 2000 presidential election marked the end of the KMT rule. The DPP candidate Chen Shui-bian won a three-way race that saw the KMT vote split by independent James Soong (formerly of the KMT) and KMT candidate Lien Chan. Chen Shui-bian garnered 39 percent of the vote. After the election, Soong formed the People First Party (PFP). The KMT, the PFP, and the New Party (NP) then formed a coalition called the Pan-Blue Coalition. Those who follow them are called Pan-Blue supporters. This coalition tends to favor a Chinese nationalist identity and endorses the One-China Principle (one China is the ROC) and a greater economic linkage with the PRC. The Pan-Green Coalition was also formed after Lee Teng-hui was expelled from the KMT in 2000 and he organized the Taiwan Solidarity Union (TSU). Contrary to the Pan-Blue Coalition, the Pan-Green Coalition (mainly the DDP and the TSU) tends to favor Taiwan independence, advocates that "Taiwan is an independent, sovereign country," and refuses to endorse the One-China Principle.

In an effort to gain wider support from the people in Taiwan, in his inauguration speech on May 20, 2000, Chen Shui-bian promised not to declare Taiwanese independence, change the national title, include the doctrine of special state-to-state relations in the ROC Constitution, nor promote a referendum on reunification or independence. In addition, Chen pledged not to abolish the National Unification Council (NUC) or the National Unification Guidelines (NUG). The above Four Noes and One Without have become an important part of ROC-U.S. relations. Several times Chen Shui-bian has had to reassure the U.S. that the Four Noes and One Without policy has not been abolished and that he is not attempting to circumvent the pledge via some of the suggested loopholes. In short, the cross-strait situation stagnated under Chen Shui-bian's governance, and there has been no success in restarting any semi-formal negotiation through formulations referred to as the 1992 Consensus, namely "one China with respective interpretations by the two sides."

During Chen Shui-bian's first term of presidency, Taiwan's economy declined sharply. One day before the March 20, 2004 presidential election, both Chen Shui-bian and Vice President Annette Lu were shot at while campaigning in Tainan City and suffered minor injuries. The 3/19 Incident is believed to have gained them enough sympathy votes to influence the result and Chen Shui-bian was reelected by a narrow 0.2 percent margin of the vote over KMT Chairman Lien Chan (with PFP Chairman James Soong as running mate). The incident also allowed Chen Shui-bian to declare martial law, preventing the police and military—who were mostly Pan-Blue supporters—from voting. The 3/19 Truth Commission was formed to investigate the shooting incident, but no reliable facts on the incident have ever been uncovered.

In the international arena, the ROC was originally recognized as the sole legitimate government of both mainland China and Taiwan by the United Nations (UN) and most nations. However, on October 25, 1971, the UN General Assembly passed Resolution 2758, which expelled the ROC and placed the PRC in the China seat on the Security Council (and all other UN organs). Most countries now recognize one China with the PRC as its sole legitimate representative. The ROC currently maintains formal diplomatic relations with only 25 countries, mainly in South and Central America, the South Pacific Islands, and Africa. Although the U.S. has been firm on its one-China policy since January 1, 1979 (when it established a diplomatic relationship with the PRC), it often takes advantage of the subtle difference between "opposing" and "not supporting" Taiwanese independence by continuing to sell weapons to Taiwan. The PRC regards this as sending mixed messages regarding Taiwan independence. The U.S. has so far taken only one explicit stand for the cross-strait political future: a peaceful "resolution" but not a peaceful "unification." Such ambiguities result in the U.S. teetering on a diplomatic tightrope with regard to the China/Taiwan issue and saber rattling at times for the two sides of the Taiwan Strait.

After this very brief overview of Taiwan's history, I would now like to discuss certain significant events related to the cross-strait relationship that have taken place in Taiwan since the new Chinese edition of the book was published in July 2004.

First, the Pan-Blue Coalition gained a slim majority in the legislative elections held in December 2004. After that, in April 2005 and in acceptance of Chinese President Hu Jintao's invitation, KMT Chairman Lien Chan made an ice-breaking trip to mainland China. The Hu-Lien meeting reached consensus on five issues for cross-strait peace, exchange, and goodwill gestures, and the KMT's popularity reached a new high. Following Lien's visit, leaders of the PFP and the NP also visited mainland China for bridge building and peace making. In the meantime, the PRC's Office of Taiwan Affairs of the State Council announced many measures of direct benefit to Taiwan. The Taiwanese people's attitude toward mainland China started to show an obvious change and the cross-strait tension gradually relaxed.

Second, led by Ma Ying-jeou, the KMT enjoyed a resounding win in the three-in-one local election held on December 3, 2005, and the DPP suffered its biggest defeat ever. Ma Ying-jeou, the Taipei mayor and the new chairman of the KMT since July 2005, is not only virtually assured of leading the KMT and Pan-Blue supporters for the 2008 presidential election, but also of being a front-runner among all potential candidates. Ma Ying-jeou made it clear that the KMT supports the One-China Principle and 1992 Consensus, but the current policy of the KMT is to keep the status quo.

The DPP's defeat in the aforementioned 2005 local election was due to the corruption of high-ranking officials and possibly even to Chen Shui-bian and his wife. Chen Shui-bian tried to keep his power by restricting cross-strait economic policies and abolishing the NUC and NUG on February 27, 2006. He not only broke his Four Noes and One Without promise, but also provoked the PRC and the U.S. government. Chen Shui-bian's cross-strait policies are under severe scrutiny by the DPP itself, where serious power struggles exist. Chen Shui-bian has become a lame duck!

Finally, I would like to turn attention to the main concept of this book: "one country, two systems." It is an idea originally proposed by Deng Xiaoping, leader of the PRC, for the reunification of China. In 1984, Deng Xiaoping proposed to apply this principle to Hong Kong during the negotiations with the United Kingdom (UK). This same principle was proposed during talks with Portugal over Macao. The principle, simply stated, is that upon reunification and despite the practice of socialism in mainland China, Hong Kong and Macao, former colonies of the UK and Portugal respectively, can continue to practice capitalism under a high degree of autonomy for 50 years after reunification.

As one consistently concerned with the future of Taiwan, I have paid great attention to the concept of "one country, two systems" since it was first proposed. I knew that such a concept was unpopular in Taiwan. In 2001, one year after Chen Shui-bian became president, I noticed that public opinion supporting reunification and "one country, two systems" had increased to a historical high. I therefore believe that as long as the political and economic trend continues pointing toward a decline in Taiwan and sustained growth in China, the material basis for reunification will only strengthen. And, since no one has proposed a better alternative, "one country, two systems" remains the only method that can ingeniously give Taiwan, under the "one country" framework, a high degree of autonomy while allowing Taiwanese people to govern themselves.

From my observation, most people in Taiwan, particularly those who strongly oppose "one country, two systems," do not fully understand the concept. I believe that as long as the two sides negotiate and resolve their differences on equal footing, many more Taiwanese people will accept "one country, two systems." To me, only "one country, two systems" can guarantee that: 1) the Chinese in Taiwan can continue to be Chinese; 2) the current lifestyle in Taiwan can be maintained; 3) the reunification of China can be completed; and 4) the safety of the Taiwan Strait can be ensured.

Frankly speaking, the Taiwan independence route and de-Sinicization promoted by Lee Teng-hui and Chen Shui-bian over the last 16 years violated the ROC Constitution. Supporting a One-China Principle and seeking the nation's reunification are legal and Constitutional acts. How can people who support reunification be criticized as not loving Taiwan? Furthermore, Taiwan is constantly crying for "democracy, freedom, pluralism;" hence, people should not be fearful about expressing their political opinions, for this important and growing minority opinion should be preserved.

I wrote this book in the hopes that all people in Taiwan and elsewhere in the world have the opportunity to better understand "one country, two systems." I hope that after open-mindedly reading this book they will find that the concept of "one country, two systems" is truly attractive and practicable.

Hsing Chi

Taipei

April 10, 2006

A Short Note from the Translator

The Taiwan independence movement reached its climax around late 2004, just before the legislative elections in December when Taiwan President Chen Shui-bian initiated a comprehensive country name change from China to Taiwan. The unexpected defeat of the DPP put an immediate stop to this widespread movement. Soon Taiwan's political climate moved swiftly in favor of the opposing Pan-Blue Coalition, which became friendlier to mainland China after the KMT Chairman Lien Chan made his historic trip to the mainland in April 2005, ending the six decades of hostility between the KMT and the Communist Party of China (CPC). Not willing to give up, in February 2006, Chen Shui-bian made his last-ditch effort to revive Taiwanese independence by announcing that the NUC established in 1990 "ceased to function" and that the NUG enacted in 1991 "ceased to apply" as a symbol of abolishing the aim of reunification with mainland China.

There is an old Chinese saying: From the fall of a leaf, you can tell autumn's coming. This adage, in my opinion, describes the falling tide of the Taiwan independence movement and the DPP's dim future. But, how can the Taiwanese people escape their historical fate of long separation from mainland China embodied by the last Chinese Civil War? I found most of my answers in Hsing Chi's book *"One Country, Two Systems" in Taiwan.*

The book outlines the specific benefits which could be enjoyed by the Taiwanese people under "one country, two systems" after reunification with China. The author warns that "'keeping the status quo' in Taiwan does not equal 'one country, two systems,'" and that the current "status quo" of "no reunification, no independence, and no war" advocated by U.S. and Taiwan politicians, including KMT Chairman Ma Ying-jeou, will not last forever. For example, in 1995, Taiwan's gross domestic product

(GDP) was 36 percent of mainland China's; in 2005 it dropped to below 15 percent, and it continues to drop by about two percent every year. This is a very frightening trend. If it continues, in ten years Taiwan's economic size may be only a few percent of mainland China's. Depleting Taiwan's economy by pressing arms sales, as the U.S. did all along to maintain a "horror balance" of the two sides of the Taiwan Strait, would further speed up Taiwan's marginalization. Therefore, the best choice for Taiwan is to reunite with mainland China. I'm reminded of another Chinese proverb: The world must separate after a long union, and must reunite after a long separation.

"Taiwan is probably the most dangerous situation in East Asia at this point," said Kenneth G. Lieberthal, former National Security Council member to President Clinton. "We could see military conflict . . . if things go badly" (*CNN*, 05/06/2004). His warning is further supported by recent and frequent maneuvers of the U.S. military force to contain China near Japanese bases (*CNN*, 03/12/2006). But, "despite the fact that peaceful reunification would have many negative impacts on the U.S., there is one big benefit, and that is its elimination of the fuse, immediately and comprehensively lowering the risk of Sino-U.S. conflicts and clashes . . . the disadvantages are much smaller than mainland China and the U.S. engaging in war," said longtime China expert Nancy Bernkopf Tucker, History Professor at Georgetown University (*China Times*, 07/18/2002). Later, former U.S. Secretary of State Henry Kissinger also advised that "conflict is not an option" and "military imperialism is not the Chinese style" (*International Herald Tribune*, 06/09/2005) when calling for a Sino-U.S. peaceful resolution of the Taiwan issue.

The Taiwan issue is the core challenge of Sino-U.S. relations. Only after this issue is resolved can these relations truly develop in a normal and cooperative way. Playing the "Taiwan card" or promoting the "China threat" theory is not a wise step for the U.S. since China's economy is already closely connected with the U.S. and with global economy. In addition, the U.S. needs a strong country like China to cooperate in many international affairs in the twenty-first century. Therefore, it would be helpful for the U.S. government and the American people to encourage the Taiwanese people to play a more active role and to accept "one country, two systems" as a springboard to leap forward into the modern world.

I express my heartfelt thanks to Alia Curtis and International Publishing House for China's Culture for polishing the English version of this book. I hope that this book will profoundly impact American politi-

A Short Note from the Translator

cians as well as the general public. This would best serve my intention of promoting peace on Earth.

Sheng-Wei Wang

April 26, 2006

PART I

The Policy of "One Country, Two Systems"

"One country, two systems" is a basic national policy set by the PRC in order to bring about China's peaceful reunification and to resolve the problems left over by history for Taiwan, Hong Kong, and Macao. Its basic content is the premise of a reunified country: Mainland China continues to practice a socialistic system, while Taiwan, Hong Kong, and Macao keep their original capitalistic systems unchanged. The two systems can coexist for a long time. Following the sequential returns of Hong Kong and Macao, the PRC is left with only the Taiwan problem to resolve. In this part of the book, the origin and development of the "one country, two systems" policy proposed by the PRC toward Taiwan and the conditions for carrying out "one country, two systems" in Hong Kong and Macao, as well as their effects on Taiwan, will be introduced.

CHAPTER 1

THE ORIGIN AND DEVELOPMENT OF THE "ONE COUNTRY, TWO SYSTEMS" POLICY

During a 54-year span, beginning from the time when the CPC established the PRC until present day, mainland China and Taiwan remained separate. In order to bring about the great undertaking of reunification, the PRC's policy towards Taiwan has gone through different stages, from "militarily liberating Taiwan" and "peacefully liberating Taiwan" to "peaceful reunification and 'one country, two systems.'"

SECTION 1
THE ORIGIN OF "ONE COUNTRY, TWO SYSTEMS"

After the KMT retreated to Taiwan and during the period from 1950 to early 1955, the collective policy of the first generation leaders of the CPC was to treat the Taiwan problem as a continuation of the civil war between the CPC and the KMT. They insisted on liberating Taiwan through military force. In July 1953, the Korean War ended and mainland China began to proceed with a large-scale construction of socialism. This was when its policy toward Taiwan entered the second stage. CPC Chairman Mao Zedong and Premier Zhou Enlai many times expressed their willingness to "peacefully liberate Taiwan" and to bring about collaboration between the CPC and the KMT for the third time.

3

In 1963, Zhou Enlai summed up mainland China's policy towards Taiwan as "one principle, four outlines." The one principle was that Taiwan must be reunified with China. The four outlines are as follows:

1. After Taiwan's reunification with its motherland, it is expected that her diplomacy would be reunified with that of the central government. At the same time, Taiwan's military forces, political powers, and personnel arrangements would remain in the hands of then ROC President Chiang Kai-shek.

2. All military, political, and economic deficits in Taiwan would be subsidized by the central government. (Taiwan had a deficit of about US$0.8 billion a year at the time.)

3. Taiwan's social reform could be delayed until conditions matured. The actual steps would proceed only after discussions with Chiang Kai-shek and while respecting his viewpoints.

4. Neither side would spy on the other side, nor conduct activities to destroy the solidarity of the other side.

The "one principle, four outlines" policy is mainly a united-front strategy aimed at Taiwan KMT's military and political personnel. However, it also exhibited an embryonic form of "one country, two systems." Mao Zedong maintained repeatedly that as long as Taiwan authorities could keep Taiwan and not let it split off from China, the Chinese mainland would not change its relationship with Taiwan. One can see that from 1953 to 1970, mainland China's Taiwan policy changed from "military liberation" to "peaceful liberation" in order to keep Taiwan away from U.S. control. Mao Zedong and Zhou Enlai repeatedly sent messengers to make contacts with Taiwan authorities to explore the possibility of a peaceful liberation. Taiwan also tried to secretly get in touch with mainland China. But no result was achieved.

After the Cultural Revolution, from the second half of 1978, mainland China's second-generation leaders collectively began to adjust their Taiwan policy. In October, Deng Xiaoping inherited the guiding principle of a peaceful liberation and the "one principle, four outlines" policy. He set forth the views of respecting Taiwan's realistic situation in solving the Taiwan problem. When mentioning the Taiwan question, the communiqué of the 3rd Plenary Session of the 11th Central Commission of the CPC for the first time used the phrase "Taiwan returns to her motherland and realizes the great reunification undertaking," thus replacing the motto "liberate Taiwan." On New Year's Day 1979, the Standing Committee of the National People's Congress (SCNPC) announced its Message to Compatriots on Taiwan, which marked the third stage of mainland

China's Taiwan policy. The key points of the document include the following:

1. Taiwan's realistic situation must be taken into account.

2. Respect Taiwan's realistic situation and Taiwanese people's viewpoints, and use fair and reasonable methods so that the Taiwanese people will not lose anything.

3. Taiwan authorities have always insisted on the one-China policy, opposing Taiwan independence. This is our common ground and basis for collaboration.

4. First, the PRC government and Taiwan authorities should engage in discussions to end the current situation of military stalemate, both sides should bring about the opening of transport and postal relations as soon as possible, develop trade, help to supply each other's needs, and engage in economic exchanges. (Later these latter points were combined into what became known as the three links.)

On September 30, 1981, Marshal Ye Jianying further proposed Ye's Nine-Point Policy for peaceful reunification. This proposal includes the following points:

1. Holding talks on a reciprocal basis between the CPC and the KMT, collaborating for the third time to realize the country's great reunification undertaking. Both sides could send messengers to fully exchange ideas before talks began.

2. Both sides provide convenience and reach related agreements for the opening of postal service, trade, transport, family visits, tourist services, and for the development of academic, cultural, and gymnastic exchanges.

3. Taiwan could become a special administrative region, enjoy a high degree of autonomy, and maintain its own military. The central government would not interfere with Taiwan's internal affairs.

4. Neither the current social and economic systems and lifestyle in Taiwan, nor Taiwan's economic and cultural relations with foreign countries would change.

5. The Taiwan authorities and representatives from various social circles could take leadership posts for national political organizations in order to participate in the nation's management.

6. If the Taiwan local economy encountered difficulties, the central government would provide subsidies accordingly.

7. Any person in Taiwan who desires to reside in their motherland would be guaranteed proper arrangements without discrimination and would further be allowed to freely move back and forth between the mainland and Taiwan.

8. The Taiwanese enterprises are welcome to make investments in the mainland and to set up economic enterprises of their choice. Their legal rights and profits would be guaranteed.

9. Taiwanese people from all provinces, arenas, and people's organizations are welcome to make suggestions and to enter into discussions on national affairs.

Ye's Nine-Point Policy was a more advanced and further development of the Taiwan policy during this new era of the CPC and the Chinese government. On January 11, 1982, Deng Xiaoping said during a speech, "The nine guiding principles were proposed under the name of Ye Jianying, but it is in fact 'one country, two systems.'" This was the first time that Deng Xiaoping proposed the concept of "one country, two systems." In December 1982, the Constitution passed by the 5th Session of the 5th National People's Congress (NPC) stipulated, "When it is necessary, the country can set up special administrative regions." This provided a constitutional guarantee for the execution of "one country, two systems" and became a basic national policy.

On June 26, 1983, Deng Xiaoping met Professor Yang Liyu of the Asia Research Institute of Seton Hall University in New Jersey and pointed out that the CPC and the KMT should jointly accomplish the reunification of the nation. Six key points resulted from that conversation:

1. A peaceful reunification is already the common language of the CPC and the KMT. It serves as the basis for further collaboration.

2. The One-China Principle must be insisted upon. There can be different systems but, internationally, China can only be represented by the PRC.

3. Taiwan's autonomy should be limited to avoid damaging the interests of the united country.

4. After reunification, the Taiwan special administrative region can practice a different social system from that of the mainland. It can hold legislative jurisdiction, judicial rights, and rights of final appeal. It can have its own military, but only to the extent of not threatening the mainland. The mainland will not send officials to Taiwan; and Taiwan's parties and political and military systems will be under the authority of the Taiwan government. The central government would even offer some positions in the central government to the Taiwanese.

5. A peaceful reunification does not imply that one side annexes (swallows up) the other. Using the Three Principles of the People to reunify China is not realistic.

6. The proper way to bring about reunification is to hold reciprocal talks between the CPC and the KMT. Foreign powers may not

> interfere. (The original text of the publication was on pages 30–31 of the third volume of *Selected Writings of Deng Xiaoping*.)

Deng Xiaoping's Six-Point Conception made the theory of "one country, two systems" more complete, concrete, and systematized. He also proposed that after the reunification, "one country, two systems" should be carried out for 50 years unchanged. Some people worried about the course that Taiwan would take after 50 years. Deng Xiaoping clarified that he meant no change for a long time, and then change only if needed and desired.

SECTION 2
THE DEVELOPMENT OF THE
"ONE COUNTRY, TWO SYSTEMS" POLICY

In June 1989, the 4th Plenary Session of the 13th Central Commission of the CPC produced a new governing body led by Jiang Zemin. The gazette of the Congress announced the following: "A peaceful reunification of our motherland and the 'one country, two systems' proposal is our basic policy." After that announcement, the Strait Exchange Foundation (SEF) of Taiwan and the Association for Relations across the Taiwan Strait (ARATS) of mainland China engaged in busy interactions, but no political negotiations were undertaken.

On August 31, 1993, the Chinese central government announced its first white paper, "The Taiwan Question and Reunification of China." The purpose of the white paper was to make the international community clearly understand the stance and viewpoint of the Chinese government for solving the Taiwan problem. The first chapter states that Taiwan is an inalienable part of China since ancient days. The second chapter explains the source of the Taiwan issue and reviews the root and development of the problem on the two sides of the Taiwan Strait. It clearly points out that the U.S. government bears some responsibility in the unsettled Taiwan issue. The third chapter details the basic guiding principles of the Chinese government towards the Taiwan issue and indicates that "peaceful reunification, and one country, two systems" is a basic, unchangeable, long-term national policy of the Chinese government. This guiding principle has a few basic points:

ONE CHINA: There is only one China in the world, of which Taiwan is an inalienable part; the central government is in Beijing. This fact, generally recognized by the entire world, is the premise for solving the Taiwan problem peacefully. The Chinese government resolutely opposes any statement or action that aims to alienate China's sovereignty and territorial integrity. It opposes "two Chinas," "one China, one Taiwan," and "one country, two governments." It also opposes any intention and action that would lead to Taiwan independence.

THE COEXISTENCE OF TWO SYSTEMS: Under the premise of "one China," the socialist system in the mainland and the capitalist system in Taiwan will coexist for a long time, develop together, and not annex one another. This consideration is mainly based on preserving Taiwan's current situation and the realistic interests of the Taiwan compatriots. This will be the special feature and important creation of China's national system after the reunification. Upon reunification, Taiwan's present social and economic systems, lifestyle, and economic and cultural relationships with foreign countries will not be changed.

HIGH DEGREE OF AUTONOMY: After the reunification, Taiwan will become a special administrative region. It will be different from other Chinese provinces as it will enjoy a high degree of autonomy. It will maintain its own administrative, legislative, independent judicial, and final appeal rights. It will manage its own party, political, military, economic, and financial affairs; enter into business and cultural agreements with foreign countries; enjoy certain rights of handling foreign affairs; and have its own military. The mainland will not send military or administrative personnel to Taiwan.

PEACEFUL NEGOTIATION: The people on both sides of the strait are Chinese. It would be extremely unfortunate for the two sides to enter into an armed clash, to hurt their own flesh and blood for the sake of a split of the country's sovereignty and territorial integrity. A peaceful reunification is beneficial to the consolidation of all the people, to the stability and development of Taiwan's society and economy, and to the entirety of China's vitalization, prosperity, and strength.

On January 30, 1995, General Secretary Jiang Zemin of the Chinese Communist Party Central Committee in a speech entitled "To Continue the Struggle for Facilitating the Completion of the Reunification Undertaking of the Motherland," made several recommendations. He offered eight propositions (abbreviated as Jiang's Eight-Point Proposals) for pushing forward the progress of a peaceful reunification of the motherland and developing the relationship between the two sides at the present stage. From this point forward, the CPC's Taiwan policy entered its fourth stage.

Following are the viewpoints and positions of Jiang's Eight-Point Proposals:

POINT 1: Beginning with the necessity to uphold the principle of "one China" as the basis and premise of a peaceful reunification, Jiang reiterated the opposition to any idea of independence or separatism and to the notion of two Chinas during a transitional period.

POINT 2: He then added that Beijing had no objection to Taipei developing non-governmental economic and cultural relations with foreign countries, provided these are not intended to enlarge Taiwan's international living space with the aim of creating "two Chinas" or "one China, one Taiwan."

POINT 3: Jiang Zemin then went on to the question of negotiations for a peaceful reunification (our persistent position), specifying (and this was new) that during the process of reunification talks, representatives from all political parties and pertinent organizations on both sides of the strait should be included. Commenting on a statement he made at the 14th Party Congress, he stressed that discussions should be of any and all problems, talks with Taiwan authorities are political negotiations, and that the venue and format of the meetings are to be agreed upon through consultations on the basis of equality.

POINT 4: Stressing that the Chinese should not fight among themselves, Jiang Zemin indicated that the use of military force would not be discarded, but would only be directed at foreign powers that interfere in the reunification process and/or engage in a Taiwan independence plot.

POINT 5: The fifth point deals with the development of economic exchanges and cooperation and the call for concrete measures to be taken to speed up the establishment of the three direct links (post, air/sea traffic, and commerce).

POINT 6: Respecting the 5,000-year-old Chinese culture—a spiritual link that holds together China's sons and daughters—is vital for reunification.

POINT 7: Jiang Zemin proclaimed that all Taiwan compatriots, whether from the Taiwan province or other provinces, are Chinese. As such, their remarks and demands will be heard. Special mention was made to the hope that all political parties promote the development of relations across the strait with a rational, forward-looking, and constructive attitude.

POINT 8: Finally, Jiang Zemin invited Taiwan's leading authorities to come for a visit in an appropriate capacity, and expressed the desire to receive an invitation to visit Taiwan. An international occasion is not needed, Jiang concluded: We ourselves must handle the affairs of the Chinese people (*Xinhua News Agency*, 01/30/1995).

On September 12, 1997, Jiang Zemin pointed out during the 15th Communist Party Congress that Hong Kong's return to her motherland marked a huge success of the "one country, two systems" concept. It symbolized that Chinese people had taken a big step forward on the path of accomplishing the nation's reunification. In the report, he solemnly advised that as a first step, the two sides across the strait should conduct talks to "formally end the state of hostility between the two sides under the One-China Principle" and reach agreement.

On January 26, 1998, during the symposium convened for the third anniversary of the publication of Jiang's Eight-Point Proposals, Vice Premier of the State Council Qian Qishen explained the One-China Principle again. He emphasized that during the cross-strait negotiations on the issue of reunification, the One-China Principle must be insisted upon. Taiwan is part of China, and the sovereignty and territorial integrity of China cannot be alienated. Under the One-China Principle, a formal end of the state of hostility between the two sides is a necessary step to further develop the relationship between them. Qian Qishen also stated that abiding by "one country, two systems" would not cause damage to the Taiwan compatriots' realistic and long-term benefits. Many Taiwan compatriots hope to maintain the current status quo; for them, "one country, two systems" is the best method for maintaining the status quo.

On October 14, 1998, the PRC's ARATS Chairman Wang Daohan told the visiting ROC's SEF Chairman Koo Chen-fu, "There is only one China in the world. Taiwan is part of China. At present, the reunification is not yet realized. Both sides should work together under the One-China Principle; conduct dialogues on equal footing to discuss reunification. The sovereignty and territorial integrity of a country cannot be alienated. The political position of Taiwan should be discussed under the premise of one China."

Wang Daohan continued, "At present, the reunification is not yet realized" and he expressed acknowledgment of the current status of the two sides. The words ". . . conduct dialogues on equal footing to discuss reunification" and "the political position of Taiwan should be discussed under the premise of one China" express three meanings: 1) Beijing agrees that Taiwan authorities should have a proper political status, but that this political status should be appropriate; 2) Beijing does not classify Taiwan as a renegade province; and 3) The political status of the Taiwan authorities should be discussed under the premise of one China.

On November 8, 1998, the Taiwan Affairs Office of the Central Commission of Chinese Communist Party and the Taiwan Affairs Office of the State Council (abbreviated as the Taiwan Affairs Office) publicized the content of Jiang Zemin and Koo Chen-fu's conversation: 1) Mainland China practices a democratic system suitable for socialism. The different systems of the two sides are not the problem. The problem is the struggle between reunification and Taiwan independence; 2) Mainland China wants to solve the Taiwan problem through peaceful reunification but is not willing to discard the possibility of using military force; 3) After the reunification of the two sides, Taiwan would practice "one country, two systems"; the mainland would not send military to Taiwan. Taiwan could send people to the Beijing central government to take official positions, but the nation's chairmanship could not be held by a Taiwanese; and 4) The meeting of political leaders of the two sides is an internal affair of China and there is no need to meet each other at international venues (*United Daily News*, 11/08/1998).

On April 6, 1999, Wang Daohan met with a delegate of the New Alliance Association from Taiwan and explained to them the content of the "one China" policy. He pointed out that, in the past, Taiwan always interpreted the cross-strait situation as "a separately governed China" and asked why it wasn't interpreted as "one China being governed separately." As for the exact definition of the political negotiation, Wang Daohan stated clearly, "It is an issue of reunification." Wang Daohan also asked his entourage to review the minutes of his conversation with Koo Chen-fu written a year earlier. He reiterated the content of those talks: "There is only one China in the world, Taiwan is part of China, but at present China has not been reunified; both sides should work together under the One-China Principle, conduct negotiations on an equal footing, and discuss reunification together" (*China Times Daily News*, 04/06/1999).

On February 21, 2000, the Taiwan Affairs Office and the Information Office of the State Council published an 11,000-word white paper entitled "The One-China Principle and the Taiwan Issue" prior to Taiwan's presidential election. The document has five parts: 1) The basis for "one China," *de facto* and *de jure*; 2) The One-China Principle is the basis and prerequisite for achieving peaceful reunification; 3) The Chinese government is a staunch champion of the One-China Principle; 4) Several questions involve the One-China Principle in the cross-strait relations; and 5) Several questions involve adherence to the One-China Principle in the international community. Apart from a strong criticism of the "two-state theory," the Two German States Formula was also inappropriate for solving the Taiwan issue due to the different nature of Germany's split after the war in comparison with the temporary separation of the two sides across the strait. The main differences are as follows: 1) The causes for the two situations are different; 2) The two situations have different positions in the international law; and 3) The existing conditions for the two situations are different. As a result, the German issue and the Taiwan issue have little in common and therefore the Two German States Formula cannot be applied to the Taiwan issue.

The white paper also raised three conditional statements: 1) "If a grave turn of events occurs, leading to the separation of Taiwan from China"; 2) "If Taiwan is invaded and occupied by foreign countries"; and 3) "If the Taiwan authorities refuse, *sine die*, the peaceful settlement of cross-strait reunification through negotiations." If any of these situations occur, then the Chinese government will be forced to adopt all drastic measures possible, including the use of force, to safeguard China's sovereignty and territorial integrity to achieve reunification. The white paper also stated, "The Republic of China has already ended its historical position in 1949," and, "The People's Republic of China naturally should fully enjoy and exercise China's sovereignty, including its sovereignty over Taiwan."

The white paper blamed the use of "the struggle of democracy and social system" as a pretext to obstruct China's reunification. Also, after the two sides of the strait realize a peaceful reunification, Taiwan's "one country, two systems" theory can be more relaxed than in Hong Kong and Macao. It would not be democratic or logical for Taiwan authorities to attempt to obstruct the reunification using the aforementioned pretext. The nature of the divergence of viewpoints between the sides is never a fight for democracy or system, but rather a fight for reunification or division (*Xinhua News Agency*, 02/21/2000).

On August 24, 2000, Qian Qishen received a visiting *United Daily News* group from Taiwan. While discussing the cross-strait relations, he voiced mainland China's "one China" statement: There is only one China in the world. The Chinese mainland and Taiwan belong to the same China. China's sovereignty and territorial integrity cannot be alienated from one another.

On July 13, 2001, Qian Qishen received the New Party's Mainland Affairs Commission and clearly cited the three adherences of the current cross-strait development: "one China, cross-strait negotiations, and direct three links as soon as possible." During discussions, Qian Qishen stated that the two systems emphasized in "one country, two systems" referred to socialist and capitalist systems. Hong Kong, Macao, and Taiwan have capitalist systems, though the three implement their systems differently. Mainland China had no intention of obliging Taiwan to copy the systems of Hong Kong or Macao.

When asked to explain the contents of "one country, two systems," Qian Qishen cited the established seven items of the "one country, two systems" contents:

1. Taiwan can continue its use of Taiwan currency.
2. Taiwan can keep its military.
3. Taiwan is a separate tariff region regarding foreign imports.
4. Taiwan can continue to keep its government structure.
5. The Chinese mainland will not take any money from Taiwan or relocate Taiwan's capital.
6. Taiwanese people and entrepreneurs will be able to maintain their individual property.
7. Taiwan has its own independent political system and mainland China will not require Taiwan to have any mainland official representation.

Concerning the New Party's suggestion of not using military force, Qian Qishen said that "our original position is to reunite peacefully" (*Central News Agency*, 07/13/2001).

On January 11, 2001, at Beijing's Zhong Nan Hai (the Chinese equivalent of the White House), Jiang Zemin met with the Alliance for the Reunification of China delegate from Taiwan. He suggested that the name fight over using the PRC or the ROC could be resolved by simply using the name China. As long as the Taiwan leaders accept the One-China Principle, they could visit the Chinese mainland any time. He, himself, could also visit Taiwan at any time. Jiang Zemin said that when he met the U.S. President William J. Clinton the first time, he told Clinton that the Taiwan problem was due to obstacles propagated by the U.S. Without this interference, Taiwan would have been reunified long ago. The Taiwan problem was in fact a Sino-U.S. problem. Jiang Zemin also said that another roadblock for solving the Taiwan problem was that some people in Taiwan would "rather be the chicken head, not the ox tail," implying the preference of being leaders in a small province than officials of a large country (*China Times Daily News*, 11/01/2001).

On January 11, 2001, Jiang Zemin made a political report during the 16th Communist Party Congress about "a comprehensive building up of a well-to-do society, setting up a new phase of socialism that has special Chinese characteristics." The eighth portion of the report, entitled "Taiwan Policy," pointed out, "There is only one China in the world, the Chinese mainland and Taiwan belong to the same China, China's sovereignty and territorial integrity cannot be alienated." This was the first time that China officially cited the One-China Principle. The report also emphasizes that the two sides could temporarily set aside certain political disputes in order to resume the cross-strait dialogues and negotiations. Both sides could talk about formally ending the state of hostility; Taiwan's status in the international arena; the matching platform for its economic, cultural, and social activities; and the political status of the Taiwan authorities (*Xinhua News Agency*, 11/08/2002).

Since the spring and summer of 2003, the candidates from the Pan-Blue Coalition and the Pan-Green Coalition for the 2004 presidential election proposed "one country on each side," a referendum, and the need to write a new Constitution. Though mainland China paid much attention to these developments, it did not interfere with Taiwan's election. It only proclaimed many times through its spokesperson of the Taiwan Affairs Office that Taiwan's referendum would lead to "gradual Taiwan independence" and that it opposed such measures resolutely.

On October 24, 2003, PRC Chairman Hu Jintao gave a speech at the Australia Congress. After the speech, he made several statements, including the following: "We will try our best to maintain the cross-strait peace. We will try our best to strive for a peaceful resolution of the Taiwan problem. But, we will absolutely not allow Taiwan independence." Also: "Taiwan independence threatens the peace of the strait and China's territorial integrity, which is a stance that cannot be accepted by any sovereign country and its people. The Taiwan problem matters for China's sovereignty and territorial integrity as well as for the nationalistic passion of the 1.3 billion Chinese people" (*China Times Daily News*, 10/25/2003).

On November 17, 2003, Wang Daohan pointed out that Taiwan's Pan-Blue and Pan-Green presidential candidates increasingly argued that the referendum and the formulation of a new Constitution had caused cross-strait relations to suffer a "serious setback." Taiwan Affairs Office Vice Minister Wang Zaixi also expressed the strongest objection. He argued that demanding democracy and promoting Taiwan independence are two different matters. If Taiwan authorities openly provoke mainland China and challenge the One-China Principle, the use of force would be difficult to avoid (*China Times Daily News*, 11/19/2003).

On November 21, 2003, the spokesperson of the PRC's Ministry of Foreign Affairs reiterated that the Chinese government insisted on the basic principle of "a peaceful reunification and one country, two systems." The spokesperson also stated that the "Chinese people wish more than anyone else in the world to peacefully solve the Taiwan problem. We will not give up the effort of a peaceful resolution. But we absolutely cannot tolerate Taiwan independence and never can allow anyone to split Taiwan from China. The Chinese government and the people's determination in protecting the nation's sovereignty and territorial integrity are firm and unshakeable." The spokesperson further claimed that the U.S. government made clear promises to the Chinese government regarding the Taiwan issue. The U.S. has prudently stated in the three Sino-U.S. joint communiqués that it has no intention of encroaching upon China's sovereignty and territorial integrity, no intention of interfering with China's internal politics, and no intention of exercising the policy of "two Chinas" or "one China, one Taiwan."

SECTION 3
THE BASIC CONTENTS OF "ONE COUNTRY, TWO SYSTEMS"

From as early as the 1980s, when mainland China proposed "a peaceful reunification and one country, two systems" as the policy of the nation's reunification, its basic principle has not changed. Although both Taiwan and the U.S. often spread rumors that mainland China will abandon "one country, two systems" in favor of "one country, three systems" or already is using a confederation system to replace "one country, two systems," these rumors have no basis in truth. On the contrary, in order to enhance Taiwan's willingness to proceed with political negotiations, mainland China's leaders and officials responsible for the cross-strait affairs have offered looser and more flexible interpretations regarding the meaning of "one China" and the specific contents of "one country, two systems."

Concerning the contents of "one China," mainland China thought that the SEF and the ARATS reached a consensus in 1992 about "both sides of the strait insisting on a One-China Principle." Qian Qishen pointed out on January 26, 1998, "In dealing with the cross-strait related affairs before the reunification, especially during the cross-strait negotiations, insisting on the One-China Principle means insisting that there is only one China in the world, that Taiwan is part of China, China's sovereignty and territorial integrity cannot be alienated." But only two years later, he redefined the One-China Principle. In August 2000 he said, "The mainland and Taiwan belong to the same China," and not, "Taiwan is part of China." In November 2002, during the 16th Communist Party Congress, Jiang Zemin formally introduced in his political report the three issues that could be discussed: ". . . talk about formally ending the state of hostility across the strait; about Taiwan's suitable economic, cultural, and social activity platform in the international arena; and about the political status of the Taiwan authorities."

Jiang Zemin's report further enriched the concept of "one country, two systems" by providing many new meanings. First, facing the new situation, Jiang Zemin no longer insisted that the KMT and the CPC negotiate; instead, he said that "the representatives from various parties and organizations on both sides are welcome to participate in the negotiation." This meant that the Chinese mainland already had given a certain degree of tacit approval of Taiwan's current status of political democratization and party politics.

Second, under "one China" all problems can be discussed. There is no longer insistence on China being the PRC or Taiwan being a renegade province. Accordingly, then, during cross-strait negotiations Taiwan's name, national flag, national anthem, and Constitution could all be discussed so that an acceptable agreement by both sides may be reached. Such an approach should not be viewed as "offering amnesty" to Taiwan, or "surrendering" by the Taiwan authorities; instead, it is a respectful and collaborative effort working towards China's future.

Third, for the first time it was stressed that while "striving for the realization of a peaceful reunification, Chinese will not fight against Chinese." This statement is aimed at foreign powers that interfere with China's reunification and that are playing with the conspiracy of Taiwan independence.

Fourth, it was reiterated that both sides could undertake negotiations to reach agreements "under the One-China Principle, formally ending the state of hostility." This is closer to the step-by-step realization of the nation's reunification proposed by Taiwan's NUG.

According to the above review, it is clear that while mainland China requested that Taiwan should revert to the 1992 Consensus, it simultaneously made adjustments in its own policy to address Taiwan's strong attitude of "one not being subordinate to the other." However, Taiwan was not impressed by China's effort. Additionally, the attitude of Taiwan's leader Lee

Teng-hui and the transformation of political power through the 2000 presidential election impaired the cross-strait relation from start to finish. Instead, the situation fell to its lowest point after Chen Shui-bian proposed "one country on each side."

As the 2004 Taiwan presidential election approached, in order to cover up poor political performance as well as to improve low election morale, Chen Shui-bian proposed a sequential referendum and the formulation of a new Constitution. This completely deviated from the One-China Principle and the cross-strait relation suffered another serious setback. Disentangling this new crisis is testing the wisdom of the leaders on both sides as well as the Taiwanese people themselves.

CHAPTER 2

"ONE COUNTRY, TWO SYSTEMS" IN HONG KONG AND MACAO

Deng Xiaoping originally targeted his idea of "one country, two systems" at the reunification of mainland China and Taiwan. After the return of Hong Kong (1997) and Macao (1999) to Chinese sovereignty, though, the policy was enforced by both regions. Due to the short distance of these two regions from Taiwan and their implementation of the policy, the Taiwan officials and people have always paid attention to the results of "one country, two systems" in Hong Kong and Macao. The international media also use Hong Kong and Macao as examples when discussing the cross-strait reunification issue. Hence, it is wise to describe the preparations Hong Kong and Macao made prior to their handover to mainland China, and the problems that occurred after their implementations of "one country, two systems."

SECTION 1
"ONE COUNTRY, TWO SYSTEMS" IN HONG KONG

July 1, 2003, was the sixth anniversary of the return of Hong Kong to Chinese sovereignty. On that day, a few hundred thousand people walked to the streets of Hong Kong to protest the Hong Kong Special Administrative Region (HK SAR) government (abbreviated as the Hong Kong government) concerning the Article 23 legislation of the Hong Kong

19

Basic Law. This attracted Taiwanese and international attention. The U.S. and Great Britain issued statements that expressed great concern about Hong Kong's freedom and human rights. In addition, the Taiwan media continuously and substantively reported the series of disturbances in Hong Kong caused by the Article 23 legislation.

The disturbances over the Article 23 legislation ended at the beginning of September 2003 when the Hong Kong government withdrew the anti-subversion legislation. Nevertheless, the entire event is important for understanding the Hong Kong Basic Law and the implementation of Hong Kong's "one country, two systems."

The Return of Hong Kong to Chinese Sovereignty and the Hong Kong Basic Law

In December 1984, the mainland Chinese and British governments signed a joint statement regarding the Hong Kong issue. The statement confirmed that mainland China would resume its sovereignty over Hong Kong. Based on Hong Kong's historical and realistic situations, mainland China established the HK SAR. While China resumed its sovereignty and implemented the "one country, two systems" policy in Hong Kong, it also enacted the Basic Law to program the political system in HK SAR.

On July 1, 1985, the Drafting Committee for the Basic Law of the HK SAR (abbreviated as Drafting Committee) was formally established. Soon after that, the mainland China and Hong Kong committee members set up five special topic teams to begin the actual drafting work:

1. The Relationship between the Central Authorities and the HK SAR
2. The Fundamental Rights and Duties of the Residents
3. The Political Structure
4. The Economy
5. The Education, Science, Culture, Sports, Religion, Labor, and Social Services.

Once the teams completed their initial drafts, they established the full task force and made any necessary adjustments and revisions.

In 1988 and 1989, the Drafting Committee promulgated the Basic Law twice to solicit a draft with different ideas. The Committee broadly sought opinions from various democratic parties, people's organizations, and related experts in Hong Kong and the mainland, and modified the draft according to expressed diverse opinions. After four years, the Basic Law of the HK SAR of the People's Republic of China (abbreviated as the Basic

Law) and its appended documents were finally passed into law. It was April 4, 1990, during the 3rd Session of the 7th National People's Congress.

On July 1, 1997, Hong Kong finally returned to mainland China's arms after being governed by Great Britain for approximately 166 years. The HK SAR was formally established with Tung Chee-hwa as the first chief executive of the Hong Kong government.

The Implementation of "One Country, Two Systems" in Hong Kong

Before the disturbance regarding Article 23, the implementation of "one country, two systems" in Hong Kong was mostly seen as positive. The basic guidance of the "Hong Kong people rule Hong Kong with a high degree of autonomy" promised by mainland China before Hong Kong's return was carried out thoroughly. Even the former last-term colonial Governor Christopher Francis Patte noted that Hong Kong's society remained stable after its return. President Clinton also said after his visit to Hong Kong that "one country, two systems" had been carried out thoroughly and that it might be a good method to resolve the cross-strait problems.

In March 2002, approximately five years after Hong Kong returned to mainland China, former British Ambassador Robert B. Mackenzie accepted an interview by the *BBC Chinese Internet*. He had previously participated in the China/Great Britain negotiations and had formulated the Sino-British Joint Declaration on the Hong Kong question. He stated that from the angle of implementing "one country, two systems," Hong Kong was a successful case. Britain always hoped that after handing over sovereignty Hong Kong could continue to enjoy a high degree of autonomy and that, regardless of its political and economic systems, everything could remain unchanged. Mackenzie also expressed much interest in Hong Kong's democratic development. He explained that during the time of mainland China and Great Britain negotiations, all Hong Kong legislators were appointed—as opposed to being elected by the people. At the time of the negotiations, Great Britain did not insist on universal suffrage. Mackenzie hoped that in the far future, the Hong Kong Parliament Members of the Legislative Council and the chief executive would all be appointed through direct elections. However, for the reform of Hong Kong's political system, he admitted it would be better to adhere to the stipulations of the Basic Law so as to avoid conflict with the Basic Law and the articles in the Sino-British Joint Declaration.

Mackenzie was in agreement with the disciplinary system for high officials as proposed by Tung Chee-hwa. Mackenzie thought that it would benefit the government to be even more responsible to the Legislative Council as well as for the officials to be more responsible to the residents. He also suggested that Hong Kong's recent economic problems were mainly caused by the influence of the Asian financial crises and that it would be difficult for Hong Kong to do well independently without taking these problems into consideration. He believed that under Tung Chee-hwa's leadership Hong Kong would successfully come out of this difficult situation. Additionally he said that Hong Kong's uniqueness and success lay in its rule by law, its incorruptible government, and its highly efficient bureaucratic framework. As a result, foreign investors had come to prefer Hong Kong as their regional headquarters. He concluded by stating that these influences conformed to the interests of Hong Kong and mainland China and that he was confident that "one country, two systems" could continue to exist effectively in Hong Kong (*BBC Chinese Internet*, 03/22/2002).

After Hong Kong's sovereignty was transferred to mainland China in 1997, the European Union (EU) Executive Committee initiated its annual report on Hong Kong's development, which included notes on its relationship with the EU and its implementation of "one country, two systems." Among the four sets of presented reports, the Executive Committee pointed out that although mainland China occasionally committed violations during its implementation of "one country, two systems," the implementation was basically successful. Hence, the committee gave a positive evaluation on Hong Kong's implementation of "one country, two systems" (*Central News Agency*, 1/28/2003).

The Disturbance Due to the Article 23 Legislation

Hong Kong's Basic Law, in essence, is considered to be its Constitution and it respects the opinions of the people as much as possible. The content of the Basic Law is also like other countries' constitutions in that it includes declared articles that express its principles. For example, if one article stipulates that the government should legislate on a particular topic, then the government must enact the required legislation in such a manner as to avoid violating the Constitution and/or taking away people's rights and benefits. Article 23 is one of the 160 articles in Hong Kong's Basic law. It reads as follows: "The Hong Kong Special Administrative Region shall enact laws on its own to prohibit any act of treason, secession, sedition, subversion against the Central People's Government, or theft of state secrets, to prohibit foreign political organizations or entities from conducting political activities in the Region, and to prohibit political organizations or entities of the Region from establishing ties with foreign political organizations or entities."

The law that protects a nation's security is generally written by the central government of that nation. Since the legal system in Hong Kong is different from that of mainland China, its social development and lifestyle are also different. During the process of passing the Basic Law, the Hong Kong government should have written its own National Security Law instead of applying the mainland criminal laws to Hong Kong. In 1976, Hong Kong signed on to the International Convention on Economic, Social and Cultural Rights and the International Convention on Citizen Rights and Political Rights positions. The Hong Kong government has the obligation to carry out these conventions, while also taking into account articles in the Basic Law that protect human rights and freedom. Hence, when talking about criminal behaviors like treason, subversion, secession, and sedition in the National Security (Legislative Provisions) Bill, the bill stipulates that only the use of force or violence, the serious violation of the law, or the initiation of riots that endangers the national security constitute criminal behavior. Talks and thoughts do not constitute a crime, and the bill keeps a reasonable balance between protecting the national security and protecting human rights.

During the process of formulating the National Security (Legislative Provisions) Bill, the Hong Kong government made broad consultations and accepted opinions from experts, scholars, political parties, and people from various social circles. After the bill was proposed, the Hong Kong government offered more than 50 suggestions for revisions, following more than 100 hours of examinations by the Drafting Committee of the Legislative Council. Even so, the legislation still caused a major dispute and led more than 100,000 people to protest in the streets. Apparently, the Hong Kong people still did not have a sufficient understanding of and were dubious about the National Security (Legislative Provisions) Bill.

Responding to the demonstration on July 1, 2003, the Hong Kong government made three additional revisions to the proposed National Security (Legislative Provisions) Bill: 1) It eliminated the regulations that were applied to local organizations, which were subordinate to those inland groups where similar regulations had already been abolished by the Central People's Government; 2) In order to increase the protection of public figures, especially those in media circles, a "protection for public interests" defense against regulations that related to "illegally revealing official secrets" was added; 3) It eliminated regulations that related to the use of the emergent investigative police power that allowed home entry without a court warrant.

After Legislator Tien Beijun of the Free Party resigned, a decision was made to put off the second reading of the proposed bill. On July 17, Tung Chee-hwa put together all of the proposed revisions and suggestions for the related Provisions Protocol Committee of the Legislation Council. On September 5, he announced that the Hong Kong government decided to put off the second reading in order to consult the public again; thus the legislation disturbance was temporarily stopped.

If one views the content of the revised National Security (Legislative Provisions) Bill as a whole, it is clear that the various stipulations are quite similar to the national security laws in other countries. Based on the Article 23 legislation of the Basic Law, the Hong Kong government must protect the safety of Hong Kong. Let's leave aside the political performance of Tung Chee-hwa for a moment, for he began his legislation work only during his second term. He did not act in haste; on the contrary, he acted most legally and responsibly.

Some people say that by the eve of Hong Kong's return and during the negotiation period for the Sino-British Joint Liaison Group to transfer the political power, Beijing had already attempted to proceed with legislation on the crimes of treason and subversion in Article 23. However, it encountered strong opposition from various Hong Kong circles and Great Britain. In order to guarantee a smooth transfer of political power, Beijing temporarily tabled Article 23 legislation. Evidently the people who spread these rumors had neither legal knowledge nor much common sense. Before July 1, 1997, the Hong Kong government was not yet in power, so the question arises: Through whom could mainland China begin legislation in Hong Kong? Article 23 of the Basic Law clearly stipulates, "The Hong Kong Special Administrative Region shall enact laws on its own." Would it not be a mistake, then, for mainland China to chance violating the yet-to-be implemented Basic Law?

During this disturbance, some Hong Kong commentators said that because the current Hong Kong laws covered treason and subversion crimes, there was no need to write new laws. These people obviously did not understand the current Hong Kong laws. In referring to the crime of treason, the law included phrases like "abrogate or force the monarch," which were no longer relevant since Hong Kong had separated from Britain. Some people say that Hong Kong was so used to freedom that it could not accept the National Security (Legislative Provisions) Bill. In fact, no country in the world can totally ignore threats to its security. Why should Hong Kong be an exception? The National Security Legislation is perhaps a good opportunity for the people of Hong Kong to learn of facets of democracy apart from simply enjoying freedom.

Some Hong Kong commentators said that since Hong Kong is part of China, there is no need to have a separate legislation. Others criticized the Hong Kong government's writing of the national security law as a violation of the "one country, two systems" principle. These contradictory arguments answer each other's questions. Precisely because Hong Kong has implemented "one country, two systems," the related mainland China's laws cannot be appropriately used in Hong Kong; hence Hong Kong must enact its own legislation. This enactment not only conforms to the stipulations of the Basic Law, but it also further presents Hong Kong's thorough implementation of "one country, two systems." The Central People's Government, from beginning to end, always insisted that national security legislation was a HK SAR matter. Any decision regarding the content or the timing of this legislation should be fully made by the Hong Kong government. All of the examples cited above show the determination of the Hong Kong government to appropriately carry out "one country, two systems."

Although the legislation disturbance ended temporarily, Tung Chee-hwa's personal popularity did not substantially rise. The Hong Kong people's demand for universal suffrage to elect their chief executive and parliament members is still strong. It is worth carefully studying exactly the specifics of the people's dissatisfactions with their government to understand why they protested in the streets.

Hong Kong People's Pleas

Before Hong Kong's return, its economic structure exhibited serious defects. Hong Kong had an inflated economy and the British government intended to take out everything and leave. Additionally, during the previous six years, Asian and surrounding countries' financial crises adversely affected Hong Kong. This caused Hong Kong to suffer economic stagnation and many residents to suffer a substantial loss of wealth. Many middle-class citizens ended up with negative assets. This economic plight and the resultant decline of living standards took a terrible emotional toll on the people and many questioned why Hong Kong's economy corroded and their quality of life diminished? They placed total blame on the government; a poor economy was the main catalyst that drove people to the streets in protest.

The pleas of the protest participants covered many aspects. Those who truly supported the democratic faction to oppose the Article 23 legislation were few. Some of the residents who participated in the demonstration came not only to oppose legislation but to make other demands as well. Indeed, most people marched because of the declining economy, the disciplinary system not being concrete, and for what was lacking in the anti-severe acute respiratory syndrome (anti-SARS) work. They blamed the government for not being effective and demanded that Tung Chee-hwa step down.

There is one more reason that completes the account for opposing "one country, two systems." The day before the demonstration, Premier Wen Jiabao visited Hong Kong and was enthusiastically welcomed by the residents. Some news media reported that the people hoped that Wen Jiabao or Zhu Rongji would become the chief executive.

Hong Kong's economic problems, indeed, are not easy to solve. The manufacturing industries gradually moved out when mainland China began the reform and opened its policies. From the mid-1990s, the software and hardware infrastructures in Guangdong were gradually completed, which prompted Hong Kong's manufacturing industries to relocate their plants. The merchandise transited through Hong Kong also gradually gave way to direct trade via Shenzhen and other ports. The service industries such as banks, aviation, and accounting offices moved to Shenzhen, Guangzhou, and other places. This relocation substantially reduced local employment opportunities in Hong Kong. In short, Hong Kong's present situation is the result of an inevitable trend. If Hong Kong had not been returned to mainland China, and if it had not implemented "one country, two systems," perhaps conditions would be even worse. Tung Chee-hwa's 2003 administrative report pointed out that in the future, Hong Kong would increase the use of mainland China's economic inland market to boost its economic development while continuing to use concrete measures to speed up the integration of mainland China and Hong Kong. In order to quickly bring Hong Kong's economy out of its plight, mainland China and Hong Kong signed the Closer Economic Partnership Arrangement (CEPA) on June 29, 2003, allowing a portion of Hong Kong's products to be sold on the mainland without tariff. Even if CEPA and other proposals yield some beneficial results, the Hong Kong people should clearly understand their circumstances and reality, adjust their mentality, and face the facts. By doing this, they will be better able to manage their lives.

Another plea made by the Hong Kong people was to demand universal suffrage for their chief executive and the Legislative Council members.

According to the stipulations of the Basic Law, after 2007 the Hong Kong people can modify the procedures for selecting the chief executive and the Legislative Council within the Basic Law. For the past few years the Democratic Party has been warning that the Hong Kong government has no intention of modifying the Basic Law, thus refusing to let the third term chief executive in 2007 and the Legislative Council in 2008 be created via universal suffrage. On August 1, 2003, the Hong Kong democratic legislator Martin Lee Chu-ming openly stated that mainland China's new leaders, Hu Jintao and Wen Jiabao, should trust themselves and the Hong Kong people. They should correct their extreme left approach in order to let the Hong Kong people implement autonomy and truly carry out "one country, two systems" (*Hsin Pao/Hong Kong Economic Journal*, 08/01/2003). The overseas scholar Zhen Hailin in Canada also published articles during July and August of 2003 in Hong Kong's newspapers stating that "Hong Kong people [should] rule Hong Kong" and that a "high degree of autonomy" has the purpose of moving in the direction of democratic development after Hong Kong's return. This kind of democratic politicking can be summarized as the free and autonomous politics of the Hong Kong people. In order to achieve the universal suffrage, the legislative organization must represent the people's will and supervise the checks and balances of the operations of the administrative organization. To be able to do this, the legislators must be selected through universal suffrage (www.epochtimes.com, 07/08/2003).

In April 2003, Hong Kong's Action for Cosignatory Declaration made two demands: 1) The Hong Kong government must openly announce the timetable for carrying out the democratic system, publicize a set of detailed consultation documents related to universal suffrage for the chief executive and the Legislative Council, and immediately begin public consultations.; 2) The 2007 third-term chief executive and the 2008 Legislative Council will be elected through universal suffrage. Participants in the movement said that their demands were similar to the spirit of the provisions of Article 45 and Article 68 of the Basic Law. The only difference was in the use of the phrase "immediately start consultations" as opposed to "proceed with the consultations gradually." As for the examination of the concrete content of the political system, the key point is to "return the political power to the people" and to accomplish the universal suffrage of the chief executive and the Legislative Council. By then, the second paragraph of Article 43, which states, "The chief executive of the Hong Kong Special Administrative Region shall be accountable to the Central People's Government and the Hong Kong Special Administrative Region in accordance with the provisions of this law," can be modified at the same time. In this way, the chief executive can be questioned while he is attending the Legislative Council and the Disciplinary System can be formally established. In the meantime, if some high officials make serious mistakes, the Legislative Council can pass a no-confidence motion to demand that he steps down, thus making the Disciplinary System worthy of its name (www.epochtimes.com, 04/22/2003).

Concerning these demands, the Committee on the Matters of Political Systems of the Legislative Council offered explanations on October 17, 2003. According to the stipulations of the Basic Law, after 2007, any modifications to the method of selecting the chief executive of the HK SAR and the Legislative Council must be passed by a two-thirds majority of Parliament Members of the Legislative Council and have the approval of the chief executive. Modifications related to the method of selecting the chief executive must be reported to the SCNPC for approval. Modifications to the method of selecting the Legislative Council must be reported to the SCNPC for the record. The Basic Law also clearly stipulates that it will reach the final goal of direct universal suffrage. Tung Chee-hwa clearly claimed that pushing forward Hong Kong's democratic development while adhering to the Basic Law is Hong Kong residents' basic demand and an inescapable responsibility of this term's government.

The Committee on the Matters of Political Systems also defined the timetable for examining the political system. During 2004, it would take another survey on the developments of the political system. In 2005, it would deal with the procedures for handling the related attachments of the Basic Law. In 2006, it would proceed with the local legislation work based on its needs. The committee also said that before the end of 2003 the Hong Kong government would make a decision about the concrete timetable on the examination of the political system and the public consultations and then brief the Legislative Council and the public accordingly (www.info.gov.hk, 10/17/2003).

Perhaps the explanations advanced by the Committee on the Matters of Political Systems will not satisfy everyone, but at least the explanations are a responsible starting point. The Hong Kong government should listen carefully and provide positive responses to the Hong Kong people's reasonable demands for democratic reforms. Concerning the efficiency of its Governance and Disciplinary System, the Hong Kong government should immediately initiate improvements and enhancements. But, at the same time, differing parties should follow the stipulations of the Basic Law and avoid arbitrarily repudiating or distorting those stipulations. While challenging the efficiencies of the executive chief and the governance of the Hong Kong government, they should take the stability of the Hong Kong political situation seriously and strive to maintain good relationships between the Central People's Government and the HK SAR. They would be wise to make constructive suggestions and avoid personal or negative arbitrary criticisms.

Discussions on the British and U.S. Positions on the Article 23 Legislation

Both Great Britain and the U.S. have historically held negative opinions about the Article 23 legislation.

GREAT BRITAIN. Even after Hong Kong's return to China, Great Britain has expressed many times that it carries some moral responsibility towards the Hong Kong society. In July 2003, the 13th Report on Hong Kong (which includes the period from January to June 2003) was presented by the British Foreign and Commonwealth Office to the British Parliament. It expressed a high degree of concern about the Article 23 legislation, the development of Hong Kong's political system, the Disciplinary System, SARS, the crackdown on illegal money laundering, and financial assistance to terrorists. In anticipation of this report, the Hong Kong government formally notified Great Britain that the operation of "one country, two systems" in Hong Kong was working well and that the people's basic human rights and freedom would continue to be protected. Still, when British Prime Minister Tony Blair visited Hong Kong on July 23, 2003, he reiterated that Great Britain still bore moral responsibility toward Hong Kong. Besides approving "one country, two systems" and the people's rule of Hong Kong, he called for the government to have universal suffrage by 2007 in order to carry out Hong Kong's democratic system. This comment seems absurd. Great Britain ruled Hong Kong for more than one hundred years: Why didn't it suggest Hong Kong's democratization during that time? Why didn't it let the Hong Kong people rule Hong Kong with universal suffrage then?

THE UNITED STATES. In June 2003, the U.S. Deputy Secretary of State met with Hong Kong Legislator Martin Lee Chu-ming, among others, and expressed deep concern about the Article 23 legislation. Afterwards, the U.S. State Department's spokesman stated again in his briefing that the Hong Kong government's legislation must conform to the people's rights and freedoms. At the end of June, the White House further declared that the U.S. opposed the Hong Kong government's adherence to the Article 23 legislation. The spokesman for the mainland Department of Foreign Affairs stated that the issue is entirely an internal affair for the HK SAR to legislate according to the Basic Law and that this is inherently mainland China's issue, with which Great Britain, the U.S., and other countries should not interfere. The U.S. stated that in accordance with the United States/Hong Kong Policy Act of 1992, it has always viewed Hong Kong as an individual economic region. The U.S. further stated, "Human rights are the basis of Hong Kong's continuous prosperity. Whether Hong Kong is prosperous or not is a matter of U.S. interest." This sort of straightforward statement is consistent with the overbearing way in which the U.S. has always acted. Hong Kong enacted its National Security Bill for the purpose of protecting its own safety. It would absolutely not hinder any foreign enterprise's economic activities in Hong Kong. Exactly, what is the worrying about?

Ever since the U.S. became the only superpower in the world it has ignored the United Nations' oppositions and has used the excuse of caring about human rights to intervene in other countries' internal affairs. On June 24, 2003, the U.S. State Department promulgated (publicized) the "U.S. Annual Report Supporting Human Rights and Democracy." This is the yearly examination by the U.S. government of human rights conditions in 196 countries and regions in the world. With the publication of its "Country-by-Country Human Rights Reports," the U.S. openly admitted that it had taken its "actions to enhance human rights and democracy" in 92 countries where "human rights conditions were not good." How could such behavior of the U.S., namely using the pretext of human rights to intervene in the internal politics of other countries, not make other countries cautious? The fact is that human rights conditions within the U.S. are deteriorating. For many years, Amnesty International has listed the U.S. as a "poor human rights country" due to its unjust judicial system in executing juvenile criminals (www.amnesty.org). After the 9/11 incident, the U.S. government clearly used the excuse of protecting national security to intrude on human rights.

Immediately after 9/11, the U.S. government illegally arrested more than 2,000 immigrants from Middle East and Muslim countries. The head of the Justice Department admitted this. Forty-five days after 9/11, the U.S. Congress passed the Uniting and Strengthening America by Providing Tools Required to Intercept and Obstruct Terrorism Act, commonly known as the USA Patriot Act. In the name of attacking terrorism, the Patriot Act gives federal investigative organizations the power to use various methods of obtaining personal information including political, social, and business activities; health and medical information; Internet behaviors and activities; credit card data; and library book borrowing records. Further, law enforcement personnel can enter private residences without search warrants to collect criminal evidence, operate comprehensive phone monitoring and recording, and install Internet tracking devices on personal computers (including e-mail tracking and Web surfing tracks). During the process of handling illegal immigrants suspected of terrorist activities, the federal judicial department can require the court to keep private the sentencing procedure and related information and can keep suspects in custody for up to six months.

The Bush administration claimed that the Patriot Act was a necessary measure for attacking terrorism and protecting the U.S. The administration also claimed that it was operating in this manner under total national support, though human rights activists and other legal circles criticized the act for its limitless power to law enforcement units. It violates the Bill of Rights, an amendment to the U.S. Constitution, and seriously intruded upon human rights, but it also contradicts the principles of the judicial system (www.abanet.org). The American Civil Liberties Union even initiated a movement to boycott the Patriot Act and demanded that the local legislative and administrative organizations execute the rights empowered by the Constitution at the local level by taking non-cooperative or resistant measures against federal enforcement personnel (www.aclu.org).

Taiwan's Responses to the Article 23 Legislation

Since early July 2003, Chen Shui-bian and the ruling and opposition parties have strongly condemned the Article 23 legislation. In mid-July, Chen Shui-bian attended a seminar entitled "One Country, Two Systems and the Hong Kong Democracy—Viewing Hong Kong's Future from Article 23 of the Basic Law" in Taipei. In his speech, Chen Shui-bian outlined the damages caused by Article 23 to the "one country, two systems" ideal and said that in the future Article 23 would seriously limit the freedoms of the Hong Kong people. He even made the statement that the Hong Kong government's legislation is an "act to drastically reverse the course of democracy."

The Foundation on International and Cross-Strait Studies presented a policy report at the beginning of August 2003 that focused on Hong Kong's proposed National Security Bill. It strongly criticized the bill, stating that the "National Security Bill has made Hong Kong's democratic route suffer a serious setback. The gap between the forms of democracy on both sides of the Taiwan Strait has continued to increase. Without a doubt, this gap has a negative impact on the relations between the two sides," and this legislation has "terminated mainland China's 'one country, two systems' support in Hong Kong and Taiwan. Mainland China declares that Hong Kong is the 'experimental window display' of 'one country, two systems.' Now, apparently the window is broken. In Taiwan the number of people who tend to favor reunification with mainland China will decrease" (*The Influence of the National Security Provisions on the Content of "One Country, Two Systems"* by the Foundation on International and Cross-Strait Studies, 2003).

On August 16 and 17 of the same year, the Taiwan Advocates led by Lee Teng-hui held a symposium in Taipei on "one country, two systems" in Hong Kong and invited several Hong Kong legislators and scholars. Lee Teng-hui spoke twice during the symposium and pointed out that Hong Kong is no longer working on internationalization and liberalization; on the contrary, it places its hope on the effectiveness of CEPA signed with mainland China. This shows that the Hong Kong people have gradually lost their direction under "one country, two systems." He also claimed that because Hong Kong has the "one country, two systems" framework, the Hong Kong government cannot avoid working under the shadow of mainland China's system. This not only has made Hong Kong lose its original independence, but also causes worry about whether mainland China's autocratic political system is being extended to Hong Kong.

Chen Shui-bian also attended the symposium. In a speech he strongly criticized Hong Kong's "one country, two systems." He also stated that the international community originally kept a reserved attitude about Beijing's promise on "one country, two systems." The formulation of Article 23 of the Basic Law inflicted serious damage to "one country, two systems." This behavior of drastically reversing democracy has aroused a high degree of doubt in the international community about mainland China's respect for its promise of "one country, two systems" (*United Daily News*, 08/17/2003).

The Hong Kong representatives who participated in the symposium were quite dissatisfied with the repeated criticisms of "one country, two systems" by the Taiwanese participants and their attitude of playing down Hong Kong. They protested on the spot. Concerning Chen Shui-bian's statement that currently Hong Kong has no freedom, one of Hong Kong's representatives Li Yi refuted, "Isn't this freedom, when half a million people can demonstrate on the street?" Li Yi said that after the July 1 protest, Chen Shui-bian continued to use words like "bankrupt" and "disillusion" when discussing Hong Kong's "one country, two systems." Ultimately what Li Yi saw was new hope for Hong Kong's fate. He stated that after the July 1 demonstration he became more optimistic and began to believe that in the next year's Legislative Council election, candidates who supported freedom and democracy would get more votes. He said, "Let's hope that Taiwan can give more blessings to Hong Kong, instead of hoping that Hong Kong will go bankrupt and become disillusioned" (*China Times Daily News*, 08/18/2003).

Hong Kong Legislator Emily Lau Wai-hing pointed out that while its people do not have the freedom to choose their government, "I will not say that it [Hong Kong] is doomed." She emphasized that certain aspects of Hong Kong life are better than those of Taiwan life. For example, public servants in Hong Kong are not corrupt and will not accept dirty money. Emily Lau Wai-hing noted that Hong Kong respects the Taiwanese people's will and expressed hope that Taiwan could support Hong Kong in its pursuit for more democracy and freedom under "one country, two systems."

Legislator James To Kun-sun said that most Hong Kong people are willing to accept "one country, two systems," especially the younger generation who believes that they are part of and that their fate cannot be separated from mainland China. They truly accept "one country, two systems" and see Taiwan as also part of China. James To Kun-sun stressed his understanding of the different lifestyles in Taiwan and Hong Kong, and that the Taiwanese people would have strong subjective views regarding change. As a Hong Kong legislator he expressed sincere hope that Hong Kong would be a good example. He said they came to Taiwan this time not for the purpose of playing down Hong Kong, but in an attempt to have Taiwan and Hong Kong learn from each other under the universal values of democracy, freedom, and human rights (*China Times Daily News*, 08/17/2003).

Apparently, the original goal of the symposium was not achieved. The general media not only publicized the Hong Kong participants' complaints, but the *China Times Daily News* and the *United Evening News* also published many articles highlighting refuted arguments.

There were those who claimed that Taiwan and Hong Kong are similar Chinese societies, both have been colonized, and that Taiwan should try to understand Hong Kong's problems instead of persistently criticizing "one country, two systems." Were Lee Teng-hui and Chen Shui-bian concerned that "one country, two systems" would bring prosperity and progress to Hong Kong to the extent that it would become mainland China's propaganda model for Taiwan (*China Times Daily News*, 08/17/2003)? Scholar Shi Zhiyu further explained the Lee Teng-hui and Chen Shui-bian mentality as having "a typical inferiority complex of the modern Chinese" (*United Evening News*, 08/17/2003).

First of all, while Hong Kong has been operating under "one country, two systems" for more than six years, it has always kept a high degree of autonomy and independence. It has always been obvious to the world that Hong Kong people rule Hong Kong. Up to the present day, Hong Kong has practiced Britain's common law system. For a lawsuit, one must hire two lawyers: a solicitor and a barrister. The lawyer fees are expensive, the pleadings must be written in English, the juror system is still in place and the death penalty is not practiced. Many complained about these details, but in order to carry out "one country, two systems," the Hong Kong legal system has remained the same. To implement Article 23, mainland China's Central People's Government has always maintained three positions: 1) solving Hong Kong's problems will be based on the Basic Law; 2) according to the Basic Law, the Hong Kong government should enact the National Security Bill; and 3) mainland China will protect Hong Kong residents' lawful rights and freedoms with every effort. When Hu Jintao and Wen Jiabao met with Tung Chee-hwa, they reiterated that the Central People's Government would insist on the basic guidelines of "one country, two systems," that Hong Kong people rule Hong Kong with a high degree of autonomy as before, and that it would fully support the SAR government to implement policies according to law. Hu Jintao also said that when Hong Kong enacts the national security law on its own, it will be the inevitable result of implementing the Basic Law. The Hong Kong government can also conduct broad consultations on the proposed National Security (Legislative Provisions) Bill in order to get the general understanding and supportive recognition of the people of Hong Kong.

Next, the various articles of the National Security (Legislative Provisions) Bill are no stricter than the regulations of civil strife crime and foreign aggression crime prescribed in Taiwan's Criminal Law and the National Security Act. In recent years, Taiwan has been involved in events such as searching newspaper offices, arresting reporters, and sentencing reporters to jail. Taiwan's freedom of press is at risk. Huang Mo, professor of political science at Soochow University, openly reminded the Taiwanese people that after the transfer of power by political parties, the high-level government officials often used the excuse of national security to strengthen the control and limitation of the media. So, in what way are these officials qualified to criticize Hong Kong's Article 23 legislation (*China Times Daily News*, 07/15/2003)?

Before Hong Kong's return to China, it had been established that British word was law. Not only was the governor of Hong Kong British, but so were the high officials. All policies gave British interests the highest priority. Since Hong Kong's return, not only has the chief executive been a local Hong Kong resident, but all legislators have been Hong Kong people as well. In the Hong Kong government, exactly what policy does not take its people's interests into account and is not supervised by the people? How could one say that with such important changes the Hong Kong government is "contrary to the democratic route?"

Finally, perhaps it can be said that the Taiwanese people need not make a big issue about Hong Kong's lack of universal suffrage. Since all official positions in Taiwan are filled through universal suffrage, during the process of conducting negotiations with mainland China, as long as Taiwan insists on preserving the system, it should not be a difficult matter to maintain universal suffrage. But both the Taiwan ruling and opposition parties state that "one country, two systems" will cause Taiwan to lose its independence just like it did with Hong Kong. What is clear, though, is that, currently, no matter who governs Taiwan, politics are conducted by accepting U.S. instructions. Taiwan cannot join international organizations, and its current international status is not even comparable to that of Hong Kong. It seems that Taiwan's fate (i.e., neither being independent nor being accepted by the international community) can only be determined after the two sides are reunified.

Section 2
"One Country, Two Systems" in Macao

Although Macao has a population of only 430,000 and occupies a small piece of land, its return to mainland China has a special meaning for Taiwan. As Jiang Zemin said in 1999 during the ceremony of Macao's return to mainland China, "The implementation of 'one country, two systems' in Hong Kong and Macao has already been and will continue to play the role of an important model for us to resolve the Taiwan problem eventually. The Chinese government and people have the confidence and the ability to solve the Taiwan problem as early as possible to realize the complete reunification of China." His speech shows that after Macao's return, Taiwan becomes the only remaining issue to be resolved on the subject of China's reunification.

The Return of Macao and Macao's Basic Law

In October 1984, Deng Xiaoping for the first time clearly proposed that "the Macao problem will be like the Hong Kong problem resolved at the same time and using the same method" and "the resolution of the Macao problem also cannot depart from 'one country, two systems.'" From then on, basic guidelines for handling the Macao problem and creating the foundation for the smooth return of Macao included that "Macao people rule Macao" and a "high degree of autonomy."

On June 30, 1986, mainland China and Portugal, the country that colonized Macao in the 16th century, held a series of talks in Beijing about the Macao issue. After four series of talks over nine months, on April 13, 1987, mainland China and Portugal signed a joint statement concerning the Macao issue in Beijing. The statement confirmed that on December 20, 1999, the Chinese government would recover sovereignty over Macao. In this historical document, the Chinese government promulgated the 12 basic policies to be implemented in Macao based on "one country, two systems" guidelines. At that point, Macao began a transition period. On March 31, 1993, the 1st Session of the 8th National People's Congress passed the Basic Law of the Macao Special Administrative Region (M SAR) of the People's Republic of China. This constitutional type of law of the M SAR is composed of one preamble, nine chapters, and three annexes totaling 145 legal articles. From the various political, economic, cultural, and social aspects the law stipulates detailed and rigorous regulations regarding the implementation of "one country, two systems" in Macao. At the same time it also provides Macao with legal protections.

There were two central tasks to complete during Macao's transition period: to guarantee a stable transition and to set up plans for the M SAR. On January 15, 1988, at the same time that the Sino-Portugal Joint Statement became effective, the Sino-Portugal Joint Liaison Team was formally established. Over nearly 12 years, the team held 37 plenary meetings, 56 formal meetings by team leaders, and countless working team meetings and specialist meetings from both sides. The broad and in-depth discussions and consensus achieved included the ceremony for the transfer of the political power, the applicability of the international treaties after Macao's return, and the continuation of certain specially operated contracts after 1999. These meetings covered a series of important matters that concerned a stable transition and the smooth transfer of political power. With the push from mainland China and the mutual work between mainland China and Portugal, the three issues that had attracted much attention were resolved, namely the nativization of the hiring of government employees, the nativization of the legal system, and the use of Mandarin as the official spoken language and Chinese characters as the official written language. From then on,

Macao had its government employee team formed by local residents, its own legal system, and Mandarin and Chinese as the official spoken and written languages, respectively.

On May 5, 1998, the Planning Committee of the M SAR of the National People's Congress was established in Beijing, symbolizing a key stage in Macao's return. Over one–and-a-half years, the Planning Committee of the M SAR held 11 plenary meetings and more than 50 small, topic meetings and made at least 20 important decisions and suggestions. The chief executive of the M SAR was elected to take his first term. The transition of the legislative organizations was completed and the Planning Committee examined Macao's 855 laws.

On December 20, 1999, Macao finally returned to the arms of mainland China. The M SAR was officially established. Edmund Ho Hau Wah became the first chief executive (*Xinhua Agency*, 12/20/1999).

The Practice of "One Country, Two Systems" in Macao

Since Macao was returned to mainland China in 1999, nearly all the Macao people and the world countries have agreed that Macao's "one country, two systems" is quite successful. The Public Opinion Survey Center of the Chinese University of Hong Kong polled people in Hong Kong and Macao about their evaluations of "one country, two systems" and the performance of the governments in the Special Administrative Regions. The surveys found that Macao people are much more satisfied than Hong Kong people. The differences between Hong Kong and Macao are related to attitudes about returning to mainland China and towards the colonizers prior to the return of these two places (www.macau.gov.cn, 12/2000).

Looking over a three year period since its return one can see noticeable changes in Macao. The security issue that had seriously affected Macao's social stability and economic development for many years has improved. Macao's previous economic plight has also begun to improve. Similarly, the overall economy has gradually strengthened and all areas of business have improved. The gambling and tourism businesses can be described as enjoying the most improvement. Both the number of tourists who visit Macao and the amount of gambling taxes collected by the government have hit historical highs. In the areas of education and culture the Macao people have gained confidence and pride, primarily due to the use of Mandarin and Chinese characters.

What's most relevant is that the Macao people give high evaluations to government officials in the M SAR, officials who not only took measures that the former government did not dare, but who also attempted reform. Among their reform experiments, the most remarkable was the first Legislative Council election. (It produced 20 new legislators to take their first term. Among these, ten resulted from indirect elections and ten from direct elections and, together with the seven legislators appointed by Edmund Ho Hau Wah, they formed the second-term Legislative Council.) The "clean election" dream came true. The policy of opening the rights of operating gambling businesses was also smoothly practiced. During the entire bidding process, the M SAR acted with fairness, justice, and openness. It refused the secret operation and interference from all sides. The results of the bidding satisfied both the Macao people and the bidders.

In addition, the M SAR keeps broad contacts with foreign countries. Most of the international treaties used satisfactorily in Macao continue to be used in the M SAR. Approximately 40 percent of these treaties have not yet been entered into by mainland China.

In mid-October 2003, Macao held an alliance meeting between China and the Portuguese-speaking countries. Participating countries showed their respect for Macao's progress since its return and expressed a desire to develop, through Macao, even closer cooperative relations with mainland China (*Xinhua Agency*, 10/13/2003).

These practices show that under the guidance of the Macao Basic Law the local Chinese can govern Macao well. The practices in the M SAR also prove that using "one country, two systems" guidelines to bring about reunification is entirely workable.

SECTION 3
THE PRACTICE OF "ONE COUNTRY, TWO SYSTEMS" IN HONG KONG AND MACAO AS AN EXAMPLE FOR TAIWAN

During the 1980s and the early 1990s, Taiwan showed a careless attitude toward the "peaceful reunification, and one country, two systems" guidelines proposed by mainland China and did very little research on its concrete content. Perhaps the Taiwan authorities and people felt that "one country, two systems" could not be carried out in Taiwan. Following Hong Kong's return, Taiwan began to feel some pressure. But, after seeing Hong Kong's emigration tide, the international community was not optimistic that, after Hong Kong's return, it could really carry out "one country, two systems" and that the Hong Kong people could effectively rule Hong Kong. Hence, Taiwan followed the trend and minimized Hong Kong's accomplishments. Surprisingly, apart from its economic decline due to the Asian financial crisis, Hong Kong had few changes. Macao's return operation was even smoother. These results satisfied the Hong Kong and Macao people as well as emigrants, who returned one by one. Observing these transitions, the international community also developed good opinions about "one country, two systems." It was at this point that the Taiwan authorities began a series of criticisms. First, the Mainland Affairs Council (MAC) in Taiwan argued that the theory of "one country, two systems" is contradictory. Later, the MAC refined its statement to saying that "one country, two systems" was not suitable for the cross-strait reunification: "Taiwan is not Hong Kong. Hong Kong is a colony; the Republic of China is a sovereign country, has its own diplomacy and national defense capabilities, and the country's future should be determined independently by its people." Soon after that, Lee Teng-hui also openly criticized "one country, two systems" as lacking democratic character and being ambiguous and contradictory in its nature.

The change of Taiwan's attitude toward "one country, two systems" sufficiently indicated the increasing pressure felt by the Taiwan authorities day by day. The implementation of "one country, two systems" in Hong Kong and Macao deserves in-depth understanding by those who care about Taiwan's future. In May 2002, the Research Center of the Cross-Strait Relations held the One Country Two Systems Symposium in Hong Kong. During the symposium, the head of the center, Tang Shubei, stated that "one country, two systems" had already been carried out successfully in Hong Kong and Macao, resulting in an inspiring effect toward solving the Taiwan issue (www.future-china.org.tw, 05/24/2002).

On the whole, the implementation of "one country, two systems" in Hong Kong and Macao offers some inspirations for the cross-strait reunification:

1. After their return, Hong Kong and Macao became special administrative regions of the PRC. On the basis of "one country, two systems," the two regions continue to carry out capitalist systems, maintaining stability and enjoying prosperity while maintaining their original social economic systems and lifestyles. Because of the differences in realistic conditions of Taiwan from those in Hong Kong and Macao, it can be said that within the framework of "one country, two systems" Taiwan can implement more relaxed policies.

2. After their return, Hong Kong and Macao achieved a high degree of autonomy, including administrative rights, legislative rights, independent judicial rights, and the rights of final appeal. Most of the laws that Hong Kong and Macao previously held were kept

intact and the basic rights and freedoms, including the freedom of public opinion of the residents, have received broad protections. Based on these facts, the Taiwanese people not only can be their own masters and rule Taiwan while keeping their current economic and cultural lifestyle, but also can broadly and directly participate in the management of all of China as well as the pursuit of peaceful development for the nation.

3. After the return of Hong Kong and Macao, the domains and scopes of foreign affairs that they handled independently remained very broad. In Hong Kong, most of its multilateral international treaties remained applicable in the HK SAR. As a member of the representative delegation of the Chinese government, Hong Kong has participated in the International Civil Aviation Organization, the International Monetary Fund (IMF), and other international organizations whose participants are sovereign states. Hong Kong has used the title "Chinese Hong Kong" to join the Asia-Pacific Economic Cooperation (APEC), the Asian Development Bank (ADB), and the International Maritime Organization. The participants of all these organizations are not limited to sovereign states. Fortune Forums and other large-scale international meetings are held in Hong Kong. The HK SAR has signed 63 bilateral treaties or agreements with other countries. By 2002, 108 countries and regions had given the HK SAR passport holders entry permits without visa requirements. These facts have greatly encouraged Taiwan to expand its international living space.

4. After the return of Hong Kong, the HK SAR has continued to keep its central position in finance, trade, and the shipping industries. It also keeps its financial matters independent, operating its own tax collection and monetary systems. It continues the free-trade policy and acts as a separate tariff region in developing external trade. The economic cooperation between Hong Kong and the mainland continues to strengthen and become closer. More than ever before, the resources, market, labor, science, and technological superiority of the mainland, which serve as its heart increase the competitiveness of Hong Kong's economy. Amid the influences of Asia's financial crisis and 9/11, the HK SAR received support from the mainland. The CEPA signed between the mainland and Hong Kong in June 2003 further raised the competitiveness of Hong Kong goods in the mainland, thereby improving Hong Kong's economy. After the realization of "one country, two systems," the cross-strait economies will be able to highly complement each other. To accomplish a better economic structure and long-term prosperity, Taiwan's economy can use the mainland as its base and sign a CEPA in order to improve its difficult economic situation.

5. Since the return of Hong Kong and Macao under "one country, two systems," many Hong Kong specialists have gone to the mainland to better use their talents. The HK SAR government also hired more than 100 specialists and talented individuals from the main-

land. These experts have contributed to the development of Hong Kong. Talented Taiwanese can go to the mainland to develop their skills, while skillful scientists and technicians from the mainland can go to Taiwan to upgrade its technology industries.

Although Taiwan can get useful inspirations from the implementation of "one country, two systems" in Hong Kong and Macao, the demonstration by the Hong Kong people on July 1, 2003 gave Chen Shui-bian, his ruling DPP government, and Lee Teng-hui the opportunity to strongly condemn mainland China for its violation of "one country, two systems." Even the opposition parties in Taiwan criticized the "one country, two systems" process without justification, and this at a time when Taiwan was suffering through the severe SARS epidemic and both the ruling and opposition parties were hostile to mainland China. Although these criticisms were unfounded and fraught with contradictions, they produced a negative impact on the Taiwanese people's attitude towards "one country, two systems." In particular, the Hong Kong Democratic Party enjoyed a big gain during the district council election in the latter part of November 2003, and Taiwan authorities made quite a story about it.

Judging from the events cited in this section, the implementation of "one country, two systems" in Hong Kong and Macao have indeed created an impact on the position of the Taiwanese people. So it is that as long as "one country, two systems" can be carried out steadily in Hong Kong and Macao, sooner or later it will serve as a model for Taiwan.

Conclusion

Mainland China proposed to use the "peaceful reunification and one country, two systems" guideline to solve the Taiwan issue during the early 1980s. Since then its position has remained the same. Of course, this insistence on peaceful reunification is due to an unwillingness to fight a war that would certainly affect China's ongoing modernization. But the main concern is that the people on both sides of the issue are Chinese and "Chinese do not fight against Chinese." The "one country, two systems" policy, which will be carried out after the reunification, is intended to reduce the resistance against reunification. It is also a gesture of respect for the Taiwanese people's lifestyle. This might not be the best approach, but it definitely can be viewed as having the best intention.

After Hong Kong and Macao's return and their implementation of "one country, two systems," mainland China cautiously abides by the principles of "high degree of autonomy," "Hong Kong people rule Hong Kong," and

"Macao people rule Macao." This latitude has received recognition from the majority of people in Hong Kong and Macao. Of course, Taiwan's problems are more complicated than those of Hong Kong and Macao. But in the past several years, mainland China has repeatedly made flexible and embracing interpretations about "one China" and has given "two systems" a more relaxed interpretation than it did with Hong Kong and Macao. If the Taiwanese people have the opportunity to understand a bit more about "one country, two systems" and are willing to carefully think about their children's and grandchildren's futures, perhaps they will come to the conclusion that "one country, two systems" is exactly the best choice for solving the Taiwan problem.

CHAPTER 3

THE MAY 17 STATEMENT AND NEW DEVELOPMENTS IN HONG KONG

Both the process and the results of the Taiwan 2004 presidential election have had a great impact on mainland China's push for "peaceful reunification and one country, two systems." Before the election, the Pan-Blue and the Pan-Green candidates competed for pro-independence, escalated the issue of referenda, and proposed the writing of a new Constitution. In addition, Chen Shui-bian proposed "one country on each side." These topics made mainland China uncomfortable. Mainland China deliberately kept a low profile so as to not influence the election but, unexpectedly, Chen Shui-bian won his reelection with the help of the March 19 shooting incident. After the presidential election, there were election disputes and street protests, but mainland China kept a low profile until May 17 when it made a formal statement expressing serious concern on the cross-strait situation and warned Taiwan's new leader about negative consequences.

After the July 1, 2003 demonstration in Hong Kong, the members of the Hong Kong Democratic Party united with those who were dissatisfied with Tung Chee-hwa and demanded that the Hong Kong government proceed with political system reform. As a result, the SCNPC of mainland China interpreted the Hong Kong Basic Law in such a way that it decided that universal suffrage for the 2007 election of the chief executive and for the 2008 reelection of the Legislative Council members would not be permitted. This interpretation of the Basic Law caused dissatisfaction among some Hong Kong people, and simultaneously gave Taiwan and the U.S. the opportunity

43

to again criticize "one country, two systems."

SECTION 1
ABOUT "PLACING HOPE IN THE TAIWANESE PEOPLE" FROM THE MAY 17 STATEMENT

When May 20 approached, mainland China finally altered its attitude of quietly observing changes. In the early morning of May 17, 2004, mainland China made a public statement to Chen Shui-bian about a "strong position on five absolute noes," and to the Taiwanese people about "seven avocations on a bright future." The statement said that in the following four years, anyone who held power in Taiwan must profess that "there is only one China in the world, [and] that the mainland and Taiwan are all part of the same China." As long as the Taiwanese people abandon the stance of Taiwan independence and put a stop to separatist activities, then cross-strait relations will immediately be associated with peace, stability, and development. If the assertations are not made, cross-strait peace, stability, and a mutually beneficial win-win situation will quickly end.

Due to the timing sensitivity of the promulgation of the May 17 Statement, it immediately gained a high degree of attention on the island. The mainstream media prominently published the full article. The political figures of various parties, scholars who specialized in cross-strait relations, and political commentators—in other words, everybody—were competing to make comments. Though the May 17 Statement contained only 1,400 words, it had so many interpretations that it received more attention in Taiwan than almost any other document in recent years.

To Eradicate the Thought of Mainland China's Playing the American Trump Card

In order not to disrupt Taiwan's election and give the DPP a chance to step down and thus reopen the door for cross-strait negotiations, mainland China sent its concerns about Taiwan via the U.S. during the presidential election. It hoped that the election propaganda and referendum pleas would not depart too far from the norm. After the election, Taiwan's disputes continued and its society went through bumps that had never occurred before. But Chen Shui-bian still clamored for the writing of a new Constitution in 2006. Mainland China once again used the military and political influences of the U.S. government on Taiwan to contain Chen Shui-bian's penchant for formulating a new Constitution and hoped that

Taiwan would not seek legal independence. The mainland Chinese leaders asked visiting U.S. Vice President Dick Cheney to ask the American government "not to send wrong messages to the Taiwan independence force." This could be considered as an attempt before May 20, 2004 by mainland China to use America's influence to contain Chen Shui-bian's inaugural speech. The strategy chosen by mainland China of handling Taiwan through the U.S. was described by the Taiwan media as "a new main theme of mainland China's Taiwan policy."

The fact is that mainland China completely understood that the U.S., for its own interests, would not disregard the cross-strait matters. However, since the U.S. established diplomatic relations with mainland China, it has always adhered to the three Joint Communiqués and the One-China Principle. The U.S., of course, has an obligation to tell the Chen Shui-bian government that a promise is not a blank check, even if the Taiwan Relations Act promises to protect Taiwan's safety. Once Chen Shui-bian walks towards Taiwan independence, in order to avoid becoming mainland China's enemy, the U.S. has no obligation to protect Taiwan. Moreover, the fact that Taiwan insists on not recognizing the One-China Principle and not beginning cross-strait negotiations simply shows that Taiwan is depending on the U.S. for its support. If the U.S. government does not state its position, the Taiwan authorities will think that luck is always on their side. Mainland China also does not want to have clashes with the U.S. over the Taiwan issue during the process of its peaceful rise to power. Based on the above considerations, mainland China has exerted pressures on the U.S. and demanded that the country keep its promises to produce an intimidating effect on Taiwan independence. This is logical and has produced a strong effect. However, viewed from the angle of striving for the Taiwan people's loyalty, this American trump card has its limitations and unpleasant side effects.

Before and after the Taiwan election, various levels of U.S. officials took turns proposing wave after wave of warnings to Taiwan authorities. However, they did not clearly state that when Taiwan holds a referendum and enacts a new Constitution the U.S. will not be obligated to protect Taiwan. The U.S. also never considered reducing arms sales to Taiwan. Furthermore, in response to Chen Shui-bian's inaugural speech, which modified the form but not the substance of his independence stance, the U.S. showed "welcome" and "approval." These facts once more proved the Taiwan people's belief held all along: that for its own interests the U.S. does not want the two sides to reunify, and that as long as Taiwan has U.S. support mainland China will not dare threaten Taiwan with force. To avoid becoming involved in the cross-strait clash, the U.S. will, as an interim solution, ask Taiwan not to provoke mainland China. In the long run, the U.S. will continue to protect Taiwan and allow it to remain in a "no reunification, no independence, and no war" state because it results in the greatest benefit to the U.S. Seeing clearly the basic contradiction in the cross-strait matters between the U.S. and mainland China, the Taiwan independence supporters blustered, "Unless mainland China can beat the U.S., it is impossible to have a reunification." Those who long for reunification painfully ask, "When will mainland China confront the U.S.?"

If mainland China continues to play the U.S. trump card, the only outcome will be to contain the rush for Taiwan independence. It will have no effect on enhancing the reunification and, on the contrary, it will create suspicion about the determination and urgency of mainland China's desire for reunification. After this presidential election, some of the Pan-Blue voters finally awoke to see that persistently defending the ROC might not enable them to continue being Chinese in Taiwan. Some people also proposed that "instead of holding ROC's blue flag, we can hold mainland China's red flag." During this period, the May 17 Statement was promulgated appropriately and assisted in the understanding of the Taiwanese people. Even if mainland China uses the American card against Taiwan independence, the leading role for pushing the reunification forward will not be handed over to any other people, and the policy of "placing hope in the Taiwanese people" remains the same.

No "One China," No Negotiation

During the presidential election, Chen Shui-bian bragged that as long as he could be reelected, mainland China would give up, and this would be helpful to the cross-strait reciprocal negotiations. After the election, the political commentators further predicted that since mainland China's "placing hopes in Taiwanese people" agenda was not effective, in the face of the escalation of the Taiwan autonomy ideology, mainland China must make more flexible interpretations of "one China." The media also took the opportunity to publish many articles based on rumor from mainland Chinese scholars that there was a possibility that mainland China would acknowledge that after 1949 Taiwan has become a separate entity. Through media manipulation, this information made more and more people believe that mainland China was in no hurry for reunification. As long as Taiwan does not change its national flag, national title, territorial boundary, and the current situation of the ROC, mainland China will continue to tolerate the situation. There are even people who believe that mainland China will no longer insist on keeping "one China" as the prerequisite for the negotiations, and that "one China" will possibly become an issue to be debated by the two sides.

Those who hope that the two sides can be reunified earlier rather than later would be happy to see mainland policies towards Taiwan become more practical, flexible, and attractive to the Taiwanese people. But, since it proposed the three-sentence theory of "one China" in August 2000, mainland China has changed its previous position of "Taiwan is part of China" to "the mainland and Taiwan all belong to the same China." For nearly four years, the Taiwan authorities did not respond to the three-sentence theory. Even the U.S. think tanks could not understand why Taiwan authorities ignored mainland China's significant expression of goodwill. Perhaps it is that prior to the May 17 Statement, most people did not know that the One-China Principle described by the Taiwan politicians as a threat of extinction was simply that Taiwan and the mainland belong to the same China. After understanding the true meaning of "one China," few Taiwanese people would not recognize themselves as Chinese. Only those who insist on separation from the mainland would consider the "one China" viewpoint tortuous. Although Taiwan leaders speak daily to the need of following the people's will, they refuse to engage in dialogues with the mainland under the guise of not being able to accept "one China." They continue to tell the people that as soon as negotiations begin, Taiwan will be downgraded, localized, and marginalized. This is curious. Why would Taiwan vanish as soon as the two sides begin to talk? In the worst case the two sides will not reach an agreement, produce no result, gain no advantage, and simply waste time! Additionally, exactly what is the meaning of being downgraded? Who will be downgraded? Taiwan's leaders must resolve these questions.

Unless Taiwan is willing to come to the negotiation table and to first express its sincere determination to resolve the cross-strait disputes mainland China does not have to rush to make concessions in the One-China Principle, as this will only make Chen Shui-bian think that his strategy is working and leave him lusting for a mile after gaining an inch. He will use the idea of "one country on each side" to fight a diplomatic war to prove that Taiwan has sovereign independence and to challenge the One-China Principle. The May 17 Statement states that it is possible to discuss issues concerning Taiwan's international living space. As long as Taiwan is willing to go through negotiations it will enjoy advantages, not suffer losses. But if

Taiwan is not willing to negotiate with the mainland, or if it wishes to continue using the U.S. to confront mainland China, it will be difficult to move ahead!

Mainland China Should Continue Attracting the Attention of the Taiwanese People

The May 17 Statement was indeed an important declaration made at a critical moment. It not only gave people a general understanding of the One-China Principle, but the seven suggestions in the statement also helped Taiwanese people to understand why Taiwan cannot walk out. It is Chen Shui-bian who controls Taiwan's mobility; it is not mainland China's unwillingness to establish the cross-strait military mutual trust mechanism. It was Chen Shui-bian's reluctance in ceasing Taiwan independence activities that caused the loss of opportunities. The statement also makes Taiwan peasants aware that their own agricultural products can be exported to the mainland. Although these suggestions have been mainland China's consistent policies towards Taiwan, due to the proper timing of their promulgation and through increased propaganda, the effect on encouraging the Taiwanese people is positive. However, mainland China cannot address the Taiwan issue just by simply making a statement. Instead, it should regularly maintain a direct dialogue with the Taiwanese people. Only by doing so can the policy of "placing hopes in the Taiwanese people" be truly carried out. In particular, the protests gradually subsided following Chen Shui-bian's formal inauguration. The media, academic, and public opinion circles have leaned towards him, causing Taiwan to suffer the surge of a more serious green terror (fascist terror) and requiring the Taiwanese people to be politically correct. If mainland China cannot continue the creation of new topics to attract the Taiwanese people's attention and initiate continuous discussions in the society, the discussions on reunification will become further marginalized and the reunification activities on the island will be more difficult to develop.

Per the May 17 Statement, mainland China should try to find a mechanism that can directly encourage and stimulate the hearts of the Taiwanese people while simultaneously making the effort to encourage Taiwan society to engage in discussions about cross-strait relations and the One-China Principle. In order to achieve this purpose, selected topics must attract the interest of Taiwan's media so that the media will compete to make reports on them. They should include topics that attract the political and academic circles to compete for discussions. Only by doing so will the Taiwanese people have the opportunity to hear and see the related discussions and understand the true content of the mainland China policies instead of blindly trusting politicians' one-sided stories.

Since Chen Shui-bian said in his inaugural speech on May 20, 2004 that, as long as it is acceptable to the 23 million Taiwanese people, any model "would be a workable model." On the next day, the MAC Chairman Jaushieh Joseph Wu, in answering a reporter's question on whether the future models also include "one country, two systems," said, "Any choice or model will not be excluded. But at the present time, 'one country, two systems' does not have a market in Taiwan." Now is the time for direct talks about the model for the cross-strait reunification. Even if Chen Shui-bian's statement was merely well expressed but superficial, why can't mainland China take the false to be true and seriously explain its reunification policy to the Taiwanese people? For example, when the Taiwan authorities declared that "one country, two systems" had no market in Taiwan, mainland China should have used the simplest and easiest method, held a position of working for the well-being of the Taiwanese people, and explained the concrete contents of "one country, two systems" to them. Naturally, in order to achieve this goal mainland China must attract those Taiwanese people who have the willingness to participate and let them take actions to challenge the so-called mainstream Taiwan dream of autonomy by breaking through the green terror within the island.

Deliberations on the Reunification Law Can Ignite Discussions

On May 9, 2004, while meeting with the overseas Chinese in London, Chinese Premier Wen Jiabao openly stated that he would "seriously consider" the research work necessary for writing a reunification law. When *Xinhua News Agency* reported that the overseas Chinese in Panama also supported this proposal, it clearly stated that Wen Jiabao showed approval of the suggestion to enact a reunification law.

In fact, quite a few mainland scholars have long suggested working out a law to serve as the legal basis for pushing forward reunification. While accepting an interview, the president of the Shanghai Institute for East Asian Studies, Zhang Nianchi, stated that the reunification law should include clear definitions on reunification and secession, or Taiwan independence. It should also set the stage for pushing forward the reunification, the definition of each stage of the process, and the methods for pushing forward. At the same time, it should also include the definition and method of anti-Taiwan independence and the legal measures against Taiwan independence actions. He also said that the benefit of formulating the reunification law is to draw clear-cut distinctions for the different stages of the reunification process. This includes different cross-strait conditions during the process and is helpful in easing the Taiwanese's fear of a "one-step solution" (*United Daily News*, 05/11/2004). Hong Kong's *Ming Pao* newspaper also reported that mainland China had already begun preparatory work for the legislation of the national reunification law and that high-ranking officials had paid attention to the draft. The Reunification Law of the People's Republic of China was completed at the end of 2003 by Assistant Professor Yu Yuanzhou of the Law School of Wuhan University at Hu Bei province (*United Daily News*, 05/20/2004). After May 20, Xin Chunying, member of the SCNPC Legal Committee in charge of research work on formulating the reunification law, revealed that while in the past the reunification law existed only at the level of academic discussions, it had entered into the early prepatory stage of legislation. The Legal Committee of the SCNPC is collecting research on suggestions proposed by different circles and is proceeding with its studies. At the present time, though, there is still no legislative timetable (*United Daily News*, 05/22/2004).

As soon as the saying "formulating a reunification law" came out, Taiwan's response was very strong. Some people worried that the reunification law would compress the flexible space that was originally available and that the possibility for seeking compromise would weaken further. Others blamed Chen Shui-bian for his proposal of writing a new Constitution. The Editorial in the *United Daily News* was more cautious. It stated that the reunification law would specify a reunification timetable, assign an "ultimate limit" for the reunification date, or clearly indicate the initiation of a forceful reunification action if Taiwan engages in certain activities (e.g., the referendum for a new Constitution) (*United Daily News, Editorial*, 05/12/2004). Also, some political commentators pretended to kindly advise the mainland Chinese. On one hand they said, "Once there is a reunification law and if someday radical people on the mainland demand that their leaders 'act according to the law,' while high level officials call for 'taking the overall situation into consideration,' wouldn't this law be inflammatory and troublesome?" On the other hand, they maliciously threatened, "If such a law really would be formulated according to the Hong Kong and Macao model by inviting Taiwan individuals as consulting members, who would dare to become a traitor like Wu Sangui in the old history?" (see Xu Shangli's article in *China Times Daily News*, 05/14/2004). Of course, there were also people who honestly said that the formulation of a reunification law was not only an excellent tactic aimed at Taiwan, but also hit "accurately the soft spot of the Taiwan Relations Act passed by the U.S. Congress. It may really work well" (see Loh I-cheng's article in *United Daily News*, 05/14/2004).

From the various immediate responses given above, it is obvious that Taiwan was nervous and mindful about "formulating the reunification law." The media was publishing follow-up reports every day. It is not difficult to imagine that as long as there is continued development, the Taiwanese people will be interested in this topic. This is also the most direct and closely related topic after the familiar terminology of "three links," and "anti-independence" that would have the greatest reaction.

The formulation of the reunification law has significant meanings. First, the reunification law is more active, clear, and practical than anti-independence and enhances reunification based on the plea for nationalism. It also has a larger appeal for the Taiwanese people. Besides, as soon as the legislative actions for the reunification law take place, not only will the reunification positions of mainland China's inner circles be more consistent, but they could also give the mainland Chinese authorities a powerful basis for taking actions toward Taiwan. Next, at this stage, formulating the reunification law is more appropriate than formulating the Taiwan Basic Law. In the past, mainland China hoped to negotiate with Taiwan authorities to achieve a consensus and then to discuss how to draft the Taiwan Basic Law to avoid being thought of as disrespecting the Taiwanese people. In addition, at this stage, formulating the reunification law would be simpler than directly writing the Taiwan Basic Law. After all, it would only involve "one China" and topics relating to the principles of the nation's reunification. As for the concrete contents of the "two systems," they could temporarily wait for later negotiations.

Although it is important to formulate the reunification law, due to its significance it must be discussed and planned thoroughly before a draft is written. After all, legal provisions are not suitable for frequent alterations. Judging from current reports in Taiwan, the drafts of the reunification law proposed by mainland scholars contain different reunification models and schedules. Such pluralistic opinions have attracted the Taiwanese people's attention, but the formulation of the reunification law should not deviate from the content of "one country, two systems" and should be realistically achievable. Furthermore, although the reunification law is internal to mainland China, the Chinese authorities can invite non-governmental Taiwanese representatives to participate in the discussions and planning of this law. Undoubtedly many people are interested in participating in such work.

The Hong Kong demonstration on July 1, 2003 to protest the Basic Law Article 23 legislation and the inefficiency of the government resulted in Hong Kong's democratic faction joining the non-governmental organization against Tung Chee-hwa and demanding universal suffrage for the 2007 chief executive election and a comprehensive direct election for the Legislative Council in 2008. In viewing the uncertainties in Appendix I and Appendix II of the Basic Law regarding the methods of selecting a chief executive and the Legislative Council after 2007, the Committee for the Constitutional Development (CCD), which was established under the Constitutional Affairs Bureau (CAB) of Hong Kong, began researching the related provisions in the Basic Law. They were responsible for collecting opinions on the constitutional development from the various societal circles.

The CCD completed its first report at the end of March 2004. Apart from expressing the Hong Kong government's opinions on legal issues related to the constitutional development in the Basic Law, they also raised five questions. These questions were sent to the SCNPC while the CCD immediately began to explain the laws. After this, Tung Chee-hwa presented his second constitutional development report. The committee voted to pass the report in late April 2004. The report determined that Hong Kong would not have universal suffrage for the chief executive in 2007 nor a complete direct election for all legislators in 2008.

The Process of Explaining and the Result of the Basic Law

This is the second time that the Hong Kong Basic Law was interpreted for the people. At the end of June 2000, the SCNPC responded to the Hong Kong government's demand for interpretations of the resident rights issue for Hong Kong residents' children who live in mainland China.

During the five-day meeting that began on April 2, the SCNPC discussed in great detail the Basic Law methods for selecting the Hong Kong chief executive and the Legislative Council. First, the main work was focused on Item 7 of Appendix I: "If there is a need to amend the method for selecting the chief executives for the terms subsequent to the year 2007, such amendments must be made with the endorsement of a two-thirds majority of all the members of the Legislative Council and the consent of the chief executive, and they shall be reported to the SCNPC for approval." Second, the work regarding Item 3 of Appendix II: "With regard to the method for forming the Legislative Council of the HK SAR and its procedures for voting on bills and motions after 2007, if there is a need to amend the provisions of this annex, such amendments must be made with the endorsement of a two-thirds majority of all the members of the council and the consent of the chief executive, and they shall be reported to the SCNPC for the record." Third, the committee answered the five questions raised by the Hong Kong government. The meeting was presided over by SCNPC Chairman Wu Bangguo. In attendance were more than 150 committee members, three Hong Kong regional representatives to the National People's Congress, and Vice Chairman of the Basic Law Committee Huang Baoxin.

On April 6, the SCNPC offered the following interpretations: 1) The "after 2007" phrase used in the two appendices actually includes the year 2007; 2) Concerning the phrase "if in need" in regards to amending the method and bills for selecting the chief executive and the Legislative Council, the correct interpretation is that voting procedures may or may not be amended; 3) The interpretation deals with stipulations in the appendices that require the endorsement of a two-thirds majority of council members, the consent of the chief executive, the report to the SCNPC for approval or for the record, and the need to apply the necessary legal procedures. These procedures are required for approving the methods of selecting the chief executive and the Legislative Council and of the passage of the Legislative Council's bills and motions. Only after going through the above procedures, including the final approval or note for the record by the SCNPC, can an amendment become effective. The need for an amendment has to first be reported to the SCNPC by the Hong Kong chief executive. Then, according to the stipulations of Article 45 and Article 68 of the Basic Law, it can be confirmed based on the actual condition of the HK SAR and gradual, ordered principles. The Hong Kong government should present amendments to the methods used for selecting the chief executives and the Legislative Council, and for the voting procedures for the legislative bills and their amendments to the Legislative Council; 4) If the methods for selecting the chief executive, forming the Legislative Council, and creating voting procedures for the bills and motions stipulated in the appendices are not to be amended, the provisions in the original appendices remain (www.xinhuanet.com, 04/06/2004).

This interpretation conforms totally to the related stipulations in the Basic Law and the general legal principles. It is a perfect interpretation of the law. First, according to the provisions of Article 158, the interpretation right of the Basic Law belongs to the SCNPC. This time, owing to some ambiguities in the appendices and in order to clarify the legal procedures to further plan election methods, it was necessary for the Hong Kong government to ask the SCNPC questions. The SCNPC responded appropriately by immediately undertaking the task of interpreting the law. Next, let's discuss laws using rules of law. The four explanations completely conform to ordinary legal principles. The criticisms that arose were either mere complaints that the SCNPC should not interpret the law or suppositions that it indicated mainland China's reluctance to allow universal suffrage to Hong Kong. No one questioned the legality and rationality of the content of the interpretation.

The Decision-Making Process for Hong Kong's Implementation of the Universal Suffrage

On April 15, 2004, Tung Chee-hwa sent CAB Secretary Stephen Lam to Beijing to present Hong Kong's second report on constitutional development to the SCNPC. Stephen Lam claimed that from January to April 2004 the CCD interviewed 86 organizations and individuals and received more than 600 opinion letters. The CCD had already turned over the letters to the SCNPC and hoped for a quick reply so that the Hong Kong government could begin research work on amending the election methods (www.info.gov.hk, 04/15/2004).

After receiving the report, the SCNPC immediately assigned its Vice Secretary-General Qiao Xiaoyang to lead a delegation to Shenzhen to listen to opinions from the Hong Kong National People's Congress, the National Committee of Chinese People's Political Consultative Conference, and people from various circles. The SCNPC then decided to convene a special two-day meeting on April 25 and 26. On April 26, before the end of the meeting, the SCNPC approved the report.

After the SCNPC meeting, Qiao Xiaoyang went on to give speeches in Hong Kong, emphasizing that he had the spirit of "seeking truth and working with realities" to talk about the reasoning behind the actions in regard to Hong Kong. He said that he knew more than 60 percent of the people supported universal suffrage but that "a responsible government should do more than listen to the opinions expressed by the polls. Public opinion is only one of the factors to be referenced, but not the only standard" (*United Daily News*, 04/27/2004).

Before the SCNPC made its decision, its members carefully read Hong Kong's second report and listened to the opinions of the people in Hong Kong's various circles. Hence, their decision was not only legal, but also fair and reasonable. Hong Kong's constitutional reform is an inevitable trend. As long as the social conditions continue to mature, universal suffrage can be expected soon.

The Response of the Hong Kong People

The Hong Kong society's responses towards the law interpretation and the absence of immediate change in election methods reflected two extremes. Tung Chee-hwa believed that the law interpretation could effec- tively calm down disputes and assist in Hong Kong's democratic develop- ment. The absence of immediate change in election methods could give Hong Kong ample time to study and plan the law amendment. Elsie Leung, the HK SAR Secretary for Justice, pleaded that the Hong Kong people not accept the Basic Law provisions selectively. Since the power of interpreta- tion of the Basic Law is vested in the SCNPC, as provided by Article 158 of the Basic Law, the Hong Kong people must accept its interpretation. The interpretation of the law does not change the law; therefore, the interpreta- tion alone cannot reduce the rights and freedoms of the residents. Once the Hong Kong government has a better understanding of the appendices, they would be able to draw on all useful opinions and research to amend the elec- tion methods to gradually develop a democratic system that suits Hong Kong's situation (www.xinhuanet.com, 04/06/2004).

The members of the democratic faction, on the other hand, maintained a high profile by claiming that the interpretation of the law damaged the high degree of autonomy of the SAR and that the negation of the 2007 and 2008 universal suffrage deprived Hong Kong people of their voting rights. After the SCNPC's voting decision, members of the Hong Kong frontier formed by the democratic faction announced that in the coming month the members would dress in black whenever they were to appear at public occa- sions in protest. Some Hong Kong media guessed that the SCNPC's inter- pretation of the law and its quick turnaround in the universal suffrage matters were achieved with the hope of closing early to avoid impacting the September Legislative Council election. The Taiwan media publicized these reports and pointed out that several of Hong Kong media's analyses indicated that Beijing's tightening of Hong Kong's democratic development was related to Chen Shui-bian's reelection in Taiwan. Since the Chen Shui-bian government planned to conduct a referendum and write a new Constitution, Beijing had to stabilize the Hong Kong political situation in order to concentrate its energy on confronting the offensive force of Taiwan independence (*China Times Daily News*, 04/07/2004).

The responses by ordinary Hong Kong citizens to the interpretation of the law and the negation of universal suffrage were not as critical as they were for the proposed national security law and the July 1 demonstration. However, some people were dissatisfied. On April 11, 2004, more than 10,000 people protested the SCNPC's interpretation peacefully in the streets. On April 20, the Public Opinion Research Program of Hong Kong University published its Public Opinion Survey, which showed that the law interpretation significantly decreased the Hong Kong people's confidence in the Central People's and the Hong Kong governments. According to the director of the Public Opinion Research Program, the Central People's and the Hong Kong governments "paid a heavy price in terms of gaining the common aspiration of the people" (*China Times Daily News*, 04/21/2004). On April 27, people stood in front of the Hong Kong government building protesting the SCNPC's decision regarding universal suffrage. Considering Hong Kong's public opinion polls over these several years, it was expected that the Hong Kong people would have a short period of dissatisfaction. However, as long as the Hong Kong government insists on reform, public opinion will turn around.

Taiwan's Responses to the Interpretation of the Law

When the interpretation of the law and the decision on universal suffrage came about, the attacks by the Taiwan media and political commentators continued nonstop. Some said, "Hong Kong cannot walk out of its caged politics." Some showed deep sympathy for "the Hong Kong people's sadness." Others said, "Mainland China disappointed the Hong Kong people," hence the Taiwanese people must treasure the democracy they have. Neither the emotional reports nor the inflammatory abuse made clear the background for the interpretation of the law and the decision on universal suffrage, thus depriving the Taiwanese people even a minimal understanding of the Hong Kong government's constitutional reform. At the very least, this looked like another comprehensive Taiwanese tactic to defame "one country, two systems."

Over the years 2000 to 2004, the Chen Shui-bian administration never missed an opportunity to sneer at "one country, two systems." Even before the interpretation of the law, he predicted that the Hong Kong people would not be able to directly elect their chief executive. On the night the interpretation of the law came out, the MAC in Taiwan criticized mainland China by stating, "Mainland China suppressed Hong Kong's democratic development. In the future, the Hong Kong people will worry more that 'one country' is real, but 'two systems' is false." Ye Guohao, a graduate student of the Institute of Sociology at Qinghua University, wrote an article to alert the Taiwan authorities. He said that the SCNPC indeed has the power to interpret the Basic Law and that Taiwan should understand clearly that even members of the Hong Kong Democratic Party support "one country, two systems" and oppose Taiwan independence. Ye Guohao also pointed out that the Taiwan government generally does not understand Hong Kong and often uses Hong Kong's economic decline after its return to China to prove the failure of "one country, two systems." Despite all these arguments by the Taiwan government, apart from their inconsistencies with the reports and the political viewpoints in the international world, they also cannot realistically tell the Taiwanese people why its government opposes "one country, two systems" (*China Times Daily News*, 04/04/2004).

The Taiwan authorities continue to oppose and laugh at "one country, two systems" but do not explain to the Taiwanese people the concept. Hence, it is meaningless to talk about supporting or opposing it. In order to enable the Taiwanese people to make choices and to express confidence in the system, the authorities must educate the people and provide them with the true picture of how "one country, two systems" is carried out in Hong Kong and Macao.

The U.S. Response to the Interpretation of the Law

Since the return of Hong Kong, the U.S. has published a yearly report stating its position on Hong Kong's democratic development and the implementation of "one country, two systems." The U.S. also has repeatedly invited Legislator Martin Lee Chu-ming and other members of the Hong Kong democratic faction to Washington, D.C. On one hand, the U.S. is collecting firsthand information and on the other hand it is establishing the legitimacy of paying attention to Hong Kong's constitutional development.

Directed at the interpretation of the law, Deputy Spokesman of the U.S. State Department, Adam Ereli, stated on April 2, 2004, that the U.S. is paying serious attention to the situation in which a government decision was made to interpret the law on this important political issue before the Hong Kong people could express opinions. Ereli also urged the Beijing authorities not to forget the promised rights and freedoms it had given to the HK SAR government and said that Hong Kong residents should make their own decisions concerning the "speed and scope of its constitutional development." The Hong Kong government immediately responded to Ereli, "The international community should have confidence in the governance of the Hong Kong government, as it continuously and strictly adheres to the Basic Law," and, "The constitutional development of Hong Kong is an internal affair of our country and it is handled by the Central People's Government and the SAR according to the Basic Law. The U.S. government should respect this position and give no intervention" (www.info.gov.hk, 04/03/2004).

On April 26, as soon as the SCNPC's decision was publicized, the U.S. consul in Hong Kong expressed regret and pleaded with mainland China to respect the democratic reform of Hong Kong. Chinese Foreign Minister Li Zhaoxing immediately responded by saying, "This is a matter for China itself. [We will] not allow a foreign country's interference; furthermore, there is no need for it." He also said that democracy is not measured by the volume of a voice or how many noises people can make. Democracy must be carried out by the people themselves, not directed by other countries. He stated that Hong Kong has a good investment environment, which is the result of the Hong Kong residents' wisdom and hard work and not attributable to the Americans and the British. The credit can only be given to the strength of Hong Kong's people; hence, the decision made by the SCNPC decision could not affect the confidence of foreign investors.

The U.S. Assistant Secretary of State for East Asian and Pacific Affairs, James A. Kelly, visited Hong Kong on May 16, 2004 and related the U.S. concern for Hong Kong's constitutional development to Tung Chee-hwa. Later, after the SCNPC negated the double universal suffrage in 2007 and 2008, Kelly told reporters that the U.S. was closely watching Hong Kong's constitutional development. At the present stage, it is too early to judge whether Beijing's decision will damage Hong Kong's autonomy. This would require more research time in order to draw conclusions (*Central News Agency*, 05/16/2004).

During the 166 years that Hong Kong was colonized by Great Britain, the U.S. never spoke to the fact that the Hong Kong people could not directly elect their governors or legislators. Whether they could enjoy democracy and human rights was never questioned. Similarly, the U.S. did not express any opinions during the long period of time when the Hong Kong Basic Law was being drafted and discussed. It was only after Hong Kong finally broke away from colonization and returned to its motherland—

and gradually began to implement democratic systems—that the U.S. has shown serious concern about the rights and benefits of Hong Kong's people. What is the intention of the U.S.? Is it possible that after Great Britain pulled out from Hong Kong, the U.S. felt uncomfortable not being able to take over the benefits left by Great Britain? Perhaps Kelly's friendly gesture in Hong Kong was the U.S. government's attempt to protect Sino-U.S. relations. If the U.S. does not want to make the entire Chinese people, including the Hong Kong people, feel antipathy against it on the subject of the Hong Kong issue, then it should change its "world police" mentality.

An Evaluation of Hong Kong's Constitutional Reform

Hong Kong's commentators said that Tung Chee-hwa's poor performance was the fuse for constitutional reform. But, perhaps the real issue was political figure competition for the directly voted seats of the Legislative Council. In November 2003, the democratic faction obtained a large victory in the District Council's election, boosting their confidence. At the present time, the Hong Kong executive chief is nominated and elected by the NPC's Grand Selection Committee made of 800 people and voted in by them. In the Legislative Council, 24 of the 60 legislators are elected directly while representatives from various organizations choose the rest. In September 2004, the number of legislators directly elected increased to 30. Those dissatisfied with the election method argued that the Grand Selection Committee members were primarily pro-China, who obviously knew Tung Chee-hwa's political ineffectiveness but still cast many votes for him. Citizens also argued that because the legislators selected by the organizations were not elected through universal suffrage, they did not have enough representation and should be eliminated. All 60 legislators, therefore, would be elected directly. In fact, the method of selecting legislators by organizations of different functions was passed by members of the Drafting Committee of the Basic Law after their long-term thinking, discussions, and final vote. It is a product of a high degree of idealism and social justice. Besides, more and more people in countries that do not adopt American-style democracy have realized that universal suffrage and every ballot being counted equally may not be the best way to select suitable legislative representatives. The purpose of using two kinds of votes is to lower the negative effect of complete universal suffrage.

Summarizing the previous discussions, the SCNPC's responsible interpretation of the Basic Law is a milestone for Hong Kong's constitutional development. After the interpretation of the law, the SCNPC examined the reports presented by Hong Kong and decided on a schedule for carrying out universal suffrage with the utmost speed. The SCNPC's actions showed that the Chinese Central People's Government attaches importance to Hong Kong's public opinion and its future constitutional development. If any political party in Hong Kong wants to push for direct election of the chief executive and all seats of the Legislative Council, it should seek a social consensus in a manner that does not violate the provisions of the Basic Law. It should avoid tarnishing Hong Kong's constitutional development by imposing oversimplified, populist slogans that incite those Hong Kong people who lack the understanding of the Basic Law to protest.

In Taiwan, those who care about Hong Kong's democracy should not overlook the Hong Kong people's recognition of mainland China and their longing for democracy. Some worry that if Taiwan implements "one country, two systems" the Taiwanese people will lose their rights of direct and universal suffrage. Such concern is unnecessary. Judging from the Taiwanese people's superstition about democracy and their fanaticism about elections, when the day comes for the two sides to negotiate the "two systems," it is certain that absolutely no one would dare to suggest changing Taiwan's election system. As to whether this kind of election can transform Taiwan into a more democratic, more just, and more harmonious society, that is a different matter!

Conclusion

The promulgation of the May 17 Statement not only took into account Chen Shui-bian's May 20 inaugural speech, but it was also mainland China's important declaration on Taiwan policy. At the most appropriate time it destroyed Taiwan's "win by chance" mentality. The May 17 Statement clearly instructs mainland China to absolutely not give its self-guiding power on the reunification task to others and to continue its policy of "placing hope in the Taiwanese people." Hopefully mainland China can continue to make direct pleas to the Taiwanese people in order to initiate the trend for discussing the reunification theory on the island.

Hong Kong's practice of "one country, two systems" has been tested and has gained much attention up to the present day. As long as Hong Kong maintains its prosperity and stability, and the government adheres to the Hong Kong Basic Law, the practice of Hong Kong's "one country, two systems" will become the example for Taiwan's implementation of "one country, two systems."

PART II

The U.S. Positions on the Cross-Strait Dilemma and "One Country, Two Systems"

Chinese reunification is an internal matter between the people on the two sides of the Taiwan Strait. Nevertheless, whether viewed from a historical or realistic perspective, one must admit that the U.S. attitude toward China's reunification will impact the cross-strait reunification. This unfortunate reality has compelled people to pay attention to China-U.S.-Taiwan relations during the past half-century and to the future development of these relations.

Over the past 50 years, the U.S. government has made several large-scale adjustments in dealing with China-U.S.-Taiwan relations. These adjustments were based on international situations, cross-strait relations, and America's strategic needs, economic interests, and security considerations. Mainland China recognizes the Taiwan issue as the most important and sensitive aspect of Sino-U.S. relations. To maintain a friendly relationship with mainland China, since the beginning of the 1990s the U.S. has maintained its position of promoting "one China, cross-strait dialogue, and peaceful resolution." However, since cross-strait relations directly affect its own interests in many ways, the U.S. has been suspected of political double-dealing.

The scope of the China-U.S.-Taiwan relations is very broad. The next chapter is an overview of U.S. positions regarding China's reunification from the 1990s to the present. Chapter 5, then, will deal with U.S. think tanks and scholars and how they have influenced the China-U.S.-Taiwan triangular relationship.

CHAPTER 4

THE U.S. GOVERNMENT'S POSITIONS ON CHINA'S REUNIFICATION

SECTION 1
A REFLECTION ON CHINA-U.S.-TAIWAN RELATIONS (1950–1990)

In June 1950, U.S. President Harry S. Truman dispatched the 7th Fleet into the Taiwan Strait and sent the 13th Aviation Brigade to station in Taiwan. On December 2, 1954, the U.S. and the ROC signed a mutual defense treaty, placing Taiwan under U.S. protection.

In order to ease the nervous cross-strait situation and to solve the dispute between the two countries, mainland China began a dialogue with the U.S. in the 1950s. From August 1955 to February 1970, the U.S. and mainland China held 136 ambassador-level talks, though they have achieved no progress on the issue of easing and eliminating cross-strait tension. At the end of the 1960s and in the early 1970s, in response to changing international developments and the growing strength of mainland China, the U.S. began to adjust its mainland China policy. A thawing of the frozen relations between the two countries gradually materialized. On October 25, 1971, the 26th UN Congress passed UN General Assembly Resolution 2758 (XXVI), restoring all lawful rights of the PRC in the UN, and expelled forthwith the representatives of Taiwan, the Republic of China. In February 1972, U.S. President Richard M. Nixon visited mainland China. On February 28, the U.S. and mainland China promulgated a joint communiqué in Shanghai (popularly known as the Shanghai Communiqué). In the communiqué, "The U.S. side declared: The United States acknowledges that all Chinese on either side of the Taiwan Strait maintain there is but one China and that Taiwan is a part of China. The U.S. government does not challenge that position."

On December 6, 1978, the U.S. government accepted the three principles proposed by China for establishing a diplomatic relationship; 1) that the U.S. and Taiwan terminate their diplomatic relationship; 2) that the U.S. and Taiwan abolish the mutual defense treaty; and 3) the U.S. withdraw troops from Taiwan. The U.S. and the PRC agreed to recognize each other and to establish diplomatic relations as of January 1, 1979. The joint communiqué on the Establishment of Diplomatic Relations between the PRC and the U.S. stated the following: "The United States of America recognizes the government of the People's Republic of China as the sole legal government of China. Within this context, the people of the United States will maintain cultural, commercial, and other unofficial relations with the people of Taiwan," and, "The government of the United States of America acknowledges the Chinese position that there is but one China and [that] Taiwan is part of China." Subsequently, the U.S. terminated its diplomatic relationship with the Republic of China.

On April 1, 1979, about three months after the U.S. and mainland China established diplomatic relations, the U.S. Congress passed the Taiwan Relations Act in an attempt to continue maintaining the relationships between the U.S. and the Taiwanese people. The Taiwan Relations Act was enacted in a style similar to that of U.S. domestic laws and the act eliminated the mutual defense treaty. However, the act stated, "The absence of diplomatic relations or recognition shall not affect the application of the laws of the United States with respect to Taiwan, and the laws of the United States shall apply with respect to Taiwan in the manner that the laws of the United States applied with respect to Taiwan prior to January 1, 1979." The U.S. government has adhered to this law, continues to provide Taiwan with arms, and guarantees Taiwan's security. According to this act, the American Institute in Taiwan (AIT), which began operating in Washington, D.C., and Taiwan, also set up the Coordination Council of North American Affairs (the current name is the Taipei Economic and Cultural Representative Office) in the U.S. to handle matters on both sides. On April 16, 1979, the AIT office in Taipei officially began its operations.

The U.S. and Chinese governments conducted negotiations and finally reached an agreement on August 17, 1982, regarding the issue of the U.S.

arms sales to Taiwan. Both unveiled the third Sino-U.S. joint communiqué, abbreviated as the China-U.S. August 17 Communiqué. In the communiqué, the U.S. government stated that "it does not seek to carry out a long-term policy of arms sales to Taiwan, that its arms sales to Taiwan will not exceed, either in qualitative or in quantitative terms, the level of those supplied in recent years since the establishment of diplomatic relations between the United States and China, and that it intends to reduce gradually its sales of arms to Taiwan, leading over a period of time to a final resolution." However, over the more than 20 years since these stipulations were set, the U.S. has continued to sell huge amounts of arms to Taiwan. Mainland China sees this as a barrier to solving the Taiwan problem.

SECTION 2:
U.S. POLICIES ON CHINA'S REUNIFICATION ISSUE AFTER 1990

Immediately before and after 1990, the East European communist regimes and the Union of Soviet Socialist Republics (USSR) collapsed. The Cold War era, which had lasted more than 40 years, finally ended. The international system transformed from two polarized superpowers to multi-faceted collaborations, and the U.S. became the sole superpower in the world. Facing this new international situation, the Sino-U.S. relationship became a key issue in America's quest to develop a worldwide strategy.

The "China card" became useless after the collapse of the USSR. America could not stop paying attention to the rising mainland China. Some Americans felt that mainland China could become the second strongest country (in economy and military forces) and play a very important role in the new world. That is, mainland China might no longer be the strategic military ally of the U.S.; it could become a long-term enemy.

The "China Threat" Theory and the U.S. Policies on Mainland China and Taiwan

In 1993, *New York Times* reporter Nicholas D. Kristof, who once lived in Beijing, became the first to point out that mainland China could fill the power vacuum left in the Asia-Pacific Region after the retreat of the U.S. and Russia, and could further expand its interests in this area and become the dominant power. British military strategic expert Gerald Segal said, "In the twenty-first century, no military strategic challenge could become more important than adjusting to the rise of mainland China." U.S. Atlantic Council researcher Mike Pillsbury suggested that if the GDP of mainland China exceeds that of

America's in 2020 as expected, then mainland China will be in a position to threaten U.S. interests. By then, mainland China may blockade Taiwan, or even initiate military attacks against Taiwan, and severely threaten its neighboring countries in Asia. Based on the aforementioned reasons, the "China threat" took shape and subsequently the "containing China" argument appeared in the international forum.

The Economist in Britain and the weekly *Time Magazine* in the U.S. continued to harp on "containing China." The July 1995 issue of *The Economist* even used "containing China" as the cover-page headline and *Time Magazine* made ripples across the ocean with its special article, "Why Should We Contain Mainland China?" by Charles Krauthammer. *The Economist* agreed with the policy of economic collaboration with mainland China but felt that mainland China had no right to threaten its neighboring countries. These policies are not contradictory: An economic link with China together with a strategic containment would make the policy complete. Krauthammer's analysis in *Time Magazine* was derived from a historic angle. He saw the general expansion of mainland China's influence as a parallel, gradual threat. This wildly ambitious strong power requires quick and rigorous containment. Richard Bernstein and Ross Munro, joint authors of the book *The Coming Conflict with China* (1997), analyzed mainland China's enormous changes in national strength, military power, and strategic thinking during this time. They also predicted that it was very likely that mainland China would attack Taiwan with force and incite a Sino-U.S. war. This book is largely viewed as a representative piece of the "China threat" theory.

In March 1997, in response to the aforementioned *Time Magazine* article, the bimonthly *Foreign Affairs* published a special issue on the "China threat" theory. Samuel P. Huntington's *The Clash of Civilizations and the Remaking of World Order* analyzed the situation from a cultural angle and stated that China could threaten Western civilization, thus providing a theoretical basis for the "China threat" theory.

It is important to note that not all Americans accept the "containing China" argument. The Cold War era diplomatic policymakers Henry A. Kissinger and Alexander N. Haig Jr. and many liberal scholars, for example, strongly question this argument. After cautious evaluations, the Clinton administration developed a "constructive engagement" policy to be used in developing relations with mainland China. In October 1995, U.S. Defense Minister William J. Perry made a speech at The National Committee on U.S.-China Relations entitled "Active Contact with Mainland China Is neither Containment nor Appeasement," in which he pointed out that active contact with mainland China would make the U.S. take constructive steps to protect its national interests.

In June 1995, President William J. Clinton permitted Lee Teng-hui to make a private visit to the U.S. for the purpose of participating in an alumni reunion event at Cornell University as a distinguished alumnus. Lee Teng-hui took the opportunity to brag about the ROC in Taiwan. Although the U.S. State Department repeatedly argued that Lee Teng-hui's visit was strictly private, mainland China saw it as the U.S. violating the "one China" policy and hence summoned its U.S. Ambassador back to Beijing in protest. Mainland China also temporarily suspended mutual visits at high levels as well as military exchanges. Afterwards, both sides went through many high-level negotiations before finally settling the political turbulence.

In March 1996, Taiwan held its first direct presidential election and the clash between the U.S. and mainland China began again. Mainland China was dissatisfied with Lee Teng-hui's repeated statements during the election about splitting Taiwan from China and announced that it would hold a missile exercise near the Taiwan Strait as a retaliation. Although mainland China informed the U.S. in advance that this exercise would not create a military threat, the U.S. still expressed "serious concern" and dispatched two fleets of combat jet aircraft carriers to cruise near the Taiwan Strait and avoid the accidental sparking of a war. The U.S. declared its determination to protect Taiwan's security and maintain peace in the Asia-Pacific region. During this period, both sides were able to keep self-control and avoid clashes. After mainland China ended its exercise, the U.S. carriers sailed away. In order to prevent a recurrence of the rift, both sides agreed to clarify their positions in a "Taiwan issue" meeting.

In May 1996, U.S. Secretary of State Warren Christopher outlined a few key points of the U.S. Taiwan policy:

1. Prevent mainland China from using force at the Taiwan Strait
2. Keep the current Taiwan Strait status quo
3. Provide Taiwan with sufficient defense weapons
4. Continue adhering to the "one China" policy and keeping active contact with mainland China using the good relations between Washington and Beijing to safeguard Taiwan
5. Confirm Taiwan's behaviors in the international community with the "one China" policy.

The Clinton administration repeatedly emphasized the U.S. "one China" policy prerequisite, that mainland China promises to solve the Taiwan issue peacefully, and Taiwan's behavior in the international community should conform to the One-China Principle. If this prerequisite is not met, the Taiwan Relations Act cannot be carried out. In short, the U.S. believes that the One-China Principle conforms to the interests of the three sides: the U.S., mainland China, and Taiwan. As a result, the U.S. cannot support Taiwan's participation in international organizations, such as the UN, whose membership requirement is "statehood." The U.S. can only help Taiwan participate in functional international organizations, such as the World Trade Organization (WTO), whose membership does not require "statehood."

Warned by the previous Taiwan Strait crisis and the intense situation on the Korean Peninsula, the U.S. revised The Guidelines for U.S.-Japan Defense Cooperation. On September 23, 1997, new guidelines were formally published. The change came in the original phrase "the U.S.-Japan cooperation when an incident takes place in the Far East" being edited to "the cooperation when an incident takes place in the region surrounding Japan and has an important impact on Japan's surrounding area's peace and security." The scope of the U.S.-Japan peace protection cooperation was expanded to the Korean Peninsula, Taiwan, and Penghu. Mainland China reacted very strongly to these guidelines, stating that Taiwan and Penghu are its territories and that the U.S. and Japan should not expand the bilateral defense zone to mainland China's territory.

Clinton and Jiang Held a Summit and the Three Noes Policy

Mainland China and the U.S. issued a joint statement on October 29, 1997, following White House talks between visiting Chinese President Jiang Zemin and U.S. President Clinton. After the talks, they held a joint press conference. In summary, they reached some degree of consensus on the Taiwan issue and then separately declared their own positions:

- Mainland China stresses that the Taiwan question is the most important and sensitive central question in Sino-U.S. relations, and that the proper handling of this question must be in strict compliance with the principles set forth in the three Sino-U.S. joint communiqués which hold the key to stable growth of Sino-U.S. relations.

- The United States reiterates that it adheres to its "one China" policy and the principles set forth in the three Sino-U.S. joint communiqués and does not support Taiwan's independence or its wish to become a UN member. The U.S. also states that it would adhere to the principles set forth by the China-U.S. August 17 Communiqué in handling the issue of arms sales to Taiwan.

At the press conference, Clinton stated that he hoped the PRC and Taiwan would soon resume a constructive cross-strait dialogue and expand cross-strait exchanges. He said that the U.S. "one China" policy could provide a solution for both sides because, within the context of the one-China policy as articulated in the three communiqués and the Taiwan Relations Act, the U.S. could maintain friendly and open relations with the people of Taiwan and mainland China. But, the U.S. understands that this issue must be resolved peacefully by the people from both sides of the strait—and the sooner the better.

Jiang Zemin stated that the Taiwan issue involves China's sovereignty. Mainland China intends to adhere to "one country, two systems" to achieve a peaceful resolution, but it cannot promise to renounce the use of force. However, this decision is aimed at the interference of foreign powers and pro-independence people, not the Taiwan compatriots.

China expert Kenneth G. Lieberthal described the Clinton-Jiang meeting as "normalization for the second time" of Sino-U.S. relations. From this time on, Taiwan could seek its own fortune only with diplomatic maneuvers. This is because, after the Clinton-Jiang talks, Sino-U.S. relations gradually stepped towards a "constructive strategic partnership."

Afterwards, U.S. Secretary of Defense William J. Perry transmitted a message to Taiwan saying that mainland China was willing to unconditionally resume the cross-strait talks. But, mainland China's Foreign Ministry spokesman Shen Guofang later clarified, "'one China' is the reality, not the condition. Both sides must recognize the 'one China' reality to be able to resume the dialogue."

In January 1998, the U.S. AIT/Washington Chairman Richard Bush made a speech at the Taiwanese-American Chamber of Commerce in Los Angeles regarding U.S. and Taiwan relations, in which he stated that the U.S. would not do anything that might harm Taiwan. He stressed that the U.S. wished for permanent peace in the Taiwan Strait and the guaranteed security of the Taiwanese people. The Clinton administration then worked hard on these unchanged goals: 1) continue to require the two sides to avoid provoking each other and to solve the source of the conflict peacefully; 2) facilitate the communications and understanding of each side by correcting each other's misunderstandings; 3) hope that both sides remain flexible in solving the problems; 4) provide a favorable environment and encourage the two sides to resume talks, increasing the likelihood of resuming negotiations.

During the second half of June 1998, Clinton visited mainland China.

On June 27, Clinton and Jiang Zemin held a joint press conference and called on the mainland and Taiwan to resume peace talks. In Shanghai on June 30 Clinton participated in the roundtable seminar, "Constructing China for the 21st Century," sponsored by the Shanghai Library. He talked about the Three Noes policy on Taiwan (no support for Taiwan's independence, no support for "two Chinas" or "one China, one Taiwan," and no support for Taiwan to enter international organizations that require statehood). He reiterated the U.S. desire to see cross-strait issues resolved in a peaceful manner. Afterwards the U.S. government emphasized that Clinton's Three Noes policy was simply a reiteration of the U.S. "one China" policy; however, this was the first time that the U.S. clearly stated its position of not supporting Taiwan independence or two Chinas or "one China, one Taiwan" or Taiwan entering international organizations that require statehood. This was a big blow to Taiwan.

The U.S. Response to Lee Teng-hui's "Special State-to-State Relationship" Talk

On July 9, 1999, Lee Teng-hui unveiled the "special state-to-state relationship." Mainland China immediately responded, demanding that Lee Teng-hui withdraw the "two-state theory" and that the U.S. adhere to the three Sino-U.S. joint communiqués and related promises.

On July 13, U.S. State Department spokesman James P. Rubin reiterated America's "one China" policy: that the cross-strait issue be solved by both sides and that the U.S. insists that the problem be resolved peacefully. On July 15, during a routine briefing, Rubin reiterated the related clauses in the Taiwan Relations Act. He pointed out that the U.S. insists on opposing the use of force, but he also emphasized that the U.S. does not support Taiwan independence.

On July 18, Jiang Zemin agreed to speak with Clinton on the phone. Clinton said that he proposed the call to Jiang Zemin in order to reiterate America's resolute promise of a "one China" policy and to emphasize that the U.S. did not change its Taiwan policy. Jiang Zemin pointed out that Lee Teng-hui openly described the cross-strait relations as a state-to-state relationship, which he described as a very dangerous step in the country's walk towards secession. It also posed a serious challenge to the internationally recognized One-China Principle. Mainland China's basic guideline for solving the Taiwan issue is still "peaceful reunification and one country, two systems." Mainland China does not promise to renounce the use of force, since there is a force trying to split Taiwan away from her motherland in Taiwan and in the international community. Mainland China absolutely will not sit back and twiddle its thumbs as Taiwan walks towards independence and foreign powers interfere with China's reunification. Jiang Zemin also said that in America, anti-Chinese opinion is still rampant. To this day, there are still people who advocate Taiwan's independence. History has proved that the handling of the Taiwan issue will directly influence the progress of the Sino-U.S. relations. Let's hope that the U.S. will earnestly adhere to the three Sino-U.S. joint communiqués and the Three Noes policy.

Clinton Vetoed the Taiwan Security Enhancement Act

In March 1999, the U.S. Congress passed a resolution bill entitled Commemoration of the 20th Anniversary of the Taiwan Relations Act. In March and May, a small number of people in the Senate and House proposed the Taiwan Security Enhancement Act, which advocated strengthening Taiwan's military power. Some U.S. congressmen were trying to bring Taiwan into the theater missile defense (TMD) system and sell Taiwan submarines and other advanced armaments. They even demanded that direct U.S.-Taiwan military contacts be established to enhance the cooperation. On February 1, 2000, the U.S. House passed this bill. The bill has six portions, including training the Taiwan military and selling defensive weapons and services to Taiwan, evaluating Taiwan's defense needs, strengthening Taiwan's defense, and reporting on the U.S. capabilities to respond to emergency situations in the Asia-Pacific region.

On February 2, Vice Foreign Minister Yang Jiechi summoned U.S. Ambassador Richard Holbrooke to engage in solemn talks about the U.S. House passage of the Taiwan Security Enhancement Act. On February 3, during a regular briefing, James P. Rubin commented on the Taiwan Security Enhancement Act, declaring the U.S. position of not supporting the act. He emphasized that the Taiwan Relations Act had operated well and that change was unnecessary. The White House also reiterated that President Clinton would veto the Taiwan Security Enhancement Act (China Times Daily News, 02/04/2000).

Clinton Signed the "Support Taiwan's Entry into the World Health Organization Bill"

In December 1999, Clinton signed for the first time the Support Taiwan's Entry into the World Health Organization Bill. From then on, the State Department would report to Congress the efforts made by the executive branch in its support of Taiwan's entry into international organizations, especially the World Health Organization (WHO). Clinton also signed the 2000 General Appropriation Act, which contained clauses for the support of Taiwan's entry into the WHO. This act stipulates that the State Department sends a report to Congress every six months and informs the various executive branches of the State Department about its efforts to support Taiwan's entry into international organizations of sovereign countries. On December 10, Yang Jiechi raised a strong protest and accused the U.S. government of acting in violation of the three Sino-U.S. joint communiqués and the related U.S. promises, a serious interference in China's reunification.

Despite mainland China's strong protest, President George W. Bush signed similar bills in 2002 and 2003. These bills have given Taiwan, which always wanted to participate in the WHO, strong encouragement. In June 2003, Taiwan used the excuse of having a severe SARS epidemic and utilized all available methods to try to become a participating member in the WHO's annual meeting. Without the support of enough countries, Taiwan was not granted admission. Chen Shui-bian hence proposed using a referendum to enter the WHO.

The Bush Administration's Policies toward Mainland China and Taiwan

On January 17, 2001, U.S. Secretary of State nominee Colin L. Powell attended a confirmation hearing at the Senate Foreign Relations Committee in the Congress. He said that America acknowledges that there is only one China and, as such, Taiwan is part of China. Within this context, the two sides of the Taiwan Strait could make decisions for themselves and resolve differing opinions using methods other than force. In the meantime, the U.S. would also support Taiwan according to the Taiwan Relations Act and the content of the three communiqués to provide Taiwan's defense needs.

On January 25, U.S. State Department spokesman Richard Boucher related the following in a routine briefing: The newly named Secretary of State Colin L. Powell met mainland China's Ambassador Li Zhaoxing in Washington on January 24 and stated that the U.S. did not treat mainland China as an unavoidable enemy; the U.S. would adhere to the One-China Principle and fulfill its obligation in providing Taiwan's defense needs; and although the U.S. and mainland China had differing opinions, its own position was clear and firm. In April 2001, the Sino-U.S. relations turned sour due to the plane collision incident. Bush publicly announced, "We will do everything in our power to assist Taiwan's defense."

In May 2002, the U.S. State Department published the report, "The Military Power of the People's Republic of China." In it, the U.S. accused mainland China of hiding its military development and warned mainland China against serious future threats to global security. In July, the U.S.-China Security Review Commission of the U.S. Congress presented its "Report on U.S.-China Relations." The report warned that investments in mainland China by the U.S., Japan, and Taiwan in high-tech industries might encourage the growth of such industries in mainland China and create a potential concern for U.S. national security. The report also stated that the U.S. China policy might encourage mainland China to become a nation that could challenge the U.S. in economic, political, and military areas. With U.S. Congressional authorization, the U.S.-China Security Review Commission was established in 2000. Its main task was to review the impact of U.S.-China economic and trade exchanges on U.S. national security. The commission was made up of 11 members, almost equally Democrats and Republicans.

On September 21, 2002, President Bush promulgated the 33-page "National Security Strategy of the United States of America" document. This report made clear that the U.S. military strategy has changed in favor of preemptive strikes against hostile states that develop large-scale weapons of mass destruction and terrorist groups. He also declared for the first time that the U.S. would definitely not allow its military supremacy to be challenged, as was seen in the Cold War era. In response to other countries' criticisms, he insisted that the U.S. would use its military and economic power to support free and open societies instead of seeking "unilateral superiority." The report describes this strategy as "a distinctly American internationalism" that reflects the union of U.S. values and national interests.

This document unveiled a powerful and offensive strategy to maintain U.S. national security; its forcefulness has not been seen since the Reagan era. The report downplayed most of the weapon nonproliferation treaties and advocated an "anti-proliferation" principle that included everything from TMD to dismantling weaponry or parts via compulsory means. It claimed that the "contain and intimidate" tactic used by the U.S. since 1940 has almost ended. In this strategy document, one of the portions that deserves in-depth attention is the passage, "We do not intend to allow the strength of any foreign superpower to catch up with the U.S. in order to keep the large-scale leading strength enjoyed by the U.S. since the collapse of the USSR over ten years ago." Further, "Our troops will be so strong as to be able to prevent potential enemies expanding their armaments in order to override the U.S. strength or be comparable with it." Since no country has had the financial strength to compete with the U.S. in its military expenditure, hence this statement was regarded as singling out mainland China. Most of the document emphasized the aspects of how to win an "ideological" war via operations of public diplomacy, foreign aid, IMF, and World Bank—including "a war for the future of Islam." Many passages in this document express that when important U.S. interests are threatened there can be absolutely no compromise. Although the U.S. promises to seek allied assistance in confronting terrorism, "if it is necessary we will take our own actions without hesitation preemptively to execute our rights of self-defense." This includes "to persuade or compel some countries to bear their supreme responsibilities, not to assist terrorists" (*China Times Daily News*, 09/21/2002).

On June 30, 2003, Richard Boucher announced that beginning on July 1, those countries not willing to sign an agreement that prevents U.S. soldiers from receiving international criminal court sentences would lose U.S. military assistance. However, this rule does not apply to some countries, including North Atlantic Treaty Organization (NATO) countries, some non-NATO U.S. allies, and Taiwan. On July 1, a Taiwanese delegate upon returning from a U.S. visit confirmed that the U.S. would continue its arms sales to Taiwan, though with some changes in priority orders. The U.S. wanted Taiwan to purchase C4ISR systems (Program of Po Sheng), anti-missile systems (Patriot III, Anti-Missile Defense Systems), and anti-submarine warfare patrol aircraft (P-3C). Note that the submarines and Aegis destroyers that Taiwan desired were not among the top three items on the list.

The Bush/Hu Meeting and the Ensuing U.S. Cross-Strait Policy

On June 1, 2003, when U.S. President Bush met with PRC President Hu Jintao in Evian, France, he declared for the first time his insistence on "one China," and he listed together "disagreeing with Taiwan independence," the three Sino-U.S. joint communiqués, and the Taiwan Relations Act. In terms of assisting Taiwan's self-defense, Bush only said that, "If necessary, the U.S. will try to help Taiwan's self-defense." Hu Jintao reported that Taiwan does not accept the One-China Principle and continues to promote alienation activities. This results in apprehension towards the cross-strait situation and the poor relationship between the two sides. China expressed hope that the U.S. would adhere to the "one China" promise, properly handle the Taiwan issue, and not give the wrong messages to the Taiwan independence supporters.

On June 5, 2003, Therese Shaheen held her first press conference after taking the post of AIT Chairperson in Washington, D.C., and said that there is no change in American policy. Bush's statement does not have any hidden information and Taipei has not done anything that requires Bush to emphasize not supporting Taiwan independence. The "one China" policy includes the Taiwan Relations Act and the three joint communiqués. If necessary, the U.S. would help Taiwan to defend itself. Shaheen concluded by stating that the U.S. has always emphasized a peaceful resolution of the cross-strait disputes and that its Taiwan policy "has absolutely not changed."

After hearing pro-independence Chen Shui-bian's announcement of a referendum vote in June 2003, the U.S. showed opposition and further reminded him to firmly adhere to the Four Noes and One Without rule stated in his 2000 presidential inauguration speech and not to let the cross-strait relations step over the "red line." Afterwards, some of the U.S. incumbent officials, former officials, and think-tank members visited Taiwan in an attempt to persuade Chen Shui-bian to withdraw his talk about a referendum. Chen Shui-bian also sent Chiu Yi-ren to the U.S. to explain that a referendum is only campaign language and that the U.S. need not worry about it.

Boucher confirmed on July 24, 2003, that Director of the PRC Taiwan Affairs Office Chen Yunlin and Deputy Director Zhou Minwei visited the State Department on July 21. There they discussed the cross-strait issues with high-level officials like Deputy Secretary of State Richard Lee Armitage and Assistant Secretary of State for East Asian and Pacific Affairs James Kelly. Chen Yunlin and Zhou Minwei reported that Chen Shui-bian's insistence on a referendum was meant to provoke "gradual Taiwan independence" and would cross the "red line" tolerated by mainland China, creating regional tension. Mainland China would not simply sit and watch. It hoped that the U.S. would also take responsive measures.

After August 2003, following Chen Shui-bian's numerous actions on the referendum and on formulating a new Constitution, the U.S. refrain of hoping "not to change the current status quo" became more frequent. On September 29, Boucher read out Chen Shui-bian's Four Noes and One Without promulgation item by item. During a White House briefing, National Security Advisor Condoleezza Rice prudently emphasized, "Nobody, nobody is allowed to change the [Taiwan Strait] status quo unilaterally."

On October 19, Bush met with Hu Jintao and, afterwards, the briefing of the White House senior officials reiterated that the U.S. "does not support Taiwan independence."

On November 19, 2003, aiming at the warning by Vice Minister of the PRC Taiwan Affairs Office, Wang Zaixi said that "Taiwan independence is war." Adam Ereli stated in a routine press briefing that he had already read mainland China's warning statement. He said, "I want to reiterate the U.S. policy on this issue: Using force to solve the cross-strait disputes is not acceptable." Ereli also stated that the U.S. "opposes" any attempt by either of the two sides to unilaterally change the current situation of the Taiwan Strait. The U.S. believes that it is necessary to have the two sides engage in dialogues to keep the peace and stability of the Taiwan Strait (*United Daily News*, 11/19/2003). Finally, Ereli said that "we oppose anyone on either side of the Taiwan Strait who attempts to change the status quo unilaterally."

On November 20, Deputy Assistant Secretary for East Asian and Pacific Affairs Randy Shriver held a special press briefing for the Taiwan reporters stationed in Washington to explain two issues. First, regarding the ongoing Taiwan election, the U.S. would remain neutral: "Any attempt to read into U.S. statements or actions and turn them into any other position is just flat wrong." Next, he said, "We firmly oppose the use of force in settling the differences between the two sides of the Taiwan Strait." Referring to the Taiwan Relations Act, he pointed out, "Any threat to use force against Taiwan is of grave concern to the United States, and . . . we will only support a peaceful approach to resolving the differences." He also said, "This is not only our law. It is embedded in our policy."

In answering reporters' questions, Shriver reiterated the U.S. position several times: "We oppose the use of force and we do not support Taiwan independence." Concerning Chen Shui-bian's referenda as well as the new Constitution, Shriver said, "We have been clear on our position regarding independence. We do not support independence. So if any of these efforts touches on Taiwan's status in a way that leads it towards independence, we're not going to be supportive of that." He stated several times that "the policy, as determined by the president, is: We do not support Taiwan independence." Shriver also said that the current situation is different from the Taiwan Strait crisis in 1996 and that, to his knowledge, no plans or arrangements were being made for special deployments or anything along those lines by the U.S. military. But, according to the Taiwan Relations Act, the U.S. must maintain the capacity to resist force that may endanger Taiwan's security, and this responsibility falls on the shoulders of its commander of the Pacific Command (*China Times Daily News*, 11/22/2003).

SECTION 3
DISCUSSION OF U.S. GOVERNMENT POLICIES
TOWARD CHINA'S REUNIFICATION ISSUE

From the manner in which the U.S. has dealt with the cross-strait affairs for more than a decade, we can understand that the U.S. cross-strait policies are continuous. Although varying somewhat—and only to accommodate its own needs and interests—the U.S. has not actually deviated from the One-China Principle.

The Basic U.S. Cross-Strait Policies Are Not Altered

President Clinton once said that "one China" is an important policy that has been adhered to for six presidential terms and by both parties. It is the basis for guaranteeing Sino-U.S. relations and the safety of the Taiwan Strait, and it need not be changed. This policy was confirmed in the 2000 American presidential election. Both candidates George W. Bush and Al Gore agreed that the two sides should engage in dialogues and find peaceful resolution. Keeping its own interest in mind, the U.S. also encouraged the two sides to keep the condition "without reunification, without independence, and without war." This, of course, will contain mainland China for the long term and also keep Taiwan as an "unsinkable aircraft carrier." The U.S. hoped to utilize Taiwan's "democratic experience" to push mainland China's "peaceful reform." However, following mainland China's growing political and economic strengths, the U.S. realized that if Sino-U.S. relations continued to deteriorate due to the unsettled Taiwan issue, the American economic and security interests would suffer serious losses. Hence, the U.S. placed increasing emphasis on China-U.S. relations rather than on U.S.-Taiwan relations. Basically, its Taiwan policy is aimed at stabilizing its mainland China policy. The U.S. also clearly realized that the only situation that could make the China-U.S. relations fall off track is a military confrontation across the Taiwan Strait. Supporting alternatives to "one China" such as "two Chinas" or "one China on each side" would result in more trouble than benefit. Although it still sells arms to Taiwan and opposes mainland China using force, the U.S. remains cautious of Taiwan moving in the direction of independence and compelling the U.S. into a military confrontation with mainland China over the Taiwan issue.

In the 1990s, facing increasingly complicated and sensitive cross-strait relations, U.S. Taiwan Strait experts suggested that keeping a vague strategy would conform best to U.S. interests. It could on one hand keep Beijing in the dark about Washington's true intention and on the other hand scare Taiwan away from acting rashly. Furthermore, by playing the "Taiwan card," the U.S. could intimidate mainland China. This kind of policy only encouraged Lee Teng-hui and provoked the 1995 Taiwan Strait tension, and eventually the Taiwan Strait crisis in the spring of 1996. In 1997, Clinton proposed the "strategic alliance" concept and in 1998 he verbally stated the Three Noes. All these attempted to revise the strategic ambiguity policy. In July 1999, after Lee Teng-hui unveiled the "two-state theory," Taiwan Strait rhetoric rose again and Washington again replaced strategic ambiguity with strategic clarity. In the later stages of the Bush presidential campaign, think-tank members, such as Paul Wolfowitz and Richard Lee Armitage, openly acknowledged the necessity for a clear strategic policy. Namely, if Taiwan declares independence unilaterally, it should not expect U.S. assistance. If mainland China attacks Taiwan for no reason, it should expect U.S. retaliation. This is similar to the policy advocated by China experts to the U.S. about having cross-strait negotiations and signing a "no independence, no force" interim agreement.

In April 2001, the China-U.S. mid-air collision incident occurred. The newly elected President Bush openly stated that he "will try all he can to help Taiwan's self-defense." The U.S. Senate and House subsequently passed bills supporting Taiwan to become an observing member of the WHO. China-U.S. relations were at a low tide. In less than two years, Bush's attitude had apparently changed. When he first met the new Chinese leader Hu Jintao, apart from reiterating that he would not support Taiwan independence, on the subject of assisting Taiwan's self-defense he only said, "If necessary, the U.S. would help make possible Taiwan's self-defense."

This Bush/Hu conversation aroused disturbances in Taiwan. Some scholars said that the China-U.S.-Taiwan triangle showed a bias and Taiwan should find a way to deal with it. Other scholars said, "The basic nature of Bush's Taiwan policy has not changed; the Taiwanese people should not worry." Regardless, all people acknowledged that the current U.S. Taiwan Strait policy was "one China, two principles," namely not supporting Taiwan independence and opposing the use of force. After these debates, the Taiwanese people could see more clearly that neither Lee Teng-hui's "two-state theory" nor Chen Shui-bian's "one country on each side" conforms to the U.S. Taiwan Strait policy. As long as mainland China does not offend Taiwan with force, the U.S. has no reason to oppose the peaceful reunification of the two sides.

As the Iraq war has shown, although the U.S. has become the only superpower in the world, it cannot solve all international problems. In particular, to resolve the crisis on the Korean Peninsula, the U.S. must get mainland China's help, thus solidifying the China-U.S. partnership. Mainland China's participation in the Korean Peninsula multilateral talks in 2003 helped Southeast Asia construct a free-trade region and improve its relations with India, and has even gone as far as assisting the operation of the Shanghai Cooperation Organization in Central Asia. Such actions have exhibited the ease and moderation of mainland China in handling its diplomatic affairs. This, of course, has much to do with its overall national strength. According to an article titled "China's New Diplomacy" written by scholars of the U.S. think-tank Rand Corporation, mainland China has already transformed itself from having a "victim mentality" as a result of being colonized in the past to having "big-country diplomacy." This kind of confidence and its accompanying ease would certainly be reflected in its cross-strait policies.

After the Bush/Hu meeting, the DPP did not improve its cross-strait relations and boldly advocated "one country on each side," a referendum, and a new Constitution. It also repeatedly challenged the One-China Principle. As for the U.S., apart from reiterating the "do not support Taiwan independence" in the Three Noes policy, it changed its position from that "we hope not to change the status quo unilaterally" to "nobody is allowed to attempt to change the status quo unilaterally" to "we oppose any side to change the status quo." However, the temporary strengthening of the U.S. attitude was due to the pressure created by the Taiwan authorities. Basically, the U.S. long-term policy has not changed.

CHAPTER 5

U.S. SCHOLARS' VIEWPOINTS ABOUT CHINA'S REUNIFICATION ISSUE

SECTION 1
U.S. THINK TANKS AND RESEARCH WORK ON CROSS-STRAIT RELATIONS

Since most scholars who research cross-strait relations work for the various U.S. think tanks, it is necessary to understand the nature of these think tanks in order to fully understand their viewpoints.

In the U.S., there are thousands if not tens of thousands of political think tanks. Most of them research public policies. The research subjects are broad, from history and social sciences to the newest technologies, from equal rights between different genders and social benefits to military tactics. Any subject can be covered. The purpose of their existence is mainly to guide, influence, or revise the specific government policies through academic and policy research.

Most of the U.S. public-policy research think tanks have two characteristics. First, they are nonprofit organizations. Through their tax-exempt status, they can raise operating funds from various social circles and at the same time strengthen the fairness of their policy arguments. Second, they are nonpartisan organizations. Their bylaws emphasize this as indication that their research results are for the interests of the country and the public at large and not for the benefit of any political party. However, the trend in the U.S. is that whenever a political party is voted out of office, the former officials often transfer to related think tanks and continue to provide recommendations or critiques of current politics. For example, if a Republican president is elected into office, ousting a Democrat, many of the former Democratic officials would likely take important jobs in the public-policy think tanks. Clearly, although the think tanks claim to be non-partisan, their viewpoints are often inevitably party focused.

The Categories of the U.S. Public-Policy Think Tanks

Though there are many public policy think tanks in the U.S., they can all be put into one of the two following categories:

1. Nongovernmental and semigovernmental think tanks: In order to broadly gather opinions from all circles to improve the quality of their policymaking, the various departments of the U.S. government often provide funds or prioritize their financial assistance to support public-policy think tanks. For example, the Rand Corporation has close ties with the U.S. Air Force and the Office of Naval Research. Rand Corporation has the status of Federally Funded Research and Development Center; that is, it can directly accept government contracts to conduct research projects. But other nongovernmental think tanks must rely on corporate or privately donated funds and contracted research for the operations. These think tanks can also accept government research contracts and related financial assistance. Many famous American universities—such as Harvard University, Stanford University, Georgetown University, Columbia University, and the University of California at Berkeley—have research centers to study Asian issues or Chinese policies. The related teaching and research work are carried out by the university professors or associated research staff.

2. Conservative and liberal think tanks: Although most of the U.S. public-policy think tanks emphasize their non-partisan character, it is clear that their financial resources, the personal bias of the leaders, and the traditions of the organizations distinguish between being conservative and being liberal. For example, Washington's Heritage Foundation and the American Enterprise Institute (AEI) are both regarded as pro-Republican conservative centers. By contrast, the Brookings Institution and the public-policy centers in universities and institutes are regarded as liberal.

The U.S. Think Tanks' Research on Cross-Strait Relations

Most of the U.S. public-policy think tanks do not have departments that specialize in research on Chinese affairs and the cross-strait relations. Such studies are performed in the Asian studies or international affairs departments. The Heritage Foundation, AEI, and the Center for Strategic and International Studies (CSIS) have Asian Research departments; the Brookings Institution has a Center for Northeast Asian Policy Studies; the Atlantic Council of the United States (ACUS) places China-related research topics with its Institute Asia/Pacific Research Center (A/PRC). The International Security Studies of CSIS places Chinese issues and cross-strait relations within its international security program.

Frequently, research staff members in the aforementioned departments were former U.S. officials who worked in the Asia-Pacific region or in defense affairs, or diplomats stationed on either side of the Taiwan Strait. For example, AEI's James R. Lilley has been Ambassador to the PRC and Director of the AIT. CSIS's Kurt M. Campbell was Deputy Assistant Secretary of Defense during the 1996 crisis over the Taiwan Strait. The Heritage Foundation's Dr. Mark Woodruff was a U.S. army officer stationed in Beijing. The think tanks that hire China experts usually have more research activities and more reports on the cross-strait relations. The angle of analysis, position, and specialized area of think tanks are often influenced by the individual bias of the hired research staff.

The main function of U.S. think tanks is to provide recommendations to the government. Hence, when the cross-strait affair becomes a main subject of the U.S. foreign policy, or when a major incident takes place—such as Lee Teng-hui's and Chen Shui-bian's visits to the U.S., the Taiwan Strait crisis, the U.S. president's official visit to mainland China, the Sino-U.S. mid-air collision incident, the U.S.-Taiwan arms sales negotiation, or Taiwan's presidential election—then the U.S. think tanks usually focus their research attention on cross-strait relations. They would either convene seminars or write policy papers to be used as references by various circles.

Taiwan pays great attention to the influence of U.S. think tanks and often actively looks for channels to be in touch with them. In order for the Taiwan media to know American think tanks and scholars, MAC Deputy Chairman Lin Chong-pin in June 2001 led a 20-member Visiting Taiwan Reporters' Visiting Delegation to U.S. Think Tanks trip to New York and Washington. They visited a few well-known think tanks such as the Brookings Institution, Cato Institute, Rand Corporation, AEI, and others. AEI's James R. Lilley met the delegation and listened to a report presented by Lin Chung-pin on Chen Shui-bian's mainland policy (*China Times Daily News*, 01/06/2001).

The Interchanges between the U.S. Think Tanks and the Two Sides

In order to enhance the research capacity on cross-strait policies, the U.S. think tanks or university research centers sometimes would invite politicians and scholars from mainland China and Taiwan to do in-house research. Sometimes they would even invite people from both sides to collaborate on certain related research topics, thus promoting cross-strait cultural and educational exchanges. For example, Georgetown University's China Policy Research Institute, the ACUS, and the Brookings Institution regularly invite scholars and military personnel from both sides to conduct research in the U.S. simultaneously. In addition, the CSIS has signed contracts with the Taiwan Defense Department to regularly invite Taiwan military officers to the U.S. (see the Huang Chieh-cheng paper presented at The National Policy Forum, p. 111–114, 12/2001).

U.S. think tanks that research cross-strait relations also frequently organize delegations to visit the two sides. On one hand, they want to understand the most recent cross-strait situation for their research; they can also at the same time promote U.S. policies or act as messengers of the U.S. government. They could meet high-ranking officials (in Taipei, they could see the president almost every time) and have their opinions taken fairly seriously. For example, in December 2000, Brookings Institution's Kenneth G. Lieberthal, A/PRC's Douglas H. Paal, and others formed a six-member U.S. Foreign Policy Visiting Delegation and met with both sides. They hoped to understand the direction Chen Shui-bian's mainland policy had taken after his inauguration. In Beijing, they met Qian Qishen and Wang Daohan and in Taipei they met Chen Shui-bian and all the high-ranking officials. As another example, in January 2002, ACUS's retired U.S. General Jack N. Merritt led an 11-member delegation (among them the former Under Secretary of Defense Walter B. Slocombe) and visited both sides. In Taipei, they met Chen Shui-bian, the secretary general of the National Security Council, the minister of National Defense, the chairperson of the MAC, and the chief of the General Staff.

In 2003, when the Taiwan presidential election was approaching and in order to win more votes, Chen Shui-bian unveiled "one country on each side," the referendum, and a new Constitution. Research staff in U.S. think tanks familiar with the Taiwan issue—such as James R. Lilley, Natale H. Bellocchi, and Richard C. Bush III—visited Taiwan one after the other in order to communicate with Chen Shui-bian. The purpose of their visits must have been related to understanding Chen Shui-bian's intentions and to deliver the U.S. government's instructions to him. During the visits, they also met and talked with Lien Chan and James Soong. The topics of all the talks concerned cross-strait issues.

In conclusion, the U.S. think tanks and scholars who conduct research on the cross-strait issue often act as official "messengers." They not only collect information, but also pass on some messages for the U.S. government. Hence, it is very difficult to define their viewpoints and positions as purely nongovernmental. For this reason alone, their statements seem particularly valuable as references. Since these scholars and think tanks publish many related papers and deliver numerous speeches that cover various topics, this chapter deals only with those that study China's reunification issue. Statements published before the mid-1990s are not considered. The scholars discussed are well known by the two sides. They often alternate between visits to both sides. Although they claim that their trips are purely "academic visits" and that their statements do not represent U.S. thinking, it is assumed that they are in fact delivering messages for the U.S. government.

Section 2
U.S. Scholars' Viewpoints on China's Reunification

In this section, I shall introduce U.S. scholars' viewpoints on China's reunification.

James R. Lilley (Former U.S. Ambassador in Beijing, Now AEI Senior Research Fellow)

In 2000, before the Taiwan presidential election, James R. Lilley came to Taiwan to observe its election situation. After returning to the U.S., he reported during a Joint Economic Committee of the U.S. Congress hearing directed at U.S.-China trade relations that mainland China was the biggest loser in Taiwan's election. The reason was that the pro-independence Chen Shui-bian had been elected, causing Beijing to lose face. But viewed from another angle, mainland China was a big winner because the anti-Beijing Lee Teng-hui would resign from the KMT's chairmanship and Chen Shui-bian had not mentioned independence since he was elected. Hence, mainland China could also declare victory. Upon evaluating the cross-strait situation after the election, Lilley thought that, realistically speaking, Beijing would not renounce the use of force. Its method of using force could be a small-scale provocation that would not attract U.S. interference. It would not shed blood, but it would satisfy Beijing's hawks and make Taiwan nervous. He said it was also possible that Beijing could be considering a more clever way by initiating small-scale, peaceful attacks (*United Daily News*, 03/25/2000).

In June 2001, Lilley met the Taiwan Reporters' Visiting Delegation to U.S. Think Tanks in Washington and told them that the U.S. would not be involved in any of the cross-strait negotiations. He also did not think that U.S. arms sale to Taiwan would lead to an arms race between the U.S. and mainland China. He emphasized that the U.S. must maintain its military supremacy and its world superpower. However, this had nothing to do with an arms race. Concerning the role the U.S. played in cross-strait negotiations, Lilley said that the U.S. could influence the future direction of cross-strait relations, but that it would not be the "mediator" for the two sides. This was explained very clearly in the six guarantees provided to Taiwan in 1994.

Concerning the U.S. attitude toward mainland China's military expansion, Lilley pointed out that mainland China said that the development of the TMD system by the Bush administration may lead to a military race between the two countries. However, he thought that, regardless of whether the U.S. would set up the TMD or not, mainland China would still continue its military expansion. According to Lilley, the TMD is a U.S. response to mainland China's military expansion and not an offensive (*China Times Daily News*, 06/13/2001).

At the end of July 2003, after Chen Shui-bian proposed his referendum, Lilley arrived in Taiwan and met with Vice President Annette Lu. After hearing her explanations on the WHO referendum, he said that he needed to understand more about Taiwan's referendum stance. He also pointed out that based on his own working experiences, Beijing should not suppress Taiwan's international living space because hygiene and health matters are humanitarian issues, not political issues. Lilley also said that, at that time, the most important matter was to make Taiwan feel more confident with the help of the U.S. He pointed out that, judging from the situations of the Philippines, Indonesia, and Hong Kong, democracy in much of Asia is developing strongly. These Asian democratic countries, along with Taiwan, are on the winning side (*China Times Daily News*, 07/29/2003).

Susan L. Shirk (Former Deputy Assistant Secretary of State for East Asia and Pacific Affairs, Now Professor for the Graduate School of International Relations at the University of California at San Diego)

At the end of 2002, Susan L. Shirk accepted an interview by Hong Kong reporters and explained the "one country, three systems" plan proposed during her term as Deputy Assistant Secretary of State for East Asia and Pacific Affairs. In 1999, Shirk attended an activity sponsored by Chinese from Taiwan, mainland China, and Hong Kong. She first said that Lee Teng-hui's "two-state theory" was well supported by the Taiwanese, and then later she suggested the "one country, three systems" with the third system to be implemented in Taiwan. This idea was opposed by many audience members. Due to her official status, some people questioned whether her idea was in violation of U.S. official statements. She stated that in order to avoid devastating results, mainland China should provide Taiwanese people with concrete incentives to enhance their willingness to get close to mainland China (www.people.com.cn, 09/07/1999).

Shirk said during the interview that she understood that the idea of "one country, three systems" was not yet a set suggestion. She proposed that idea in a Washington activity sponsored by some Chinese in order to emphasize that future cross-strait relations should be more flexible and that the Beijing government should have a better reunification plan. She thought that "one country, two systems" was not attractive to the Taiwanese people, despite Beijing's talk about giving Taiwan's "one country, two systems" more living space and lenience (neither of which produced a strong enough motivation for the Taiwanese people to accept). Hence, she suggested that the Beijing government should present a new plan: "one country, three systems."

Shirk continued to say that mainland China's "one China" policy had become more lenient for more than a year. "One China" includes mainland China and Taiwan, as opposed to the old phrase, "One China Is the People's Republic of China." However, mainland China still has not done enough in realistic terms. In Shirk's opinion, mainland China is a fast-growing, large country that should be full of confidence—and with that should show a more amiable and humble attitude as it moves towards reunification.

Shirk said that the Clinton administration always encouraged the two sides to engage in dialogue. In her opinion, engaging in dialogues does not necessitate agreement. Both sides can continue their dialogues until they find the issues on which they can agree. In addition, she suggested that the two sides strengthen their economic ties and enhance their economic developments by analyzing the model of their economic corporations.

Richard C. Bush III (Former AIT/Washington Chairman, Now Director of the Center for Northeast Asian Policy Studies at Brookings Institution)

Richard C. Bush III was invited to speak at the 20th International Asian

Affairs Studies at St. John's University in November 2002. There he stated that mainland China always misinterpreted Taiwan's resistance to "one country, two systems" and its attempt to increase international living space as ways to permanently segregate from mainland China. These are the main reasons for the cross-strait stagnation.

Bush said that some Taiwan people hope for permanent segregation from mainland China, but "I don't believe that was Lee Teng-hui's policy during his presidency or what Chen Shui-bian is seeking now." He said that what Lee Teng-hui and Chen Shui-bian care most about is whether in the reunified China the Taiwan government would still have true sovereignty. The reason for Chen Shui-bian's refusal to fall into the "one China" trap was his fear that it would acknowledge the One-China Principle, which is the equivalent to making a big concession before the negotiation. Besides, the DPP's internal pressure would only make him even more cautious. Since the Beijing government knows Taipei's emphasis only too well, it is not willing to conduct negotiations with Taiwan on an approximate reciprocal basis. Hence, the two sides could only play their "increasing escalation" games: Beijing used tactics such as increasing its military preparation, playing "economy pressuring politics," and "making friends with Taiwan conservative factions" to pressure Taiwan, which caused Taiwan to increasingly seek U.S. assistance.

Bush said that he did not know how the game would end, but that the possibility of a China-U.S. war due to the Taiwan issue was becoming greater and greater. He further stated that it is not that mainland China has no other choice; for example, it could bear more with Taiwan. Unfortunately, as long as Jiang Zemin was in power there would be no bold goodwill gestures toward Taiwan from Beijing. He said that since mainland China's fourth generation of leaders had just stepped up to their political platform, one could not determine when they would be able to make their own political decisions. Generally speaking, mainland China's power transformation was smooth. However, "policy continuity does not guarantee stability."

Bush thought that if mainland China proceeded with broad political reforms and abandoned the "one country, two systems" policy on Taiwan, cross-strait and China-U.S. relations would have a stronger foundation and the possibility of conflict between China and the U.S. would be reduced. In responding to audience questions, he emphasized that the common consensus of the major Taiwan political parties was to strive for Taiwan's legal status. Even if the Pan-Blue parties were in power, mainland China would not be able to gain any advantage.

As for whether Chen Shui-bian's reelection and his push for referendum would trigger mainland China to attack Taiwan, Bush attempted to answer the question as well as he could. He described Chen Shui-bian as a clever man who knows Taiwan's interests and who is aware of "what can be done and what can't." If reelected, he does not have the power to do whatever he wants. Taiwan is a democratic society, so any arrangement concerning Taiwan's future must be accepted by the Taiwanese. The long-term U.S. interest is to create an environment that "avoids mainland China challenging the U.S." and "encourages the coexistence of both sides" (*Central News Agency*, 11/16/2002).

Harry Harding (Dean of the Elliott School of International Affairs at George Washington University)

On November 1, 2000, Harry Harding attended a symposium in New York on the subject of Mainland China-Taiwan-U.S.A. Dilemma: Legacy of the Cold War. During the symposium, he openly proposed that the essential point in handling the cross-strait issue was to have both sides design a *modus vivendi* (interim agreement) together and eventually establish a cross-strait "confederation."

Harding emphasized that designing a *modus vivendi* was a top priority of cross-strait discussions since that time was certainly not the right moment for solving the Taiwan problem. A *modus vivendi* would provide a buffer and serve as a transition. During this period, the two sides could expand economic and cultural exchanges, and establish and enhance mutual understanding. In Taiwan, people could reach a wider consensus on the cross-strait topics and hope for Beijing's renouncement of using force in response to Taipei not seeking independence. Through a *modus vivendi* buffer, both sides could proceed with the final solution of Taiwan's problem—the formation of a confederation. Harry Harding's proposal of forming a confederation gained support from Chiu Hung-ta at the New York symposium.

After the symposium, Harding agreed to an interview by the *United Daily News* and further explained the concepts of *modus vivendi* and confederation. He pointed out that although *modus vivendi* was interpreted by Taipei as an "interim agreement" that favored Beijing, the concept was actually similar to the framework of a "peace mechanism" proposed by Lee Teng-hui. The main purpose of the *modus vivendi* would be to serve as a transition mechanism to gain time and living space. He pointed out that the cross-strait problem certainly could not be resolved in a single attempt in the foreseeable future, and might even take a few decades. At that time, the two sides should think creatively and work out a *modus vivendi* to establish more interchanges, develop a deeper mutual trust and dependence, and to engage in dialogues to ease the cross-strait tension and eventually form a confederation (*United Daily News*, 11/01/2000).

Nancy Bernkopf Tucker
(History Professor at Georgetown University)

Nancy Bernkopf Tucker is a research specialist on China-Hong Kong-Taiwan issues. During 1986–87, she worked at the China desk of the State Department and the American Embassy in mainland China. In June 2002, she published a 14-page article entitled "If Taiwan Chooses Unification, Will the United States Care?" in the *Washington Quarterly*. In her article, she reminded the U.S. government, that due to the increasingly apparent trend toward cross-strait economic integration and Taiwan's growing economic dependence on mainland China, a "peaceful reunification" was no longer entirely out of reach. America should begin thinking seriously about the impact of such a reunification on U.S. strategic interests in Asia.

Tucker further declared that if the Taiwanese people voluntarily or unknowingly moved toward reunification with a mainland China that was not friendly with the U.S., that would in the long run become a serious problem for the U.S. Mainland China was seen as a strong and growing power and the "China threat" theory was held by more than a few members of the U.S. government. Tucker pointed out that once the two sides were reunited China would have more national defense resources and its strategic goals would thereby change. At the same time, the Chinese Air Force and Navy could project more military capabilities externally, which would give mainland China more control of the Taiwan Strait, which would put the U.S., Japan, and Australia in an uneasy position. After cross-strait reunification, the U.S. would lose an important intelligence station—Taiwan. Moreover, with economic integration or reunification, U.S. military technologies exported to Taiwan might be passed on to mainland China, which would be of considerable concern to the U.S. Another area of concern to U.S. politicians would be regarding arms sales to Taiwan, which could become harmful to the U.S. Given all of the above, although peaceful reunification would avoid a China-U.S. war, if after mainland China reunifies Taiwan and is not satisfied with American forces stationing in Asia, then reunification would not conform to U.S. interests. Moreover, after reunification, Taiwan's contributions to China's economy, science, technology, and military would be very appreciable.

Tucker concluded, "Despite the fact that peaceful reunification would have many negative impacts on the U.S., there is one big benefit; and that is its elimination of the fuse, immediately and comprehensively lowering the risk of Sino-U.S. conflicts and clashes. China's reunification undoubtedly is not advantageous to certain U.S. interests, but the disadvantages are much smaller than mainland China and the U.S. engaging in war" (*China Times Daily News*, 07/18/2002).

David Shambaugh (Director of the China Policy Program at George Washington University)

David Shambaugh stated in his article "Facing Reality in China Policy" that was published in the January/February 2001 issue of the bimonthly periodical *Foreign Affairs* that at that time the stagnated cross-strait situation was full of danger. The new U.S. administration should actively seek opportunities to bring the two sides to the negotiation table. Any cross-strait dialogue must begin with the One-China Principle, and the two sides forming a confederation was the best hope for eventually solving the cross-strait issues (*Central News Agency*, 01/2001).

David Shambaugh declared at the end of 2002 that mainland China's Taiwan policy is "economic integration, political absorption, international strangling, and military threat." Unless better methods could be found, this "standard operational procedure" would continue. He believed that after more than a decade in power Jiang Zemin had built a solid power foundation. Most of the high-level military commanders were promoted by Jiang Zemin, and he was more able to control the military. In contrast, Hu Jintao did not have strong military connections. Regarding the cross-strait crisis, in order to show his nationalism and determination to the military, Hu Jintao may have been inclined to use bold and rash actions (*Central News Agency*, 12/24/2002).

Robert A. Scalapino (U.S. Senior Specialist on China Issues and Professor at the University of California at Berkeley)

In March 2000, during an interview with the *China Times Daily News* reporters, Robert A. Scalapino stated that the U.S. was under great pressure from the cross-strait issues. In particular, on the subject of arms sales to Taiwan, it faced pressures both from Congress about strengthening arms sales to protect Taiwan's security and from Beijing, which expressed strong opposition. The U.S. hoped that Chen Shui-bian could maintain a moderate attitude and try to engage Beijing in some kind of dialogue. However, the U.S. government was concerned even more about whether Taipei could maintain domestic political stability in the new situation. That was, if during the transition period the new Taipei government suffered serious internal conflicts, especially on the subject of cross-strait issues, it would be very difficult for it to deal with Beijing coherently.

On the topic of whether the cross-strait talks should return to the One-China Principle, Scalapino thought that this was precisely the serious gap to be faced by the forthcoming cross-strait talks. Beijing still insisted on "one China, Taiwan is part of China, a province of China" (but was willing to consider "one country, three systems" to be differentiated from Hong Kong and Macao), whereas Taiwan insisted on its having a separate government and a sovereign political entity. Scalapino thought that, theoretically speaking, there were two workable solutions. The first method was for both sides to agree to begin negotiations based on "one China, but not clearly defined." The other method was to push for the concepts of federation or confederation and to use this framework as a political pipeline for dialogues of both sides, not trying to hurriedly solve the sovereignty issue now. However, it was still impossible for Beijing to accept these viewpoints; therefore, reaching a political agreement was impossible. Too, he said that because mainland China's military and national strength would indeed grow stronger, Taiwan should seek more and better arms for self-defense.

Scalapino suggested that Taiwan should do two things simultaneously: 1) It should devote efforts to engage in dialogues with Beijing; and 2) It should seek to be in balance militarily with mainland China's military power. What the U.S. could do is to first push for dialogues between the two sides and remain cautious that arms sales to Taiwan not exceed Taiwan's defense needs (see *China Times Daily News*, 03/22/2000).

Scalapino stated in June 2001, upon meeting a Taiwan Reporters' Delegation, that the biggest difference between the Bush administration's present mainland China policy and that of the past was Bush's use of the phrase "strategic clarity." Notwithstanding the fact that it was possible to support Taiwan more, the U.S. did not wish to damage its relations with mainland China for the sake of Taiwan. Hence, Bush's mainland China policy would still adhere to the following basic principles:

1. Mainland China cannot use force against Taiwan.
2. Taiwan cannot declare independence.
3. Under the prerequisite that Taiwan does not declare independence, if mainland China precipitately uses force against Taiwan, the U.S. will express serious concern.

Scalapino stressed that these points were, in fact, the same mainland China policies followed during the Clinton era. Hence, the Sino-U.S. relations would not undergo any dramatic change (*China Times Daily News*, 06/20/2001).

Ramon H. Myers (Senior Fellow of Asia/Pacific Research Center, Hoover Institution, Stanford University)

From 1990–1991, Ramon H. Myers was a visiting professor at the National Taiwan University. He is very familiar with the cross-strait issues.

In March 2000, the *China Times Daily News* published a translated version of one of Myers' articles on the issue. In the article, he questioned why Chen Shui-bian did not propose his own confederated model after Beijing leaders did based on "one country, two systems" to reunify China. This, Myers argued, would not only guarantee Taiwan's democracy and prosperity, but it would also satisfy the Beijing leaders' argument that Taiwan was still part of China.

Myers thought that instead of visiting Beijing to express goodwill, Chen Shui-bian could have used the confederated model proposal as a negotiating chip for solving the China problem. The content of the model would be that both sides could enjoy together the "greater China confederation" sovereignty. The confederation would be composed of territories under the jurisdiction of Taiwan authorities, along with territories under the jurisdiction of mainland China authorities and those under the jurisdiction of Macao and the Hong Kong SAR.

Myers argued that the "greater China confederation" would not create a threat to Taiwan, the U.S., or other countries. Such a "one China" would allow different economic integration as well as social and cultural exchanges. Such a creative diplomacy would hopefully leave Chen Shui-bian's name in history as the "designer who enhanced the peace and promoted the Great China's modernization and democratization" (*China Times Daily News*, 03/19/2000).

In June 2001, Myers stated during his meeting with a Taiwan Reporters' Delegation that the "three new sentences" in Qian Qishen's "one China" statement revealed the new concept that Beijing was willing to share sovereignty with Taiwan. For this reason alone, Taiwan should sit down and talk with mainland China. He thought that Qian Qishen was saying that Taiwan and the mainland are both part of China and, therefore, share the sovereignty. This was a tremendous compromise, and extremely different from mainland China's position in 1992. It would be a very good opportunity for Taiwan, but Taiwan's new government did not seem to be interested and did not offer an enthusiastic response (*China Times Daily News*, 06/20/2001).

On June 9, 2003, the School of Oriental and African Studies of London University invited Myers to speak at its annual lecture on Taiwan matters. Myers pointed out that Taiwan had not responded positively to mainland China's definition of "one China" as both Taiwan and the mainland being part of China. He also reported that the reason was because Taiwan authorities did not think mainland China was sincere.

Myers suggested that the Taiwan authorities proposed a set of legal explanations of "one China" according to its own Constitution. He thought that it would be helpful for the Taiwan authorities to first accept Beijing's new definition of "one China" and then demanded that Beijing prove with concrete actions that the two sides of the strait are companions that can share mutual interests, benefits, and sovereignty on an equal footing.

Myers said that the most urgent matter for Taiwan should be a suggestion to Beijing to reduce the military threat by removing missiles aimed at Taiwan from the mainland coast and to make the Taiwan Strait a demilitarized zone. After that, representatives from both sides could sit down and discuss practical matters like the three links. Beijing should also actively assist Taiwan in becoming an observing member of the WHO. Myers also suggested that both sides begin negotiations about practical matters instead of the reunification issue. There was no need to research the possibilities of the two sides forming a confederation or federation because the most important matter for the two sides at this time was to establish mutual trust. Myers believed that the question of reunification could be left to later generations to deal with (*Central Daily News*, 06/11/2003).

Kenneth G. Lieberthal (Former Special Assistant to the President for Asia and Senior Director for Asia on the National Security Council, Now Professor, Distinguished Fellow and Director for China at the William Davidson Institute, Research Associate of the Center for Chinese Studies, University of Michigan)

Kenneth G. Lieberthal is the former special assistant to President Clinton on national security matters and former Senior Director for Asia on the National Security Council. He is one of the most famous China specialists in the U.S.

In January 1998, Lieberthal suggested that the two sides sign an "interim agreement" to keep the status quo unchanged for 50 years. The main points of the agreement were: 1) Taiwan declares itself to be part of China and does not seek independence; 2) Mainland China renounces the use of force against Taiwan; 3) Prior to reunification, both sides govern their own internal politics and foreign relations, as limited by the two previous points; 4) Both sides of the Taiwan Strait regularly hold high-level talks; the subject of Taiwan's arms purchases can be discussed, but it must be coordinated with mainland China's military planning; and 5) Both sides discuss name changes to reduce tension between the two sides. For example, the People's Republic of China could be changed to "China," and the Republic of China to "Taiwan, China." Perhaps both sides could develop similar phrases like "Greater China." The authorities on neither side responded to Lieberthal's interim agreement.

At the beginning of 2001, in a policy recommendation, Lieberthal advocated that the "loosely-held formal combination" established through long-term negotiations between Taiwan and the mainland would be a new form of government to be called China, instead of the PRC. He advocated that inside this form of government neither Beijing nor Taiwan could control the other side and that the international community should guarantee that neither side violate the new relations between them.

Lieberthal also suggested that the new U.S. government administration delay the sale of disputable arms that are part of the U.S.-Taiwan arms sales meeting to be held in April 2001. Instead, the U.S. should push for limiting the mainland's missile deployments in exchange for Taiwan abandoning its missile defense capabilities. He stated that either Washington or Taipei should discuss signing an agreement on military restrictions with Beijing, and that any agreement should include inspection and verification procedures (*United Daily News*, 01/05/2001).

The Washington think tank Nixon Center published its "U.S.-China Relations in a Post-9/11 World" document in the middle of 2002. Lieberthal was invited to comment on it in September 2002. He pointed out that the U.S. seeking mainland China's cooperation in the anti-terrorist war allowed mainland China to gain an "opportunity for a strategic break." Mainland China obviously decides to work with the U.S. in keeping stable collaborative relations and regards the U.S. as a cooperative partner.

He stated that, although the resolution of the Taiwan issue is one of mainland China's top priorities, he believed that what mainland China wanted at this time was to "lower the cross-strait temperature" and stabilize the cross-strait relations for the long term. Reunification was not at the top of the list of goals that must be realized rapidly. Solving domestic problems was mainland China's top priority. He suggested that the U.S. government must encourage the two sides to talk to each other and actively foster an environment suitable for establishing mutual confidence. He enthusiastically declared that the U.S. hoped the two sides would develop more economic and trade exchanges (*United Daily News*, 09/20/2002).

Thomas J. Christensen (Professor of Politics and International Affairs, Princeton University)

Thomas J. Christensen once studied at the University of Foreign Economic Trade, Beijing. He has made frequent visits to both sides of the strait in recent years.

He stated at the symposium on "China at a Major Turning Point," sponsored by the Carnegie Endowment for International Peace and the Council on Foreign Relations, that mainland China's becoming a democratic country would be good for the U.S. As for the reason for his believing in mainland China's future democratization, he said that the Chinese people are very clever and will be able to see this as clearly the best way, but the "problem is how to achieve this goal." Christensen observed mainland China as modifying its current systems. However, its entire political systems must undergo basic reforms to become democratic. He pointed out that mainland China being completely democratized would be the worst nightmare for pro-independence people. For a very long time, "anti-Communism" and "opposing non-democratic mainland China invading democratic Taiwan" have been the most powerful arguments for U.S. support of Taiwan. If both sides were democratic, Bush would have the dilemma of which one to choose.

Christensen also commented that China's confidence was increasing gradually as it began to understand that attacks by words and threats of force would only create effects opposite of what it desired. Hence, the situations of 1996 and 2000 during Taiwan's presidential elections would not reoccur. He believed that Hu Jintao would keep a low profile and create Taiwan policies that are more practical (*China Times Daily News*, 09/26/2003).

Joseph S. Nye Jr. (Former Assistant Secretary of Defense for International Security Affairs, Now Dean, John F. Kennedy School of Government at Harvard University)

In December 1999, Joseph S. Nye Jr. accepted an interview with the *China Times Daily News* reporter Ran Liang. During the course of the interview he said that since Lee Teng-hui's declaration of "special state-to-state relationship," the cross-strait tension had been rising steadily and might continue until after the 2000 Taiwan presidential election. The recent competition in the area of missile weaponry also added a "fair degree of danger." However, he believed that both Taipei and Beijing had enough common sense not to let the situation deteriorate to the stage of direct confrontations.

Nye also showed optimism about twenty-first-century Sino-U.S. relations. Although mainland China continuously develops military power, strengthens its high-tech combat capabilities, and opposes the U.S. "hegemony," he thought that mainland China's pluralistic trend and gradual democratization would eventually change the character of its system. He even said that he believed mainland China would eventually associate with the U.S. peacefully. He argued that the key element and a practical resolution of the cross-strait issues was to maintain dialogues and exchanges instead of using force. In addition, Nye's "Beijing does not use force, Taiwan does not seek independence" framework, proposed earlier, still made good sense because it would turn the negative cycle of military races into a positive cycle. Regarding the U.S. attitude in the event of a war erupting between the two sides, Nye gave a candid answer. He said that neither the statements made by the president in ordinary times nor public opinion polls are reliable. "It will completely depend on the situation at that moment," he said (*China Times Daily News*, 12/28/1999).

In July 2001, Nye came to Taiwan for academic research and was invited by the Institute for National Policy Research to speak. During his speech he said that the U.S. position had always been maintaining the status quo (i.e., Taiwan does not declare independence and mainland China does not use force against Taiwan). Although the U.S. was willing to protect Taiwan's democracy and human rights, it would not take the risk of getting involved in a war if mainland China invaded Taiwan by force due to Taiwan's declaration of independence.

Nye then mentioned that in his March 8, 1998, article "A Taiwan Deal" in *The Washington Post* he stated that three positions should be taken by the U.S. in dealing with the Taiwan issue (*The Washington Post*, 03/08/1998):

1. The U.S. should clearly state its opposition in regards to formal Taiwan independence. It should also specify that if Taiwan declares independence, the U.S. would actively discourage other countries from recognizing it. At the same time, however, Washington would express its objection to mainland China's use of force against Taiwan.

2. Once Taiwan forswears independence, the U.S. would ask mainland China to permit Taiwan's participation in more international organizations and to give Taiwan more international living space. The U.S. would also ask that mainland China's Taiwan policy be based on the Hong Kong "one country, two systems" approach.

3. The U.S. should demand that Taiwan pledge decisively not to formally declare independence.

Although the publication of this theory was immediately and severely attacked by pro-independents, Nye maintained that it was the most effective proposal for maintaining cross-strait stability, peace, and balance. The U.S. had its own moral insistence: "The United States has always been willing to protect the hard-earned fruits of Taiwan democracy and human rights. But she will not get involved in a war for the symbolic ideology sought by some people here."

Nye's opinions were again refuted by the strong Taiwan independence supporter Koo Kuan-min who was in attendance. Koo Kuan-min challenged Nye to prove the existence of the 1992 Consensus. Nye reiterated that his position did not represent mainland China but rather U.S. interests. The U.S. was willing to strive for the protection of Taiwan's democracy and freedom as long as Taiwan did not take on the role as the provocative side. "Taiwan of course can declare independence through referendum, but the U.S. will not fight a war for this. Why should the U.S. take that kind of risk?" Nye indicated that whenever there was any misjudgment on either side of the strait, the U.S., mainland China, and Taiwan would get into trouble. At that time, the two sides already had a 1992 Consensus as a basis, even though they had different definitions of it. Viewed from a long-term perspective, both sides should try to find a peaceful resolution. This may take a long time, but the crucial matter was to find a framework that promoted peace (*Central News Agency*, 07/06/2001).

Peter Brookes (Former Deputy Assistant Secretary
of Defense for Asian and Pacific Affairs, Now Director,
Asian Studies Center, the Heritage Foundation)

In January 2003, Peter Brookes was invited by Taiwan to give a speech entitled "Taiwan's Defense: the Challenges and Needed Reforms." In his speech Brookes summarized the five challenges for Taiwan in facing the mainland Chinese military forces:

1. Mainland China's military modernization is making rapid strides and is changing the cross-strait military situation.

2. Taiwan's isolation in the international community is limiting Taiwan's ability to obtain advanced armaments and concepts.

3. The conservative style of the Taiwan military in resisting reform is preventing creativity and development.

4. Taiwan's bureaucratic military and political system is causing a diversity of policies and limiting the speedy response needed while facing a war.

5. Taiwan's economic decline is shrinking the military budget and affecting arms procurement.

In the areas of needed reforms, Brookes made four suggestions:

1. Taiwan should expand its defense strategies against limited offense and prepare broader military plans to counter Beijing's threat.

2. Taiwan's military strategic planning, procurement, and military budget should be disbursed in good and clear order.

3. Taiwan should strengthen its military modernization and give priority to forecasting, surveillance, and tri-service joint combat.

4. Taiwan should strengthen military and non-military relations and let civilian think tanks participate in defense matters.

Finally, Brookes stated that the reason for the U.S. providing Taiwan with necessary defense capabilities was based on the mutual interests of the U.S. as well as Taiwan and the entire region. If war erupts, Taiwan must bear the first blow initiated by mainland China; therefore, Taiwan should make adequate preparations (*China Times Daily News*, 01/20/2003).

The Reports of the Rand Corporation

On November 11, 2000, Rand Corporation's David A. Shlapak, David T. Orletsky, and Barry A. Wilson together wrote a research report entitled "Dire Strait? Military Aspects of the China-Taiwan Confrontation." They called on the U.S. government to assist Taiwan in raising its military capability and to interfere with mainland China's global targeting and command systems in order to gain the initiative. The U.S. should also assist Taiwan in improving the quality of her pilots and equip them with advanced air-to-air missiles in order to strengthen Taiwan's Air Force fighting power (www.rand.com).

According to a report in the *China Times Daily News*, some of mainland China's military experts were very upset with the above pleas made by the Rand Corporation. The Ships and Vessels Web site encouraged the U.S. to remember the lessons from its defeats in the Korean War and the Vietnam War and from the Chinese Civil War between the Nationalists (which the

U.S. supported), and the Communists. Assisting Taiwan, it urged, may not guarantee success. At the same time, the mainland's *The Global Military Affairs* pointed out that the intensified U.S. military deployment in the Asia-Pacific Region was clearly directed because the U.S. said that as soon as the mainland Chinese military procured various new equipment and weapons, the mainland Chinese would be able to cope with American aircraft carriers (*China Times Daily News,* 11/18/2000).

The *Rand Review,* published in 2001 by the Rand Corporation, contains proposals on global recommendations to President Bush. It was written by the Transition 2001 Panel, which consisted of 54 renowned U.S. foreign affairs and national defense experts. On the subject of the Taiwan Strait, they suggested that the U.S. and its allies adopt a combined policy of containing mainland China as well as associating with mainland China. If mainland China were cooperative within this international system and gradually democratized, then mainland China should be regarded as a partner. If mainland China became a regional hegemonic and hostile country, the U.S. should change the combined policy to a containing policy (*United Daily News,* 03/31/2001).

Rand Corporation's scholars Evan S. Medeiros and M. Taylor Fravel published an article in the bimonthly *Foreign Affairs* (the 11/01/2003 issue) entitled "China's New Diplomacy." The article begins by explaining the role that mainland China played during the six-party talks when it broke the deadlock between North Korea and the U.S. The article goes on to give a detailed list of mainland China's achievements through its practical and new open diplomacy. For example, the 2001 signing of the Sino-Russian Good-Neighbor Treaty of Friendship and Cooperation has stabilized China's northern territory. By signing the Treaty on the Southeast Asia Nuclear Weapon-Free Zone, which will establish a free-trade region by 2010, China has set up the embryonic form of an economic entity that will be able to compete with the European Union. Furthermore, mainland China has solved territorial disputes with surrounding countries and established the Declaration of Shanghai Cooperation Organization in Middle Asia, thus solving any future worries that may arise from its western territorial boundary. Mainland China signing the Nuclear Non-Proliferation Treaty and the Chemical Weapons Treaty, and even its participation in the UN's peacekeeping actions in East Timor and Congo, are further indications of how China was fulfilling its international obligations. The entire article pays attention to important issues and prompts one to deep thought; in particular, it should ring a bell for Taiwan. The article also pointed out that mainland China had already transformed its "victim mentality" formed after years of being colonized to "big country diplomacy" described earlier in this book. This kind of confidence and the accompanying easing would certainly be reflected in its cross-strait policies (www.rand.com).

Section 3:
DISCUSSIONS OF U.S. SCHOLARS' VIEWPOINTS ON CHINA'S REUNIFICATION

By summarizing the above articles and statements by scholars and think tanks, one can see that, although their viewpoints on cross-strait affairs are not entirely identical, they basically all take the position of representing American interests; that is, the hope for continued arms sales to Taiwan so that Taiwan can keep a certain military strength to confront mainland China and the hope to maintain cross-strait peace so the U.S. can avoid military clashes with mainland China. Although the models for China's reunification are not the highest concern of these scholars, some of them do propose "one country, three systems," some an "interim agreement" first followed by "confederation," and a direct "confederation."

In order to facilitate the analysis, the opinions of the aforementioned scholars and think tanks have been organized and will be discussed as separate special topics in the following section.

The Chinese Reunification Issues

On July 9, 1997, Lee Teng-hui unveiled the "special state-to-state relationship." Clinton immediately talked with Jiang Zemin on the hot line, repeatedly stated the Three Noes policy, and sent Richard Bush to Taiwan to confront Lee Teng-hui face-to-face. Two months later, Susan L. Shirk, who worked for the State Department, attended an activity hosted by Chinese in the U.S. and surprisingly stated that the people in Taiwan supported Lee Teng-hui's "two-state theory." The fact that a government official dared to openly oppose her own national policy indicates that the U.S. cross-strait policy is full of hypocrisy and contradictions.

In November 2002, Richard Bush made an even more undisguised statement. He said that there are people in Taiwan who hope to be permanently segregated from mainland China, but "when Lee Teng-hui was the president, he did not seek segregation from mainland China; Chen Shui-bian is not doing that either." It seems that Bush has intentionally failed to see Lee

Teng-hui's 12-year segregation effort. He also said that Chen Shui-bian's unwillingness to negotiate with mainland China was due to the fear of falling into the "one China" trap. Since Chen Shui-bian thinks "one China" is a trap, isn't that pro-Taiwan independence? Bush's statement was somewhat menacing, since he talked on many occasions about the possibility of Sino-U.S. clashes. He called mainland China's Taiwan policy a power game and said that even if the Pan-Blue Coalition won the presidential election, mainland China would not have an advantage. In his and other U.S. scholars' eyes, Chinese reunification means that mainland China is trying to take the advantage. But whose advantage is mainland China taking? Couldn't it be said that the U.S. would lose its current advantage after Taiwan returns to mainland China?

Nancy Bernkopf Tucker, alternately, is honest in saying that acknowledging mainland China's reunification would create many negative impacts for the U.S. However, she thinks that reunification can eliminate the fuse and reduce Sino-U.S. conflicts and clashes. This is enough to compensate for all the disadvantages. Obviously, she is quite sure that if the U.S. supports Taiwan independence and interferes with mainland China's reunification, mainland China will pay the price in the form of a war. In addition, her reminding the U.S. to prepare psychologically suggests that the U.S. indeed never seriously considered how to push for cross-strait reunification in order to maintain cross-strait safety.

Concerning mainland China's reunification models, all scholars except Nye oppose "one country, two systems" but give no clear reasons why. It seems that opposing "one country, two systems" is a universal standard not worthy of deeper investigation. Tucker said that "one country, two systems" does not give Taiwan any attractive benefits so, naturally, Taiwan should not accept it. Such an argument suggested by an American would inevitably make people think the following: 1) After reunification, the Taiwanese people could no longer be controlled by the Americans and the Taiwan leaders would no longer have to sit on the sidelines while talking to some lower-rank U.S. officials; 2) The Taiwan president and vice president would no longer have to regard their transit visits to the U.S. as an honor; 3) Taiwan would no longer have to procure arms by spending large sums of money to defend U.S. security; 4) The Taiwan people would hear no more public statements made by their high-level officials, such as, "How could it work without embracing the Americans?" Aren't all of these huge and attractive benefits?

After opposing "one country, two systems," Scalapino and Shirk proposed "one country, three systems." Shambaugh and Myers proposed the "confederation," while Lieberthal and Harding proposed to first sign a modus vivendi and then follow up with a "confederation."

Concerning these three suggestions, several points can be made. First of all, the "one country, three systems" proposed by Susan L. Shirk and others is a result of either not completely understanding the origin and content of "one country, two systems" or opposing "one country, two systems" simply for the sake of opposing it. Mainland China already said that Taiwan is different from Hong Kong and Macao and that in the future Taiwan's "one country, two systems" would not be the same as for Hong Kong and Macao. From some of the more concrete proposals of the past few years, we know that Taiwan's "one country, two systems" will be quite different from those in Hong Kong and Macao. Furthermore, the label "one country, two systems" implies that mainland China will not force Hong Kong, Macao, and Taiwan to implement one system—the socialist system of the mainland. It also does not mean that Taiwan will practice the same system that Hong Kong and Macao do. As such, "one country, three systems" is only terminology used to describe an idea that is in fact not very meaningful.

Next, Shambaugh's "confederation" and Myers' "greater China confederation" do not offer any special or unique opinions that are worth further discussion here.

Finally, Lieberthal and Harding proposed, one after the other, to first sign a *modus vivendi* (also known as an "interim agreement," "temporary agreement," or "transitional agreement"). The purpose is to push for a compromise, namely, "Taiwan does not seek independence, the mainland does not use force," in order to ease the hostility of the two sides. This would also maintain a situation of "no reunification, no independence" for a longer period of time so that U.S. interests could be protected. Both sides have discussed this viewpoint. It was said that after Chen Shui-bian took power in 2000, some scholars showed much interest in this proposal. However, they were afraid that Taiwan would be tied up by the One-China Principle and would, in the future, move in the direction of reunification. Hence, they offered no response. On the mainland Chinese side, although the official authorities did not present any formal response, some officials said that the first step in achieving reunification is "to end the hostility on both sides." However, one should not talk about maintaining peace without also pointing out that the only real guarantee of peace in the future is reunification. Although the discussions of *modus vivendi* went nowhere, "to end the hostility on both sides" is certainly an important topic to be discussed by the two sides in future dialogues.

The "China Threat" Theory and the Analysis of Cross-Strait Military Strength

The "China threat" theory suggests that both the U.S. and mainland China are strong countries and that their confrontation is inevitable. However, many examples in history have shown that two strong countries do not necessarily have to fight with each other. The U.S. concern lies in the fact that it has not been able to rid itself of the influence of traditional geopolitical theory for global dominance. In brief, since the disintegration of the Soviet Union, the U.S. does not want to see any strong country rise in Europe and the Asia-Pacific region.

Next, the "China threat" theory utilizes the clash-of-civilizations principle initiated by Samuel P. Huntington in his book, *The Clash of Civilizations and the Remaking of World Order*. The "China threat" theory argues that the American and Chinese cultures and political systems are different, particularly in that Chinese leaders are not selected by democratic means. In order to keep the legitimacy of their governance, the Chinese must regard the U.S. as an enemy. This kind of argument indicates that the U.S. judges others by their own values. The "China threat" theory is based on American culture, thinking, and habits. America does not understand a "benevolent government." It just so happens that in this world the only country—China—that might be able to catch up with the U.S. has this type of government, and has for more than 2,000 years. The benevolent spirit still exists within the Chinese culture, and the "merciful way" is always superior to the "tyrannical way." If mainland China becomes stronger and more prosperous it not only will not become any country's threat, it will also be a benefit to the entire world.

There are a fair number of retired military officers, former officials of the Defense Department, arms merchants, and related people among the think tank researchers who work on cross-strait relations. They naturally have a special interest in the analysis of the cross-strait military strengths.

When Peter Brookes spoke in Taiwan, he stated that mainland China's military strength was developing quickly. Two reasons were presented: 1) Taiwan has had difficulties in procuring advanced armaments from other countries; and 2) Taiwan has suffered an economic decline, which has led to shrinkage of the military budget and changes in cross-strait military strengths. Brookes proposed that Taiwan should enlarge its defense strategies against mainland China's possible limited offense, prepare broader military plans to respond to Beijing's threat, and make reasonable disbursements in programming military strategies, arms procurement, and military budgets.

How would Taiwan officials feel listening to Brookes' naked promotion of the sale of U.S. armaments? He frankly admitted America's regional interests in providing Taiwan with the necessary defense. But in case a war really takes place, Taiwan has to bear the threat of the first attack from mainland China.

The joint report entitled "Dire Strait? Military Aspects of the China-Taiwan Confrontation," by the Rand Corporation's three researchers, not only called on the U.S. government to assist Taiwan in raising its military intelligence capability, but also to interfere in mainland China's global targeting and command systems in order to master the initiative. This report was met with strong opposition by mainland China. The global recommendations written by the Transition 2001 Panel and published by the Rand Corporation in 2001 suggested that the U.S. and its allies adopt a combined policy of containing mainland China as well as associating with it. Although this suggestion is less hostile than the previous one, it again shows a mentality of hegemony: No matter how diplomatically the U.S. may act, it actually still regards mainland China as a potential enemy and will not stop pushing other countries to accept U.S. values and judgment.

Conclusion

Since the summer of 2003, U.S. resistance to the Taiwan independence position seems to have strengthened. At least it has added statements like, "We oppose attempting to move toward Taiwan independence." Mainland China hopes the U.S. can further exert its influence, constrain the development of the Taiwan independence movement, and restrain itself from "doing certain things" such as stopping arms sales to Taiwan and discontinuing high-level military exchanges between the U.S. and Taiwan.

In fact, the U.S. has always kept its position on the cross-strait policy consistent. However, while the U.S. asks mainland China not to use force, it is not willing to simultaneously reduce its arms sales to Taiwan—and even openly complains that Taiwan's arms procurement is too modest and too slow. Due to this contradictory policy of saying one thing while doing another, it is no surprise that Taiwan politicians do not believe that the U.S. will truly give up Taiwan. The Taiwanese people are also certain, no matter what their politicians say or do, that Taiwan will still receive U.S. protection.

The U.S. government must know that if it sends troops to protect Taiwan once war is declared by Taiwan politicians, the number of injured and dead American soldiers would far exceed those of the various recent wars initiated by the U.S. Hence, scholars like Joseph S. Nye Jr. have pointed out that if Taiwan declares independence by referendum, the U.S. will not come to its aid and fight a war over it. Why should the U.S. take such a risk? The only reason arms sales have continued is that U.S. arms merchants are very powerful and are friendly with U.S. politicians. It is not easy for the U.S. to give up arms sales to Taiwan. The U.S. has repeatedly warned Taiwan that it opposes either side of the strait attempting to change the status quo. If Taiwan ignores the warning and provokes a war, it is likely that the U.S. would only verbally call for a cease-fire and do nothing else. After all, those who die would not be Americans.

CHAPTER 6

RECENT DEVELOPMENTS IN CHINA-U.S.-TAIWAN RELATIONS

The China-U.S.-Taiwan triangular relations before and after the Taiwanese 2004 presidential election once again prove that the U.S. is the source of the Taiwan problem and that the Taiwan issue is the most central and most sensitive problem in China-U.S. relations.

Before the election, the U.S. paid strong attention to the referendum and the advocacy for a new Constitution by both the Pan-Blue and Pan-Green camps. The candidates on both sides competed to become the U.S. favorite. In particular, Chen Shui-bian repeatedly told the U.S. that the March 20 referendum statements were only "campaign language." Once reelected, he would change them back again. After the election, street protests by the Taiwanese people made the U.S. delay its congratulations for Chen Shui-bian's reelection. However, after April, the U.S. basically acknowledged that Chen Shui-bian would be inaugurated and listened attentively to his inaugural speech.

After Chen Shui-bian sent Chiu Yi-ren and Tsai Yin-wen to the U.S. for advice he was able to design a speech that pleased the U.S., and Taiwan-U.S. relations seemed to improve. However, mainland China was obviously dissatisfied with the anti-independence role played by the U.S. before and after the election; therefore, it adopted a more direct and unyielding Taiwan policy. This suggested that Chen Shui-bian's pro-independence line, which has always depended on the U.S., would face more severe challenges.

Section 1
The Most Recent Developments
in China-U.S.-Taiwan Triangular Relations

In the 2004 Taiwanese presidential election the candidates as well as the elected were clearly pro-independence. This has caused cross-strait tension and greatly changed China-U.S.-Taiwan relations.

The U.S. Attitudes before and after the Election

At the end of November 2003, as soon as Chen Shui-bian announced a referendum for March 20, 2004, Bush administration officials sternly denounced Taiwan independence. In early December 2003, Bush sent his envoy James F. Moriarty with a sealed letter to persuade Chen Shui-bian to change course. He did not receive a positive response. When Bush met Chinese Vice Premier Wen Jiabao, Bush personally and harshly criticized Chen Shui-bian's push for a referendum and writing a new Constitution as provocative. After the presidential election, the U.S. was very dissatisfied with Chen Shui-bian's announcement of a timetable for formulating a new Constitution when Chen was interviewed by a *Washington Post* reporter on March 29, 2004. After sending another secret envoy to Taiwan and receiving no positive response, the U.S. asked Japan to send a secret envoy to Taiwan to attempt a similar persuasion. After achieving nothing by their actions, on April 21, 2004, U.S. Assistant Secretary for East Asian and Pacific Affairs James Kelly issued a written statement at the hearings of the 25th anniversary of the enactment of the Taiwan Relations Act. He pointed out that Taiwan's continuous provocative words and actions increased the possibility of a cross-strait military confrontation. The U.S. had always adhered to the Taiwan Relations Act and hoped to protect the cross-strait peace, but if Taiwan insisted on moving toward independence, the U.S. would unconditionally refuse to protect Taiwan by confronting mainland China. Kelly stated at the same time that the U.S. did not support Taiwan independence, opposed a unilateral change by any side of "the status quo as we define it," resolutely opposed mainland China using force against Taiwan, and insisted on peacefully resolving the cross-strait disputes. On April 26, during a ceremony in commemoration of the 25th anniversary of the enactment of the Taiwan Relations Act, AIT Taipei Deputy Representative David J. Keegan read out this identical text once again.

On May 4, 2004, AIT Taipei Director Douglas H. Paal was invited to give a speech at the Center for East Asian Studies at Stanford University.

There he said that the U.S. did not support Taiwan independence or either side changing the status quo unilaterally since this would make Taiwan's hard-earned gains vanish overnight. He warned that it would be irresponsible for Taiwan to take mainland China's warning lightly. He pointed out that the voting rate of Taiwan's presidential election was above 80 percent, indicating active voter participation. Despite the questionable incident on the eve of and the protests after the March 20 presidential election, he described the election as "free and fair." He also said that Taiwan residents' consciences were emerging more each day and even though the number of people who opposed the reunification was increasing, the majority of the Taiwanese people within Taiwan still hoped to maintain the status quo (United Daily News, 05/06/2004).

On May 20, 2004, the U.S. sent a delegation led by Congressman James A. Leach to Taipei to celebrate Chen Shui-bian's inauguration and express their approval. On June 2, during a hearing in Washington, Leach reiterated that the content of Chen Shui-bian's inaugural speech was "thoughtful, statesman-like, and helpful." He hoped that the speech could help initiate the cross-strait dialogue. In answering questions, Leach said that the U.S. encouraged mainland China to engage in dialogues with Taiwan, but did not welcome mainland China's military threat against Taiwan and its development of military force to implement this threat. At the same time, the U.S. did not support Taiwan independence and opposed either side taking unilateral actions to change the status quo of the Taiwan Strait (*United Daily News*, 06/03/2004).

Comments on the U.S. Attitude When Dealing with the Taiwan Issue

The U.S. attitude toward Taiwan became increasingly stern before and after the completion of Taiwan's presidential election, resulting in the Taiwanese people generally growing uneasy about the decline of U.S.-Taiwan relations. Some political commentators said that the Taiwan government continuously manipulated the autonomy ideology and directly challenged the U.S. long-term "one China" policy. This created contradictions between the basic policies of Taiwan and the U.S. and led to tensions in their relationship. Hence, they suggested that Taiwan be considerate about the U.S. position of hoping to pay the smallest price to protect U.S. interests. Taiwan, for its own security, should try to make compromises with the U.S. in order to repair the declining relationship. Others commented that the cracks in the U.S.-Taiwan relationship were caused by Taiwan's actions being too crude and tricky. For example, regarding the policies of "one country on each side," the referendum, and even a new Constitution, Taiwan not only failed to actively communicate with the U.S., but it also ignored U.S. warnings and opposition. This caused many high-level U.S. officials who were once extremely friendly toward Taiwan to change their attitudes. They suggested that in order to prevent the U.S. government, which was playing the role of balancing and mediating the two sides, from leaning towards mainland China, Taiwan must act responsibly, rationally, and maturely to regain U.S. trust.

Although the U.S. claimed to oppose any form of Taiwan independence and any action that would destroy the status quo of the Taiwan Strait, it immediately announced its plan to sell new arms to Taiwan right after the election. Similarly, the U.S. questioned the referendum while at the same time declaring Taiwan a democratic society that should decide for or against a referendum itself. The U.S was well aware that Chen Shuibian's inaugural speech was an act but expressed welcome and approval nonetheless. These incidents show that the U.S. has not changed its policy of using Taiwan to contain mainland China nor its strategy of maintaining the two sides as "no reunification, no independence, and no war." Furthermore, whenever the U.S. blamed Taiwan, it never forgot to mention the Taiwan Relations Act and "solving the Taiwan issue peacefully." It is not surprising that the U.S. accusation did not work. More recently, when the U.S. advocated that the two sides should maintain the status quo, it added unexpectedly, "the status quo as we define it." On what basis does the U.S. decide the status quo of the two sides? The U.S. should have known that the 1.3 billion Chinese people on the two sides will not allow any foreign country to do that.

A Forward Look at China-U.S.-Taiwan Relations

The Taiwan Pan-Blue political commentators and scholars often like to talk about the stern U.S. attitude toward Chen Shui-bian, as if the U.S. would give up Taiwan if Chen Shui-bian does not listen to the U.S. more carefully. In fact, America would never give up Taiwan. On the surface, Chen Shui-bian seems not to listen to the U.S., but the U.S. knows clearly that Chen Shui-bian relies on U.S. power to display his own strength. The tougher his manner, the more chips he gives the U.S. to bargain with mainland China. If mainland China wants to ask the U.S. to square away Chen Shui-bian, it has to agree with the American suggestion; for example, signing an interim and open-ended agreement with Taiwan. Of course, the idealized calculations of Chen Shui-bian and the U.S. may not necessarily work. In the future, the U.S. will depend more rather than less on mainland China in dealing with international matters. Since the reconstruction of Iraq has not been smooth and the worldwide terrorist attacks have not been stopped, perhaps the U.S. does not want to provoke mainland China. As a result, even though the U.S. for its own interests does not want to see the two sides reunified, exactly how big a price the U.S. is willing to pay to prevent reunification is difficult to estimate.

Seemingly, the U.S. would declare a war only if victory is certain. During the two world wars, the U.S. only declared war when it knew that the opponents were poor and worn out. The wars that the U.S. initiated—for example the conquests of Granada and Panama—are cases of a large country invading small countries. At the beginning of the Korean War and the Vietnam War, the U.S. strength also far exceeded that of its opponents. Considering that the U.S. does not really want to fight a war without an assured win, it is not clear whether the U.S. would really want to fight against mainland China over the Taiwan issue.

Section 2
A Closer Look at the U.S. Policy
to Resolve the Taiwan Issue Peacefully

Before the 2004 Taiwan presidential election, the U.S. condemned Taiwan independence while repeatedly advocating the peaceful resolution of the Taiwan issue. After the election, the U.S. position became even clearer. On May 26, 2004, U.S. Secretary of State Colin L. Powell pointed out that the Taiwan issue was indeed an issue between the U.S. and mainland China, and Washington was collaborating with Beijing to deal with the disputes peacefully (*China Times Daily News*, 05/28/2004). On June 1, the U.S. State Department reiterated its opposition against mainland China resolving the cross-strait disputes with force and clearly stated that the U.S. had always supported a peaceful resolution. State Department spokesperson Richard Bauer stated during a routine news briefing that it was U.S. policy to collaborate with mainland China on those subjects on which both can collaborate. However, the U.S. was also clear about the differences of the two countries. With respect to the Taiwan Strait issue, the U.S. policy of supporting a peaceful resolution was always very consistent. Bauer reiterated that the U.S. opposed the use of force in resolving the cross-strait conflicts and believed military threats to be counterproductive. In addition, the U.S. believed that mainland China's military buildup and missile deployment

111

against Taiwan would cause an unstable situation (*United Daily News*, 06/03/2004).

The U.S. has always advocated solving the Taiwan problem peacefully. However, what exactly is its policy for resolving the Taiwan issue peacefully? The impact of that policy on mainland China's reunification method is worthy of further investigation.

The Origin and Development of the U.S. "Peaceful Resolution" Policy

The U.S. "peaceful resolution" policy appeared for the first time in the 1972 Shanghai Communiqué. Apart from publicly announcing that it recognized that the Chinese on both sides of the Taiwan Strait agree that there is only one China and that Taiwan is part of China, the U.S. also "reiterated its position on Chinese resolving the Taiwan problem by themselves peacefully." On the surface, the U.S. "peaceful resolution" policy and mainland China's "one country, two systems" idea are not contradictory. However, when the Cold War ended, the U.S. policy was given a new meaning. The U.S. no longer needed mainland China to contain Russia, but it wanted to maintain the existing order in the Asia-Pacific region and use the separation of the two sides to contain mainland China's rise.

During the two Taiwan Strait crises in 1995 and 1996, the U.S. sent two aircraft carrier battle groups, thus associated the Taiwan Relations Act with new military content and increased the U.S. attention to "resolve the Taiwan issue peacefully." In 1997, after Lee Teng-hui proposed his "two-state theory," the U.S. maintained its pressure on mainland China and demanded China to pay attention to the U.S. "peaceful resolution" policy. However, President Clinton adopted an ambiguous policy in maintaining a "peaceful resolution" position. He did not make it clear whether force would be used to defend his policy. When George W. Bush took office, he created a policy that again leaned towards Taiwan. Not only did Bush announce the largest arms sale to Taiwan since 1992, but he also threatened to "take any measure to protect Taiwan."

As soon as this message reached the Taiwan independence force, Taiwan's pro-independence people called for action. They even proposed "one country on each side," thereby challenging the cross-strait status quo—in violation of the U.S. policy aim of "no reunification, no independence, and no war." The Bush administration toned down its rhetoric and moved toward a more balanced position as a result. During many meetings with the mainland Chinese leaders, Bush repeatedly clarified the need to adhere to the "one China" policy, the three joint communiqués, and not supporting Taiwan independence. Mere words do not indicate that the U.S. made fundamental adjustments to its Taiwan policy in favor of mainland China. The Bush administration not only repeatedly emphasized that the Taiwan issue should be "resolved peacefully" and that the U.S. would continue to insist on the Taiwan Relations Act, but it also called for the strengthening of Taiwan's defense capabilities. The U.S. policy towards Taiwan also turned from passive to active interference. The U.S. increased its arms sales to Taiwan and enhanced U.S.-Taiwan military interchanges. It also improved personnel and intelligence exchanges in order to push for the integration of the U.S. and Taiwan military.

According to a research report by the mainland scholar Wang Gonglong, the U.S. "peaceful resolution" policy held inherent contradictions from its execution, whether it was Clinton's "strategic ambiguity" or Bush's "strategic clarity." The "peaceful resolution" policy, in fact, became a "peaceful no resolution" policy. On one hand, the U.S. claimed non-participation in the cross-strait relations and on the other hand, it continued to exert pressure on mainland China. The U.S. used "peaceful resolution" as it attempted to freeze the cross-strait status quo in order to maintain its dominant position in East Asia. The more the U.S. attempted to increase its arms sales to Taiwan for cross-strait peace, the more likely it was delivering objectively erroneous messages to the Taiwan independence movement. As a result, the Taiwan independence supporters became more fearless in challenging the "one China" policy (*Research-Taiwan*, a bimonthly journal published by the Institute of Taiwan Studies of the Chinese Academy of Social Sciences, 2nd volume, 2004).

Based on its development after the Cold War, the U.S. "peaceful resolution" policy indeed has become more dominant. The U.S. took advantage of this policy to participate in cross-strait affairs and seriously violated the basic position insisted on by China, that "reunification is China's internal affair; other nations have no right to interfere." It also went in the opposite direction from the mainland policy, according to which "the Taiwan problem cannot be dragged out for an unlimited period of time," thus creating a big obstacle for reunification. The U.S. "peaceful resolution" policy also did not conform to the desire of the Taiwan independence movement to seek independence by destroying the status quo. It seems that the U.S. "peaceful resolution" policy would not necessarily fulfill U.S. interests. The U.S. had to wake up completely if it no longer wanted to be dragged and become exhausted by the Taiwan independence movement and its efforts to avoid misunderstandings by mainland China. Reunification or not is an internal matter between the Chinese on the two sides of the strait. The U.S. really does not have the obligation or the right to interfere.

The U.S. Increases Arms Sales to Taiwan

The U.S.'s advocacy of peacefully resolving the cross-strait issue had become the most favorable pretext for increasing arms sales to Taiwan. Taiwan authorities, of course, welcomed this policy. On June 2, 2004, a meeting at the Executive Yuan (see explanation for Yuan in Glossary) in Taiwan passed A Major Military Procurement Budget Proposal and Major Military Procurement Regulations. The Executive Yuan spokesperson Chen Chi-mai said that despite the year-by-year increase of mainland China's military expenses, the national army's expenditure had been declining. The Executive Yuan decided to purchase three types of armaments from the U.S. under a 15-year special budget arrangement that totaled US$18 billion. The army would appropriate about US$4.3 billion to buy 388 Patriot PAC-3 missile systems, the navy would appropriate about US$12.1 billion to buy eight diesel-powered submarines, and the air force would get about US$1.6 billion to buy 12 anti-submarine planes. This was the first time that the DPP proposed a super-budget military procurement. It was also the largest in Taiwan's military procurement history. The government noted that the money to finance the special budget would come from several sources: about US$2.8 billion from the release of shares of state-owned enterprises, about US$2.9 billion from the selling of state-owned land, and the raising of the national debt by about US$12.4 billion.

As soon as the Executive Yuan passed the budget proposal, both the KMT and the PFP parties described it as humiliating the country by forfeiting its sovereignty, similar to paying the U.S. a protection fee, being highly overpriced, and not meeting Taiwan's military needs. The PFP Legislator Lin Yu-fang solemnly stated that forcing the Legislative Yuan to pass this rushed, crude military procurement proposal would be "as difficult as a human flying like a bird." The DPP Legislator Lee Wen-chung pointed out that the three military procurement proposals were determined by the Taiwan-U.S. Military Procurement Meeting. However, he also agreed that the price of the submarines was a few times higher than that for equivalent submarines in the international community. The Independent Legislator Sisy Chen, on the contrary, said that the KMT and the PFP had already suffered a big defeat in the past on the Submarine Manufactured by Taiwan Special Budget Proposal, and that the Pan-Blue camp should have learned a lesson from that case. Especially when Taiwan needed an impartial U.S. participant in handling the March 19 shooting incident, the Pan-Blue should not oppose the special defense budget. She said that Taiwan's military strength had a serious imbalance compared to that of the mainland. If the KMT and the PFP insisted on opposing the proposal, achieving balance would be impossible and they would make the U.S. unhappy (*China Times Daily News*, 06/03/2004). Chen's statement clearly exposed her position.

In order to pass the huge military procurement proposal smoothly, the U.S. changed its approach of only dealing with the military to increased persuasion of Taiwan's Legislative Yuan. In June 2003, Legislative Yuan President Wang Jin-pyng led a visiting delegation to the U.S. for the first time. Later, the Kidd-class Destroyer budget was unfrozen, after Wang Jin-pyng communicated with the KMT and the PFP legislators. The Long Range Radar Space Surveillance System budget was also approved. Wang Jin-pyng would again lead a delegation in June 2004 to visit Washington and Hawaii. Although he emphasized that the Legislative Yuan was going to safeguard the people's pocket and play the role of "good guy," the media was not so optimistic about the ability and willingness of the Legislative Yuan to protect Taiwan from being trampled by others.

The U.S. expansion of arms sales to Taiwan seriously violates the China-U.S. August 17 Communiqué signed between mainland China and the U.S. Item 6 of the communiqué, which was signed in 1982, makes this clear: "The United States government states that it does not seek to carry out a long-term policy of arms sales to Taiwan, that its arms sales to Taiwan will not exceed, either in qualitative or in quantitative terms, the level of those supplied in recent years since the establishment of diplomatic relations between the United States and mainland China, and that it intends to reduce gradually its sales of arms to Taiwan, leading over a period of time to a final resolution." This communiqué was signed more than 20 years ago, but the U.S. never executed it strictly. Now the U.S. is trying to sell advanced weapons to Taiwan under the stressful cross-strait situation, which only aggravates the condition. Mainland China repeatedly made it clear that once the two sides resumed talks, the cross-strait hostility would be eliminated immediately. However, the Taiwan authorities would rather procure arms by borrowing money and placing a very huge burden on the Taiwanese people. This does nothing to lower the intense cross-strait situation and is simply not wise. Hopefully those legislators who object to paying the "protection fee" or who think that the U.S. is taking advantage can form their positions and fight until the end. Broad awareness of the Taiwanese people is required to properly solve the problem of procuring armaments from the U.S. They should resist Chen Shui-bian's military procurement proposal and not vote for those legislators who support arms procurement.

U.S. Scholars Suggest Again That
the Two Sides Sign an Interim Agreement

In the middle of April 2004, Kenneth G. Lieberthal and David M. Lampton jointly published an article in *The Washington Post* entitled "Heading off the Next War," in which they advocated for an improved interim agreement between Taiwan and mainland China. The original version was proposed by Harry Harding and Stanley Roth (former Assistant Secretary of State for East Asian and Pacific Affairs and member of the House International Relations Committee, Asia and the Pacific Subcommittee). The essential viewpoints of this improved interim agreement are that mainland China does not use force, that Taiwan does not seek independence, and that both sides maintain the status quo for a few decades. They also suggested that both sides establish a mutual trust mechanism as soon as possible and that mainland China continue to insist on the One-China Principle but must renounce the use of force against Taiwan. Taiwan could emphasize being sovereignly independent, but it must give up seeking *de jure* independence—namely each side can express its own position. The improved interim agreement did not include a reunification blueprint, but it did include suggestions such as assistance by the international community in Taiwan returning to international organizations.

Taiwan scholar Tsai Wei paid close attention to the interim agreement proposed by the U.S. After the aforementioned scholars published their articles, he wrote a piece in which he claimed that "Beijing initially also did not exclude the idea of an interim agreement." Taipei and Beijing should grasp the opportunity to "consider or accept this new improved interim agreement, under the condition that the two sides not seek independence and not use force, each side tells its own story, trying to stabilize the cross-strait situation as soon as possible. Let the U.S. be a passive witness that allows Taiwan to have more international living space and allows both sides to collaborate further toward establishing a mutual trust mechanism. Perhaps this would be the ideal result for the two sides and three parties" (*China Times Daily News*, 04/26/2004).

Agreeing with Tsai Wei's opinion is difficult. Regardless of whether mainland China intended to accept the original version of the interim agreement, after Chen Shui-bian's reelection China's attitude was quite obvious. Unless Chen Shui-bian recognized "one China," it was fundamentally impossible for mainland China to negotiate with him. Hence, it was pointless for the U.S. to suggest signing the interim agreement. The U.S. only focused on demanding that the two sides begin negotiations unconditionally, while totally ignoring the "one China" prerequisite insisted on by mainland China. On top of this, the improved interim agreement did not include the hoped-for reunification blueprint, which made it even less favorable to reunification than the original interim agreement. No matter what had been said, mainland China could not accept it. If the U.S. truly wanted to bring about a cross-strait peace, it would not interfere with other countries' internal affairs, not use scholars to release influential speeches, and not assume that all people in the world accept its suggestions.

Mainland China Changed Its Taiwan Policy

Mainland China became increasingly dissatisfied with the U.S. Taiwan policy. On May 30, 2004, the *Xinhua News Agency* published a long report, which did not point specifically at Assistant Secretary of State James Kelly's Congressional hearing, but which accused the U.S. of "defining" the status quo of Taiwan. Kelly's statements not only seriously violated the One-China Principle and the three joint communiqués, but also interfered with mainland China's internal affairs. The report indicated that in the world there is only one China and that Taiwan is part of China. This is the whole history and the current situation of Taiwan. At that time, the biggest threat to the peace and stability of the Taiwan Strait region was the divisive activities of the Taiwan independence movement, which were approved by the Taiwan authorities. If the U.S. really wanted to protect the peace and stability of the Taiwan Strait region, it had to clearly recognize the divisive nature of Taiwan independence and not use any method to send wrong messages to the Taiwan independence movement. The U.S. should not talk nonsense about mainland China's military arrangements, let alone use it as a pretext to continuously sell arms to Taiwan. The report also said that the U.S. argued that the reason for selling arms to Taiwan was to make Taiwan authorities "feel safe" in communicating with the mainland. However, the reality is just the opposite. The continuous selling of U.S. weapons to Taiwan made Taiwan's activities for a divided China appear increasingly frenzied; Taiwan's move towards independence felt more secure due to strong backing and its attitude swelled with growing arrogance. In conclusion, the U.S. acted inexcusably and bears a great deal of responsibility for the current state of development of the cross-strait situation (*China Times Daily News*, 05/31/2004).

On June 1, 2004, during a routine press conference, the Chinese Foreign Ministry spokesman Liu Jianchao also accused the 2004 annual report on the Military Power of the People's Republic of China promulgated by the U.S. Department of Defense of deliberately exaggerating mainland China's military strength and expenditures, and reiterating the old rhetoric of the "China threat" theory. He said the report clearly had other motives. Liu Jianchao emphasized that Chinese people love peace; mainland China pursues an independent peaceful foreign policy on its own, executes a defensive warfare policy, and insists on a path of peaceful development. As a sovereign country, in order to protect its national safety and territorial integrity, it is natural for mainland China to pursue the buildup of its national defense (*China Times Daily News*, 06/02/2004).

The mainland scholars did not think highly of what the U.S. did to prevent Taiwan independence. Yan Xuetong at the Institute of International Studies, Tsinghua University, pointed out that the U.S. hoped Taiwan would be "independent peacefully" and that the two sides would be "not reunified, not independent, not at war." The difficulty for the U.S. in supporting Taiwan independence was Taiwan's lack of military capability. Hence, the Sino-U.S. relationship could maintain its status. If in a year or so the U.S. can lower the temperature in Iraq, it will be able to turn around and support Taiwan independence. By then, Chen Shui-bian will have increased his pace toward Taiwan independence. He estimated that in the next two years (2004-2006) mainland China and the U.S. would have more serious clashes over the Taiwan issue. However, Chu Shulong at the Institute for Strategic Studies, Tsinghua University, said that although the two sides have obvious fundamental differences on the prerequisite of the Taiwan issue, they are still in "cooperation rather than divergence." The May 17 Statement shows that Beijing is strengthening its resolute determination and capability for reunification. In order to prevent a crisis occurring in the Taiwan Strait, the U.S. should give Taiwan a clear signal: If Taiwan's behavior seriously affects U.S. interests in the West Pacific Ocean, the U.S. would act to prevent trouble from happening (*United Daily News*, 05/31/2004).

Kenneth G. Lieberthal, the American scholar who knows much about cross-strait affairs, repeatedly warned Taiwan—perhaps because he understands all too well about the Chinese authorities' and people's resolute position on reunification. In early June 2004, he was at the East Asian Institute of the National University of Singapore and said, "If pressured by the situation, mainland China will pay any price to use force against Taiwan." As a result, Taiwan should not have the misconception that at a moment of necessity, the U.S. would definitely provide Taiwan with military assistance. Taiwan should not continuously test the mainland's baseline (*China Times Daily News*, 06/05/2004).

It would be fairly difficult for the U.S. to abandon its policy to "resolve the Taiwan issue peacefully." After all, this policy concerns practical interests of the U.S., and the arms sales to Taiwan affect the huge profits gained by arms merchants and government officials. However, the U.S. realizes that mainland China has the real strength and determination to affect the reunification. As a result, apart from continued adherence to the "one China" policy and the three joint communiqués, the U.S. should also focus on not giving wrong signals to Taiwan. As for the arms sales to Taiwan, the U.S. will not be able to give them up. The profits are huge. Fortunately, mainland China knows this and will play a leading role to prevent Taiwan independence and push for reunification.

Conclusion

Because of its interests in the Asia-Pacific region, the U.S. will not abandon its concern and interference in the cross-strait matters. However, mainland China has shown its determination for and capacity to achieve reunification. It expresses clearly that the U.S. has violated its promise, thus leading to the growth of Taiwan independence. If mainland China maintains a tough stance, the development of China-U.S.-Taiwan triangular relations will not be favorable toward Taiwan independence. However, as long as Taiwan realizes clearly that a direct dialogue with mainland China is more useful than depending on the U.S., there is still the prospect for expecting a turn for the better.

PART III

Taiwan's Attitude toward Reunification and "One Country, Two Systems"

The "one country, two systems" principle has been around for 20 years. During this period, mainland China often enhanced the policy with various concrete proposals, but it was not clear how the Taiwanese people viewed it. In recent years, the MAC of the ROC always included questions about "one country, two systems" in its public surveys. Newspapers, TV stations, polling organizations, and academic institutions have conducted polls concerning the cross-strait policy and the "one country, two systems" stance. These organizations put out very different surveys and the results varied from time to time. It is not yet clear exactly how the Taiwanese people view "one country, two systems," and this question deserves further investigation.

This part of the book will introduce and discuss separately the attitudes of Taiwan authorities and various political parties toward reunification and "one country, two systems." Their positions may not represent all Taiwanese people; however, keep in mind that during recent years the Taiwan people's information about "one country, two systems" came mostly from the propaganda of their government, various political parties, and scholars. Hence, their positions and viewpoints deserve to be introduced one by one. In this English version, for brevity, we'll omit the detailed discussions on Taiwanese scholars' viewpoints that are included in the Chinese version.

CHAPTER 7

TAIWAN AUTHORITIES' ATTITUDES TOWARD REUNIFICATION AND "ONE COUNTRY, TWO SYSTEMS"

In this chapter, I shall discuss the Taiwan authorities' attitudes toward reunification and "one country, two systems."

SECTION 1
A REVIEW OF TAIWAN'S MAINLAND POLICY

Taiwan's scholars have differing opinions about whether the ROC government had a mainland policy before granting Taiwan people visiting rights to their mainland relatives in 1987. Those who believe that there was a clear and firm mainland policy prior to 1987 further believe that the policy can be divided into two periods. The first period was between 1949, during which the ROC moved to Taiwan, and 1979, when the PRC and the U.S. established a formal diplomatic relationship. The second period was between 1979, during which China announced its Message to Compatriots in Taiwan, and 1987, when the Taiwanese people were allowed to pay family visits to the mainland (refer to the publications by Taiwan scholars Chang Wu-yueh and Shaw Chong-hai). Of course, during these two periods, numerous important turning points occurred. Some of these changes were related to the mentalities of the Taiwan power wielders and internal political power transformations. Others were related to international circumstances, in particular to changes in China-U.S.-Taiwan relations.

Before 1979, the Taiwan government's positions went through many changes, from "counterattack on the mainland to recover China," to "a good guy will not go hand in hand with a thief," to "unify China by the Three Principles of the People." But the position of making counterattacks to recover the country had never been shaken. In April 1979, President Chiang Ching-kuo proposed the Three Noes policy (no openings of transport, trade, or postal services). In April 1982, the 12th Kuomintang National Party Congress passed The Proposition to Unify China under the Three Principles of the People. In November 1987, the Taiwanese people were granted permission to pay family visits to the mainland. In July 1988, the 13th Kuomintang National Party Congress adopted The KMT's Mainland Policy at the Current Stage. In June 1989, indirect telephone calls and telegram communications were liberalized and the handling process for postal communications was simplified.

On May 20, 1990, in his inaugural speech as the eighth ROC President, Lee Teng-hui said, "If mainland authorities can adopt democracy and a free market system, renounce the use of force in the Taiwan Strait, and not interfere in our pursuit of foreign relations under the one-China premise, we will be willing to establish communication channels on an equal footing to fully liberalize academic, cultural, economic, scientific and technological exchanges." In October of the same year, he convened a meeting with representatives from major political parties and civilian organizations to establish the NUC under the presidential office and formulate the NUG.

At the end of January 1991, the MAC was formally established to function as the statutory administrative agency under the Executive Yuan responsible for the overall planning and coordination of policy related to the mainland. In March of the same year, the Executive Yuan adopted the NUG as the guiding principle of the government's mainland China policy. On May 1, 1991, the ROC government declared the termination of the Period of General Mobilization for the Suppression of the Communist Rebellion.

The main purpose of this book is not to introduce the mainland policies of the ROC government during the last half-century; instead, it is to probe the government positions on defining Taiwan's status, the nation's reunification, and "one country, two systems" issues from 1990. Hence, the relevant policies before the 1990s and many important policies after 1990, such as the three links and direct transport, are not discussed.

Because Lee Teng-hui was also the party chairman of the KMT during his terms as president, the KMT's decisions at the time were often also government policies. After the political power transformation in 2000, Chen Shui-bian held a concurrent position as the DPP Party Chairman. The policies of Chen Shui-bian's government, then, overlapped with DPP political positions. In this discussion, the positions of the government are intentionally omitted from the positions of the parties, which will be discussed in Chapter 8. Some overlap is unavoidable, however.

SECTION 2
THE STANCE OF TAIWAN AUTHORITIES TOWARD REUNIFICATION AND "ONE COUNTRY, TWO SYSTEMS" FROM 1990 TO THE PRESENT

The discussions of the Taiwan authorities' political stance on these topics are as follows:

The Executive Yuan Adopted the National Unification Guidelines (03/14/1991)

In March 1991, the Executive Yuan adopted the NUG passed in February of that year to be the highest guiding principle of the government's mainland policy.

I. Introduction

The reunification of China is meant to bring about a strong and prosperous nation with a long-lasting, bright future for its people. It is the common wish of Chinese people at home and abroad. After an appropriate period of forthright exchange, cooperation, and consultation conducted under the principles of reason, peace, parity, and reciprocity, the two sides of the Taiwan Strait should foster a consensus of democracy, freedom, and equal prosperity as they together build a new and unified China. Based on this understanding, guidelines have been specially formulated with the expressed hope that all Chinese throughout the world would work with one mind toward their fulfillment.

II. Goal

The goal of reunification is to establish a democratic, free, and equitably prosperous China.

III. Principles

The four principles surrounding reunification are as follows:

1. Both the mainland and Taiwan areas are parts of the Chinese territory. Helping to bring about national reunification should be the common responsibility of all Chinese people.

2. The reunification of China should be for the welfare of its entire people and not be subject to partisan conflict.
3. China's reunification should aim at promoting Chinese culture, safeguarding human dignity, guaranteeing fundamental human rights, and practicing democracy and the rule of law.
4. The timing and manner of China's reunification should first respect the rights and interests of the people in the Taiwan area, and protect their security and welfare. Reunification should be achieved in gradual phases under the principles of reason, peace, parity, and reciprocity.

IV. Process

There are three phases to reunification, as described below.

1. Short Term: A Phase of Exchanges and Reciprocity

   a. The short-term process is to enhance understanding through exchanges between the two sides of the strait and to eliminate hostility through reciprocity. Both sides must establish a mutually benign relationship by not endangering each other's security and stability while in the midst of exchanges and by not denying the other's existence as a political entity while in the midst of effecting reciprocity.

   b. The short-term processes are to set up an order for exchanges across the strait, to draw up regulations for such exchanges, and to establish intermediary organizations so as to protect the rights and interests of people on both sides of the strait. In addition, both sides must gradually ease various restrictions and expand people-to-people contacts so as to promote social prosperity.

   c. In order to improve the people's welfare on both sides of the strait with the ultimate objective of reunifying the nation, in the mainland area economic reform should be carried out forthrightly. The expression of public opinion should gradually be allowed, and both democracy and the rule of law should be implemented. In the Taiwan area, efforts should be made to accelerate political reform and promote national development to establish a society of equitable prosperity.

   d. The two sides of the strait should end the state of hostility and, under the principle of one China, solve all disputes through peaceful means. Furthermore, they should respect, not reject, each other in the international community as they move toward a phase of mutual trust and cooperation.

2. Medium Term: A Phase of Mutual Trust and Cooperation

a. Both sides of the strait should establish official communication channels on an equal footing.

b. Direct postal, transport, and commercial links should be allowed. Both sides should jointly develop the southeastern coastal area of the Chinese mainland, and then gradually extend this development to other areas of the mainland in order to narrow the gap in living standards between the two sides.

c. Both sides of the strait should work together and assist each other in taking part in international organizations and activities.

d. Exchange visits by high-ranking officials on both sides should be promoted to create favorable conditions for consultation and reunification.

3. Long Term: A Phase of Consultation and Reunification
A consultative organization for reunification should be established through which both sides jointly discuss the grand task of reunification and map out a constitutional system to establish a democratic, free, and equitably prosperous China. This must be achieved in accordance with the will of the people in both the mainland and Taiwan areas, and while adhering to the goals of democracy, economic freedom, social justice, and the nationalization of the armed forces.

The National Unification Council Adopted the Definition of "One China" (08/01/1992)

The NUC adopted the definition of "one China" at its eighth meeting in August 1992. The contents of this definition are as follows:

1. While the two sides of the Taiwan Strait agree that there is only one China, they have different opinions as to the meaning of "one China." To Beijing, "one China" means the People's Republic of China with Taiwan as a "special administration region" after reunification. Taipei, on the other hand, considers "one China" to mean the Republic of China, founded in 1911 and with *de jure* sovereignty over all of China. The ROC, however, currently has jurisdiction only over Taiwan, Penghu, Kinmen, and Matsu. Taiwan is part of China, and the Chinese mainland is part of China as well.

2. Beginning in 1949, the division of China under two separate governments on either side of the Taiwan Strait is seen as a temporary, transitional phenomenon in Chinese history. This has been an objective reality, and propositions seeking reunification cannot ignore the existence of such a reality.

3. In order to seek the development of nationalism, the country's

prosperity, and people's well-being, the ROC Government already enacted the NUG in 1991. It actively looks for common views to begin the steps for reunification in the hope that the Chinese authorities will be pragmatic by giving up prejudices and dealing with concrete problems. Through mutual collaborations the two sides may pool wisdom and efforts, working together to create a China of democracy, freedom, and equitable prosperity.

The MAC Promulgated the Relations across the Taiwan Strait White Paper (07/05/1994)

In response to the 1993 PRC white paper, the MAC promulgated a mainland policy white paper entitled "Relations across the Taiwan Strait" toward the end of its working meeting on the mainland issues. It clearly points out that there is "only one China" and that "Taiwan and the mainland are both part of China," but that "one China" refers to China as a historical, geographical, cultural, and racial entity. The white paper states, "The Beijing regime is not equivalent to China." Prior to reunification, China is ruled by two separate governments, which should have the right to participate alongside each other in the international community. The white paper quoted the NUG and proposed the "one China, two equal political entities" structure to define the cross-strait relations.

Lee Teng-hui Issued a Six-Point Proposal (04/08/1995)

After Jiang Zemin promulgated the Jiang's Eight-Point Proposals, ROC President Lee Teng-hui issued a statement at the NUC and made six points, which came to be known as Lee's Six-Point Proposal. Specifically, the points are to:

1. Pursue China's reunification based on the reality that the two sides are governed respectively by two governments;
2. Strengthen bilateral exchanges based on Chinese culture;
3. Enhance trade and economic relations to develop a mutually beneficial and complementary relationship;
4. Ensure that both sides join international organizations on an equal footing and that leaders on both sides meet during their participation of such organizations;
5. Adhere to the principle of resolving all disputes by peaceful means; and
6. Jointly safeguard prosperity and promote democracy in Hong Kong and Macao.

The Response of the Taiwan Authorities on
Hong Kong's Reverting to Mainland China

Hong Kong reverted to mainland China on July 1, 1997. On June 16, the MAC promulgated The Republic of China's Stance and Policy Statement toward the Hong Kong Handover and expressed disapproval at mainland China's downgrading the ROC to a "local government." The statement points out that "the ROC is a country of independent sovereignty, practicing democratic constitutionalism, possessing adequate judicial systems, conducting independent diplomacy and is capable of national self-defense. Its long-term separation from the mainland is due to the Civil War. Furthermore, mainland China has never administered jurisdiction over Taiwan. Hence, the ROC absolutely disallows mainland China to downgrade the ROC to a local government. The so-called "one country, two systems" proposed by mainland China, by its basic nature, makes the ROC surrender to mainland China. It is an effort to make the Taiwanese people abandon the democratic free system they enjoy after a fixed period of time. As a result, we resolutely oppose mainland China's use of the term reunification to actually annex the ROC."

On June 30—one day before Hong Kong reverted to mainland China—Lee Teng-hui agreed to be interviewed by an American *CNN* reporter and stated, "China has to be reunified under a system of democracy and equitable prosperity. We absolutely cannot accept the so-called 'one country, two systems.'" Lien Chan agreed with the interview and stated that the reunification of the two sides should be under "one country, one system" (i.e., one country with one good system) instead of "one country, two systems." He emphasized that the two sides should build mutual trust, collaborate with each other, and achieve the aim of reunification through political negotiations. The cross-strait reunification should not be a unification of only the territory or jurisdiction, but a unification of political ideologies.

Lien Chan Issued a Special Statement
on the Cross-Strait Relations (02/29/1998)

Lien Chan issued a statement entitled "From 'Three Noes' and 'Three Wants' to Explore the Cross-Strait Future" in the *United Daily*. He offered interpretations on the Three Noes and the Three Wants as the basis for future reunification. The Three Noes are: no Taiwan independence, no reunification, and no confrontation. The Three Wants are: peace, exchanges, and a win-win situation. Lien Chan pointed out that if the mainland does not reform, mainland China has no hope, and if neither side of the strait promotes exchange, Taiwan has no future. The larger the reformation on the mainland, the faster the cross-strait exchange can proceed. Then the positive interchange of reform and exchange can emerge in earnest.

Lien Chan also pointed out the reasons for the cross-strait opposition: first, there is a serious imbalance of constitutional development; second, the differing political ideologies have created internal political constraints; third, there are competitions in diplomacy between the two political governments. The source of the cross-strait clash still has its roots in the political systems. The reduction of the differences in political systems requires political courage on the mainland side and patience and time on the Taiwan side. Hence, both sides should try their best to think about how to get along with each other from the Three Noes and the Three Wants.

Statements Relate to China's
Democratic Reunification (07/12/1998)

Lee Teng-hui's "Democratic Reunification" proposal at the NUC meeting on July 22, 1998, urged the two sides to negotiate and reach a peace treaty under the principle that China has separate governments. At the 3rd Convention of the 3rd National Assembly on December 8, Lee Teng-hui defined the "New Taiwanism" as identification with the land, a common goal to fight for the ROC, and a sense of general community, regardless of the time of arrival in Taiwan, language spoken, or native province.

MAC Vice Chairman Lin Chong-pin emphasized that the ROC government's insistence that the mainland's democratization must take place prior to reunification was based on four considerations:

1. Regional stability: Reunification without a democratic mainland would arouse suspicion from neighboring countries and leave China vulnerable to the negative impact of regional threats.

2. Humanitarian considerations: Taiwan cares very much about the well-being of the mainland people. If mainland China does not reform politically and legally, its economic reform will not be able to continue.

3. Legal considerations: History suggests that when two governments sign an agreement and one government is not democratic, then there is a high probability for that government to breach the agreement.

4. Domestic reality: Taiwan is a democratic society. Any political party leaders who decide to reunify with the mainland before Beijing becomes democratic will certainly lose the people's support in the next election.

Lee Teng-hui Proposed a "Special State-to-State Relationship" (07/09/1999)

Lee Teng-hui gave an interview to a delegate from the Deutsche Welle Radio and said that since 1991, when the ROC Constitution was amended, cross-strait relations have been defined as "state-to-state" or at least a "special state-to-state relationship." Cross-strait relations should not be an internal relationship of "one China" in which there is a legal government versus a rebel regime, or a central government versus a local government. China has been a sovereign and independent country since the establishment of the ROC in 1912. Hence, the characterization by Beijing authorities of Taiwan as a "renegade province" is historically incorrect. Lee Teng-hui emphasized that one cannot look at issues related to the two sides simply from the perspective of reunification or independence. The key issue is the different "systems." Progression from an "integration of systems" to a "gradual political integration" is the most natural and suitable choice for ensuring the welfare of all Chinese people.

The MAC held a press conference on July 11 and confirmed that during Lee Teng-hui's interview with German reporters he said that the cross-strait relations should be defined by a "special state-to-state relationship" and that his pronouncement contains three meanings.

First, it is practical. The PRC has never ruled Taiwan, Penghu, Kinmen, and Matsu, all of which have been under the jurisdiction of the ROC. It is a fact that the two sides of the Taiwan Strait are under the administrations of different governments of the PRC. The ROC is an indisputable political reality and legal fact. Second, it has continuity. This pronouncement serves mainly to clearly state the current cross-strait situation; it does not change the mainland policy itself. Third, it is creative. The cross-strait relations should be free from the "one China" dispute. On the basis of reciprocity, both can talk about all of the problems they are facing.

In a SEF-arranged briefing on July 30, Chairman Koo Chen-fu emphasized that the cross-strait relationship is a "special state-to-state relationship." Koo Chen-fu stressed that the special relationship is the ROC government's position made in line with the 1992 Consensus that the One-China Principle can be subject to the interpretation of the two sides. However, ARATS completely rejected his interpretation.

The Response to Jiang Zemin's Speech
at the Macao Handover Ceremony (12/21/1999)

During the Macao Handover Ceremony, Jiang Zemin pointed out that "one country, two systems" will be a showcase for Taiwan. Foreign Affairs Minister Chen Chien-jen responded with the following points:

- Taiwan is completely different from Hong Kong and Macao. Neither the Taiwan people nor its government can accept "one country, two systems."

- According to public polls, most Taiwanese people are not willing to accept "one country, two systems." As such, Jiang Zemin's talk has little impact on the situation.

- Macao is a colony in which "people had no choice then and have no choice now." However, Macao does have a Constitution, the power of self-defense, and democracy. They have independent "strength, public opinion, and our own choice." It is absolutely inaccurate to use Hong Kong and Macao as Taiwan's "model."

- Since Hong Kong reverted to mainland China in 1997, it has had little impact on cross-strait relations. Macao is even less important than Hong Kong and it is not expected to have a major impact on cross-strait relations.

- The MAC also made strong statements by pointing out that "one country, two systems" in Taiwan is "humiliating" and "provoking." It is not only useless to the cross-strait reunification, it is also harmful.

The Response to Mainland China's
Second White Paper (02/21/2000)

Mainland China promulgated its second white paper on the eve of Taiwan's 2000 presidential election. The responses of Lee Teng-hui and Taiwan authorities were low-key. Only the MAC officials briefed the outside world according to mainland China's past operations. This time it expressly pointed out that Taiwan's maintaining the status quo is considered a kind of Taiwan independence; if Taiwan does not want to negotiate with mainland China, mainland China will use force. These statements meant that mainland China would definitely take the next step.

U.S. officials in Taiwan stated that Taiwan's cold response to the three "ifs" in the white paper was not understandable. During a special topic meeting of the National Committee on U.S.-China Relations in Washington, the American Ambassador in the PRC, Joseph W. Prueher, stated that the timing, the content, and the tone of the white paper were irrelevant in the peaceful disentanglement of the cross-strait conflicts. As far as the U.S. was concerned, whether there was a white paper or not it would keep its promise to support Taiwan and hoped that both sides could peacefully disentangle the conflicts.

Chen Shui-bian's Inauguration Speech (Four Noes and One Without) (05/20/2000)

After Chen Shui-bian and Annette Lu were sworn in as the tenth-term President and Vice President of the Republic of China, Chen Shui-bian made his inauguration speech. Concerning the cross-strait relations, he pointed out that "the people across the Taiwan Strait share the same ancestral, cultural, and historical background. While upholding the principles of democracy and parity, building upon the existing foundations, and constructing conditions for cooperation through goodwill, we believe that the leaders on both sides possess enough wisdom and creativity to jointly deal with the question of a future 'one China.' As long as the CPC regime has no intention to use military force against Taiwan, I pledge that during my term in office, I will not declare independence, I will not change the national title, I will not push forth the inclusion of the so-called 'state-to-state' description in the Constitution, and I will not promote a referendum to change the status quo in regards to the question of independence or reunification. Also I have no intention of abolishing the National Unification Guidelines and the National Unification Council." (The above is the so-called Four Noes and One Without.) On such a basis, as long as the governments and people on both sides of the Taiwan Strait can interact more, following the principles of "goodwill reconciliation, enthusiastic cooperation, and permanent peace" while simultaneously respecting the free choice of the people and excluding unnecessary obstacles, both sides of the strait can make great contributions to the prosperity and stability of the Asia-Pacific Region. Both sides will also create a glorious civilization for the world's humanity.

The MAC Pointed Out That the 1992 Cross-Strait Discussion Achieved No Consensus on the Issue of "One China" (05/31/2000)

Concerning whether the 1992 discussion achieved any consensus, MAC Chairperson Tsai Ing-wen met Koo Chen-fu and she said in a press interview that with regard to the 1992 Consensus, the understanding of the SEF and the ARATS towards this historical event is that both sides of the strait did discuss the issue of "one China" then, but did not achieve a consensus. Therefore, "each side has its own interpretation of 'one China.'" Each side tells its own story. She emphasized that "the 1992 Consensus is 'no consensus,' which is 'not different' from 'each side has its own interpretation of 'one China.'" Tsai Ing-wen said that both she and Koo Chen-fu hoped that ARATS Chairman Wang Daohan could visit Taiwan. Such a visit would not only have symbolic meaning, it would also draw the two sides closer.

The SEF Secretary-General Hsu Hui-yu also emphasized that in 1992, when the SEF and the ARATS met in Hong Kong, "one China" was not a consensus. "Each side tells its own story" was the consensus. No consensus on the "one China" issue was reached, including the phrase "each side has its own interpretation of 'one China.'" Hence, the statement, "the SEF repudiated the cross-strait one-China consensus in 1992" is a misnomer.

The Cross-Party Task Force Achieved Consensus (06/12/2000)

In June 2000, Chen Shui-bian called for the creation of a Cross-Party Task Force based on designated tasks directed at the different opinions of the incumbent and opposition parties about the 1992 Consensus and cross-strait relations. On August 5, Academia Sinica President Lee Yuan-tseh was appointed Chairman of the task force. The 25 team members held heated debates on "one China" and the 1992 Consensus during the third session. The task force agreed to set up a Designated Team for Studying the One-China Question. On November 26, the Cross-Party Task Force convened its seventh session and arrived at a concrete consensus: the Three Acknowledgments and Four Recommendations. The three acknowledgments are as follows:

1. The current state of cross-strait affairs is the result of historical development.

2. The PRC and the ROC neither mutually represent one another nor belong to each other. The ROC has established a democratic system. Any change to the current cross-strait situation should be approved by the people of Taiwan through democratic procedures.

3. People are the pillar of a nation and the purpose of a nation is to guarantee the people's security and benefits. Seeing that languages on both sides of the strait are similar and the physical distance between the two is small, the people on both sides of the strait should work to uphold and enhance these ideals.

The four recommendations in the statement are as follows:

1. To improve cross-strait relations, to deal with cross-strait disputes, and to deal with Beijing's One-China Principle according to the ROC Constitution;

2. To create a new mechanism or adjust current measures to continually coordinate the differing opinions on national development or cross-strait relations, that includes all political parties as well as the public;

3. To appeal to mainland China to respect both the dignity and the "space" of Taiwan and to end military threats and work with Taiwan to sign a peace agreement, thus establishing a win-win situation; and

4. To declare to the world that the government and people of Taiwan insist on peace, democracy, and prosperity as cornerstones to cooperate with the international community. With this in mind, Taiwan will construct new cross-strait relations with sincerity and patience.

Chen Shui-bian's New Year's Day Message Mentioned "Political Integration" (01/01/2001)

In his New Year's Day message in 2001, Chen Shui-bian said, "According to the Constitution of the Republic of China, 'one China' is originally not a problem," and, "We hope the other side of the strait can understand deeply what the anxieties of Taiwanese people are." He also said that he would respond to the suggestion to "seek leeway in the Constitution and establish a new mechanism" to handle cross-strait relations. But, he did not offer a more positive and direct response to the Three Acknowledgments and Four Recommendations previously proposed by the Cross-Party Task Force. He also suggested that the cross-strait problem could be resolved through "political integration to achieve permanent peace."

The mention of "political integration" was greeted positively by the opposition alliance but prompted a torrent of analysis and reactions in the DPP. The fundamentalists in the DPP attacked the statement as too great a concession to the PRC. Chen Shui-bian then changed his statement to "political integration can mean reunification or independence." The political integration theory ended there.

Ten Years after the Promulgation of the National Unification Guidlines, the Government Affirmed Its Function (02/23/2001)

Concerning the dispute between the incumbent and opposition parties about whether the NUG should be modified, Premier Chang Chun-hsiung said at the Legislative Yuan that the NUG is an important document for cross-strait relations. There were changes in cross-strait interaction and trends, and there was indeed a need for the reconsideration of some matters. However, there was no immediate need to adjust the NUG. MAC Deputy Chairman Lin Chong-pin stated during the regular press conference on the same day that the NUG and the convening of the NUC are all presidential powers. Chen Shui-bian already said in his May 20 inauguration speech that the abolition of the NUG would not be an issue. The cross-strait relation is a highly political subject. If we use the law to legalize the cross-strait relation and the NUG, then the cross-strait relation would lose its flexibility.

ROC President Chen Shui-bian on "One Country on Each Side" (08/03/2002)

The 29th annual meeting of the World Federation of Taiwanese Associations took place in Tokyo. In a live video link from the Office of the President, Chen Shui-bian delivered the opening address and emphasized that Taiwan is a sovereign state and is not part of any other country, nor is it a local government or province of another country. It can never be another Hong Kong or Macao because it has always been a sovereign state. Taiwan and mainland China stand on opposite sides of the strait and are, in fact, "one country on each side." He declared that mainland China's so-called One-China Principle or "one country, two systems" would change Taiwan's status quo and cannot be accepted by Taiwan. He "encouraged everyone to seriously consider the importance and urgency of legislation for a referendum."

On August 5, MAC Chairperson Tsai Ing-wen represented the government in stating four points to explain Chen Shui-bian's statement on "one country on each side" as follows: 1) The central idea of the government's mainland policy remains unchanged; 2) The promotion of cross-strait trade and economy policies will continue; 3) The constructive cross-strait interaction remains unchanged; and 4) Taiwan hopes mainland China will stop testing the baseline of its policies by resorting to actions that are destructive to cross-strait relations.

The Taiwan Affairs Office made an announcement that strongly protested the statement of "one country on each side" and called upon Chen Shui-bian to return to "one China."

Chen Shui-bian Announced the Need for a Referendum (05/10/2003)

On May 20, 2003, Chen Shui-bian announced that a referendum would be held on deciding whether Taiwan would enter the WHO and on the construction of the Fourth Nuclear Power Plant.

The U.S. and mainland China immediately voiced objections. However, the MAC saw the referendum as necessary for democratization. Taiwan would still strive to maintain cross-strait stability and would not change the Four Noes and One Without promise. Taiwan felt regret toward mainland China's narrow-minded viewpoint in dealing with Taiwan's pushing forward for a referendum.

Chen Shui-bian repeatedly stated that the referendum for the Fourth Nuclear Power Plant was not only his political stand, but also the promise kept by the incumbent party to the Taiwanese people. Since the time was ripe for a referendum, he prudently announced that, before the next presidential election, the government would hold referenda for the Fourth Nuclear Power Plant and other important issues.

After that, the Taiwan authorities offered explanations on Taiwan's position to the U.S. officials and think-tank members who went to Taiwan to express their concerns. Chiu Yi-ren was sent to the U.S. to privately state that the referenda were held to promote the ruling party's election campaign. However, the U.S. still favored the Three Noes attitude. The U.S. was not affected by the Fourth Nuclear Power Plant referendum, it did not understand the WHO referendum, and it would not comment on the reduction of the legislator seats by one-half.

The Taiwan Authorities Respond to Lee Teng-hui's Suggestion to Change the Name of Taiwan

ROC's former President Lee Teng-hui openly announced that "the ROC doesn't exist anymore," "the ROC is only a name, not a country," and that "Taiwan's name should be changed." In response to these statements, MAC Chairperson Tsai Ing-wen stated at an Executive Yuan session that according to the ROC Constitution, a national title change must be determined by all people and must proceed with democratic procedures. At that time, the highest goal was to maintain cross-strait stability and any political action or viewpoint must be carried out with these objectives in mind. Tsai Ing-wen also emphasized Taiwan's democratic society, spoke of the proposed name change to the Republic of Taiwan, and stated that there were also voices of support for "one country, two systems." All of these propositions had to go through legal processes. If most people in the nation made decisions according to the law, she thought that mainland China should also show respect for these decisions.

In a meeting with a group of U.S. scholars and experts on cross-strait issues, Chen Shui-bian expressed his views: "We advocate, think, and insist on Taiwan being a sovereign state. The ROC is a sovereign state; Taiwan and mainland China being one country on each side of the strait is a clear reality without any doubt." He also emphasized that according to the current Constitution, "our country's name is the Republic of China." For three years, he had been the ROC's president, working hard to protect the country's sovereignty, dignity, and security while abiding by the ROC's Constitution and seeking the highest benefit for Taiwan's 23 million people (*United Daily News*, 08/27/2003).

After President Chen Shui-bian (also DPP's chairman at the time) announced that a new Constitution should be enacted at the 17th DPP anniversary celebration in the later part of September 2003, he, as the president, further made it clear that after repeated modifications, the current Constitution had many contradictions and was no longer usable. Taiwan needed a new Constitution. This act had nothing to do with reunification or independence. After that, Chen Shui-bian proposed various changes related to the modification of the provisions of the Constitution, such as adopting a presidential system, reducing the legislators by one-half, and changing the election method. He also repeatedly stated while in Taiwan and New York that no matter if it were referendum or amending the Constitution, it had nothing to do with reunification or independence and would not violate the Four Noes and One Without promise. The purpose of formulating a new Constitution was to deepen the democratic system.

In November, the Executive Yuan drafted a referendum law, which was equivalent to writing a new Constitution, and sent it to the Legislative Yuan. On November 27, the Legislative Yuan passed the version of the referendum law revised by the Alliance of the KMT and the PFP, which stated that referenda would not be suitable for sovereign and territorial verifications. Also, those referenda that relate to changing the status quo must be modified by a higher standard equivalent to the amendment of the Constitution. However, the Defense Referendum proposed by the Executive Yuan was passed.

SECTION 3
DISCUSSION OF TAIWAN'S MAINLAND POLICIES

From the above introduction, it can be observed that Taiwan's mainland China policies have certain characteristics, which will now be discussed.

The Policies Are Not Continuous, but Are Often Contradictory

Taiwan's mainland policies and its positions on the country's reunification do not have continuity and often are in opposition with each other. First of all, in 1992 the NUC formulated the NUG according to the ROC Constitution. It insisted on the One-China Principle, although its "one China" content and acknowledgment differed from that of mainland China. It clearly implied the reunification of the country, such that at the end of 1992 the Hong Kong meeting could reach the 1992 Consensus and the Wang-Koo Meeting could convene smoothly in 1993. The people who attended the meeting and made decisions that year, apart from Hsu Hui-yu, all acknowledged the consensus that "each side tells its own story." Washington was pleased at the consensus reached then by both sides of the strait. However, after the DPP took power in 2000, it immediately reversed the original consensus and, playing word games, stubbornly refused to acknowledge the original consensus.

Next, the NUG contained the highest guiding principles of the mainland policy. But, soon after Chen Shui-bian attained power, the Office of the President and the DPP insiders engaged in debates about the guidelines and the functionality of the NUC. Chen Shui-bian also said in August 2000, "The NUG do not necessarily regard reunification as the only aim." Subsequently, he stated many times during speeches that the NUG had to be amended. Due to enormous disputes on the island, finally at the tenth anniversary of the promulgation of the NUG, the premier stated that such guidelines "indeed have to be thought through, but at the present time, there is no urgency to amend the NUG."

Finally, Lee Teng-hui established the MAC in 1991 and repeatedly made public announcements about the One-China Principle and insisted that both sides resolve all disputes by peaceful methods. Yet, in 1994 he surprisingly published the New Taiwanese Ideology and in 1999 he worsened the situation by describing cross-strait relation as a "special state-to-state relationship." Chen Shui-bian began with his Four Noes and One Without promise as goodwill, and then he proposed political integration. But, within two years (in 2003), he went from "Taiwan is a sovereign state" and "one country on each side" to proposing a referendum and writing a new Constitution. Taiwan's mainland policies have gone through multiple contradictory changes that are difficult for Taiwanese people to follow.

Words Inconsistent with Thoughts

Taiwan's mainland policies are typical words inconsistent with thoughts (act in one way, but speak in another). The leaders brag boldly about no Taiwan independence, though, in fact, they are taking steps towards independence. Lee Teng-hui openly objected to Taiwan independence during his term and reiterated more than 200 times that he would not support Taiwan independence. In actuality, he worked hard to promote the concepts of nativization and democratization to carry out "de-Sinicization" and to establish the Republic of Taiwan. Chen Shui-bian, meanwhile, painted himself on the surface as a people's president who remains neutral, yet he never tried to eliminate the Taiwan independence guideline included in the DPP party charter. On the surface, he said, "I am the President of the Republic of China. Of course I will follow the ROC Constitution." In reality he did not care about the Constitution or the law, as evidenced by his often arbitrary interpretations of the Constitution. In public he said, "Never join the rally for rectifying the name of Taiwan." In private he said, "If I were not the president, I would bring my grandchildren to the rally." The inconsistencies of words and actions by Lee Teng-hui and Chen Shui-bian made people wonder what was true and what was false.

The reason Taiwan leaders acted in one way but spoke in another was most likely due to cheating for votes or concern about opposition from mainland China and the U.S. Their behavior has already made Taiwanese people angry and confused about their nation's recognition, thereby obstructing the cross-strait reunification progress. Besides, during the middle and later parts of Lee Teng-hui's term, Taiwan stepped on the path of "reunification in name, but independence in reality." Hsu Li-nung, Hao Po-chun, Lin Yang-kang, Wang Chien-hsuan, and a very few administrative officials either voluntarily resigned or were forced to step down due to their positions against Lee Teng-hui's independent line. Other politicians, including the vice president and Taiwan's governor, and government officials of various departments also held the same opinions. It warrants further investigation to discover whether the large group of silent people who did not or were not willing to see clearly in fact agreed with Lee Teng-hui's line, or simply tried to keep their positions. After Lee Teng-hui finally took off his mask and proposed the "two-state theory" in 1999, these officials not only did not protest, but they even announced to the outside world that the government had never changed its mainland policy. Many have regretted, after Lee Teng-hui left his presidency and resigned from the KMT's chairmanship, that they had not seen it clearly or that they had had difficulties in opposing Lee in order to keep their jobs. However, who can guarantee that these people will not change their opinions again?

Exploring the historical truth may not be helpful in turning the trend in Taiwan, but it is true that many Taiwanese people have gradually given up hope for the nation's reunification after Lee Teng-hui's 12 years in power. Even their honor and pride as Chinese are gradually fading. In the end, with the help of Lee Teng-hui, the DPP that supports Taiwan independence took power in 2000 and further moved along the line of "Taiwan is a sovereign state" and "one country on each side."

Ignoring the Benefits of the Taiwanese People

Taiwan's mainland policy only exhibits the leaders' personal ideology and the ideology of their political parties. Taiwan's current situation and the rise and fall of the cross-strait economies and political strengths are totally absent from the considerations of the government. During Lee Teng-hui's mid to late term, he already knew from the bottom of his heart that Taiwan's economy depends on mainland China, yet he insisted on a "go slowly and exercise patience" policy. In particular, after the DPP took over the power and Premier Tang Fei stepped down, there was a series of disruptions: the Fourth Nuclear Power Plant trouble, extra-marital affairs, the impeachment disturbance, the big drops in stock and real estate markets, enterprises moving out, students choosing to study in the mainland, heated waves of real estate purchases and exchanges with the mainland, a rising unemployment rate, declining personal income, and an increasing gap between the rich and the poor. All of these caused Chen Shui-bian's popularity to steadily decline. But Chen Shui-bian's government entirely ignored the fact that the mainland had already become the support of Taiwan's economy. His government never wanted to make a change, adjust policies, and initiate the three links to facilitate both sides resuming talks to rescue Taiwan's economy. On the contrary, the government deliberately used politics to interfere with the economy and, as such, the two sides of the Taiwan Strait from beginning to end could not resume talks. Taiwan's economic depression became worse with every passing day. Such a political regime totally ignores the people's best interests, so if it could still use the "one country on each side" and "long live the Taiwanese" slogans to win the 2004 presidential election, where is the justice?

People often say, "A particular kind of voter will elect the [same] kind of politicians." Though this saying makes some sense, if used in Taiwan, the politicians' responsibilities should be much greater than those of politicians in other countries. Taiwan's politicians often say that they abide by the voters' viewpoints. Taiwan's mainstream public opinion objects to "one country, two systems," yet few ask how this mainstream public opinion was produced. The government and various parties for a long time despised the "one country, two systems" policy, which raises the following questions: When did they give the people the opportunity to understand its content? If the people do not even understand the contents of "one country, two systems," how can they oppose it? The government uses the excuse of the people's objection to disallow the three links. Taiwan continues to "go slowly and exercise patience" until the moment this policy cannot be used any longer, at which time another policy name will be substituted to continue interfering with the Taiwanese merchants' investment in the mainland. Do people really object to the three links? Are MAC's public polls truly reliable?

The DPP government and most politicians, apart from teaching people to hate mainland China and object to "one country, two systems," take the opportunity of each election to brainwash the voters. The so-called "localist faction" candidates in both the Pan-Green and Pan-Blue camps like to arouse people's reunification or independence emotions, provincial consciousness, and ethnic oppositions using methods of division and accusation to attack the opponents. They go so far as to deface mainland China, exaggerating its appearance to show that they love Taiwan and are not afraid of mainland China and the U.S. Moreover, they encourage the Taiwanese to elect Taiwanese: Taiwanese must be their own bosses. It is shameless for these politicians to incite the voters for their own selfish interests, but it is more horrible to see how people are affected after long-term brainwashing. The cross-strait economy has made the two sides inseparable and the exchanges on both sides have deeply affected every facet of Taiwan society. Hence, the cross-strait reunification is a general course of development that cannot be resisted; no one can obstruct it any longer. If the government and politicians are truly concerned with Taiwan's future, they will stop hating mainland China or denouncing the "one country, two systems" statement!

Ignoring International Reality

Taiwan's mainland policy has completely ignored the international reality. When George W. Bush became the U.S. president, Taiwan hoped that the Republican would be friendlier to Taiwan than former, Democratic administrations were. Indeed, soon after the Sino-U.S. mid-air plane collision incident in April 2001, Bush said that he "would try his best to assist Taiwan's self defense." However, when Bush met with PRC President Hu Jintao, he stated for the first time that he not only "does not agree with Taiwan independence," but he also mentioned the three China-U.S. communiqués with the Taiwan Relations Act at the same time. In terms of assisting Taiwan's self-defense, Bush only said, "If necessary, the U.S. will assist Taiwan in having the best possible self defense." Afterwards, the U.S. administrative officials in charge of Taiwan affairs repeatedly stated that the U.S. Taiwan policy remained unchanged. However, U.S. scholars thought that, in order to avoid Taiwan authorities being misled by the U.S. policy, the U.S. cross-strait policy should change from strategic ambiguity to strategic clarity. Chen Shui-bian's DPP government seemed to turn a blind eye to this policy change.

In order to win the election, beginning in the summer of 2003 the ruling DPP party began to propose the "one country on each side" concept, the referendum, and the formulation of a new Constitution by initiating stronger and stronger waves of attacks. Beginning in June, the U.S. repeatedly stated that Taiwan authorities should not step over the line and unilaterally change the status quo. Yet, the DPP government did not stop the clamor and frequently sent messengers to the U.S. to explain that all this propaganda were only campaign statements and nothing to worry about. The DPP government insisted on writing a new Constitution in the autumn of 2003. Then the U.S. clearly stated after November that it was in "opposition" to either side of the strait unilaterally changing the status quo. Even the high-ranking Taiwan officials in the U.S. verified that U.S.-Taiwan relations had become very "sensitive and complicated" and needed to be dealt with carefully. However, the DPP government still held the attitude that "say Four Noes and One Without to the U.S. and remain ambiguous domestically" could fool everyone.

Perhaps Chen Shui-bian didn't mind being called the next "troublemaker" after Lee Teng-hui, but he made Taiwan's safety the campaign tool of his administration. What kind of behavior is this for leaders who repeatedly declare that they love Taiwan? Furthermore, in order to keep U.S. support, how much of the taxpayers' hard-earned wages must be spent on purchasing arms specified by the U.S.? If this is the price that the Taiwan's mainland policy has to pay, isn't the bill too high?

CHAPTER 8

TAIWAN'S POLITICAL PARTIES' STANCES TOWARD REUNIFICATION AND "ONE COUNTRY, TWO SYSTEMS"

In order to understand Taiwan's stance on reunification and "one country, two systems," each political party's position must be examined. At present, there are more than 100 registered political parties in Taiwan, though not many of them are actually in operation. Even fewer parties get more than five percent of the votes in legislative elections and receive the government's party financial subsidies. In this chapter, the positions towards reunification of five political parties that have met the five percent criterion are introduced; among these, the New Party had once received 13 percent (1.5 million) of the votes but failed to pass five percent in the 2001 legislative elections.

SECTION 1
THE CHINESE NATIONALIST PARTY

For the 50 years since the Nationalist government moved to Taiwan until May 2000, the KMT was the ROC's ruling party and its party mainland policy was the government mainland policy. Although the KMT has had members of its Central Standing Committee, Central Committee, and Party Representatives since the Chiang Kai-shek era, the party chairman's power has always been supreme. This situation did not change much after

Lee Teng-hui became the president in 1988 and the concurrent KMT chairman. Hence, when the KMT's government officials and people's representatives felt dissatisfied with Lee Teng-hui's gradual move towards Taiwan independence, they had no way to change the mainland policies of the KMT or the government. They could only walk out of the KMT or suffer the fate of being deprived of their party memberships. Lien Chan became the party chairman after the DPP won the presidential election in March 2000, and Lee Teng-hui later resigned from the KMT chairmanship.

This section will only discuss the KMT's positions after 1990. Before 1990, the KMT basically believed in reunifying China using the Three Principles of the People. The 12th KMT National Party Congress, held between March 29 and April 15 in 1981, adopted the proposition to reunify China under the Three Principles of the People. In July 1988, the 13th KMT National Party Congress adopted The Mainland Policy at the Current Stage and announced that the KMT's mainland policy should "base itself in Taiwan, look beyond the mainland, and care about the whole of China." The basic policies were: 1) Protect the ROC Constitution; 2) Oppose Marxist-Communism; 3) Ensure the safety of Taiwan as the recovering base; 4) Support mainland compatriots to strive for freedom, democracy, and human rights; and 5) Strengthen the actions called for by the Three Principles of the People to reunify China.

The KMT Strongly Condemned the DPP's Passing of the Proposition of Taiwan Independence (10/16/1991)

The KMT Central Standing Committee discussed the DPP's Proposition of Taiwan Independence that was included in DPP's party charter and passed four resolutions blaming the DPP for deliberately creating a national crisis and ignoring the nation's security, social stability, and the people's benefit. The KMT reiterated its opposition against any positions that violated the Constitution for splitting the nation's territory and insisted on supporting the government to severely punish the DPP. The KMT openly promulgated this decision through heated discussions after the Central Standing Committee's meeting, though Lee Teng-hui only briefly stated the conclusion without reading out the decision.

The KMT Promulgated the Meaning of "One China" (12/03/1992)

The KMT promulgated the meaning of "one China" as follows: "At the present time, our nation is temporarily in a state of separation. Owing to the different cross-strait political systems and ideologies, economic development and living standards also exhibit disparities. This is not the right time for reunification, and the conditions for implementing it are missing." The promulgation continued by saying: "In the future, the process of seeking the nation's reunification should be based on insuring the Taiwan area's safety and the people's benefit, under the prerequisite of rationality, peace, reciprocity and mutual benefit, abiding by the NUG to achieve the goal of the nation's stepwise reunification."

The "Special State-to-State Relationship" Statement in KMT Documents (08/29/1999)

The 2nd Plenary Session of the 15th Central Commission of the KMT incorporated the "special state-to-state relationship" statement into the Project for the Nation's Construction across the Century to be used as a guiding principle for KMT's future mainland policy. The project also clearly indicates that in the future the NUG and established policies would be used to push cross-strait normalization and to seek a peaceful future and a democratically reunified, new China.

The KMT's Response to Jiang Zemin's Speech about Macao's Handover

Jiang Zemin said during the handover ceremony of Macao sovereignty that the implementation of "one country, two systems" in Hong Kong and Macao had an important, demonstrable effect with respect to solving the Taiwan issue. Chang Jung-kung, director general of the KMT's Department of Mainland Affairs, stated the following: 1) The mainland lacks economic prosperity and freedom for the people and can take inspiration from Hong Kong and Macao. Taiwan has made more progress in political democracy and this is something that the mainland can't afford to ignore on its path to democracy; 2) The "one country, two systems" policy proposed for the cross-strait reunification is in turn carried out in Hong Kong and Macao first, implying the difficult and long-term nature of the cross-strait relations. Its implementation absolutely cannot be controlled by the subjective desire of the mainland Chinese. The situation is different from the sovereignty handover of Macao, which was destined by history.

The KMT's Central Policy Committee Unveiled
the Draft Package of Policy Guidelines (06/28/2001)

The KMT's Central Policy Committee unveiled a draft package of policy guidelines during its policy guideline forum of the 16th KMT Party Congress. The draft platform says, "We will follow the National Unification Guidelines, shelve the debate on independence or reunification, push for steady development of cross-strait relations, set up a mechanism for bilateral military exchanges as well as the formulation of a Taiwan Strait peace zone based on the 1992 'one China with respective interpretations by the two sides' consensus." The KMT adds the confederation concept to the party platform in addition to enshrining Lien Chan's confederation proposal. The draft platform also calls for the opening of three direct cross-strait links (trade, mail, and transport) and relaxes the policy of "go slow and exercise patience" on mainland China-bound investments. Meanwhile, the platform proposes that Taipei takes the initiative to develop double golden triangular relationships—Silicon Valley-Taipei-Shanghai ties as well as Tokyo-Taipei-Shanghai ties—to consolidate Taiwan's pivotal role in the global economic and trade system.

Lien Chan Stated That the KMT Wanted to Be
a Neutral Party Committed to the "Middle Road" (07/05/2001)

The KMT Chairman Lien Chan agreed to a *New York Times* interview and pointed out that after a political party's power transformation, mainland China had doubts about the DPP government's Taiwan independence inclination. As an opposition party, the KMT had responsibilities to make mainland China understand that Taiwan independence was not the mainstream opinion. The KMT advocated that both sides should restart negotiations to enhance the cross-strait dialogue and exchange, and act together positively.

With respect to Taiwan's recent public opinion poll, which indicated that the Taiwanese people increased their interest in "one country, two systems," Lien Chan thought that the emergence of such a phenomenon was due to the DPP's mainland policy having only "things not to do" without "things that should be done," and due to its being vague and directionless. The KMT would absolutely not accept "one country, two systems." Lien Chan was worried about the polarization of the Taiwan independence and reunification dispute. He said that the KMT insisted on being a neutral party committed to the "middle road." Only ideologies such as under the "one

China, but not yet" principle—making an effort to construct Taiwan and allowing the people to enjoy democracy, prosperity, and freedom—are part of the mainstream opinion of the Taiwanese people.

The KMT's Think Tank, the National Policy Foundation, Unveiled the New Policy Paper on the Confederation System (07/07/2001)

The KMT's think tank, the National Policy Foundation, unveiled a new policy paper on the confederation system. The paper emphasizes that the confederation is an important segment in the mid- to long-term mainland policy. It is neither an immediate goal nor an end solution to resolve cross-strait relations. At the same time, the paper listed the three basic contents of the confederation: 1) The cross-strait confederation should abide by the principles of equal treatment, separate regimes, gradual peaceful progression, and taking care of the Taiwanese people's desire to be their own masters; 2) The cross-strait confederation is neither Taiwan independence nor immediate reunification. It is based on the principle of two separate regimes building a common roof. It is not another form of Taiwan independence. However, since two sides co-exist under the same roof, it is also not an immediate reunification; and 3) The confederation is neither a league of nations nor a federal system. Both sides are under the common roof on the basis of separate regimes and neither is subordinate to the other. Incorporating the confederation into the NUG agenda, a "five-stage reunification theory" was proposed: acknowledge the 1992 Consensus, resume the cross-strait talks, set up cross-strait peace- and stability-keeping mechanisms, enter the confederation stage, and achieve the aim of reunification.

The KMT Unveiled Taiwan's Political and Economic Environment Paper: The Cross-Strait Relations' Topics (03/12/2002)

A summary of Taiwan's Political and Economic Environment Paper: The Cross-Strait Relations' Topics follows:

The KMT can act as a "bridge" to connect the mainland with the international world. This would on one hand assist mainland Chinese entering the international world and on the other hand assist foreigners entering mainland China.

Although the KMT advocates nativization, it is never limited by nativization. On the contrary, it seeks to open to the mainland and the world. It absorbs nutrition from and provides nutrition to the mainland and the world. The KMT sees mainland China as a "threat" as well as an "opportunity." However, mainland China does not have to be an eternal enemy. For Taiwan's future and the cross-strait relations, the most important matter is not independence or immediate reunification; rather, it is "peace, democracy, and prosperity." If the two sides cannot resume talks and negotiations, then building a stable relationship to guarantee the cross-strait peace will be impossible.

According to the ROC Constitution, the Republic of China is China. The ROC's government is China's central government. At the present time, the KMT only has effective jurisdiction on Taiwan, Penghu, Kinmen, Matsu, and others. It has never given up its sovereignty on the mainland. Based on the ROC's original territory, it should include the mainland region. The people who live in Taiwan are the ROC's people, and they are also Chinese. "Taiwan first" and "localization" do not mean "de-Sinicization." These terms also do not mean segregation from mainland China; on the contrary, they refer to influencing mainland China and enabling all Chinese people to enjoy freedom, democracy, and human rights, and to someday be ruled by law.

The KMT thinks that the 1992 Consensus is not "one country, two systems." The 1992 Consensus is "one China with respective interpretations by the two sides" reached in 1992 by the two sides to relax the cross-strait tensions and to create a state of reciprocity. "One country, two systems" is mainland China's unilateral plan to downgrade Taiwan. It does not treat both sides of the strait equally. Hence, the KMT has always opposed it (www.kmt.org.tw).

The KMT's Position on Referendum Law Implemented into the Constitution (05/11/2003)

In order to avoid being accused of being anti-democratic, after Chen Shui-bian proposed the Referendum Law in May 2003, the KMT and the PFP followed in his steps and also discussed and pushed for the legislation of the Referendum Law. In September 2003, during the Legislative Yuan's meeting period, the KMT and the PFP legislators continued to draft the Referendum Law.

On October 24, 2003, the KMT's legislative caucus presented the KMT and PFP version of the Draft of a Proposed Referendum Law. It clearly prescribes that the referendum should be initiated by the people, not by the government. It also advocates that the scope of the referendum excludes topics like formulating a new Constitution, changing the national title and the national flag, territorial change, specific ethnic matters, and others. The draft also stipulates that a referendum should not be held on the same day as the presidential or city and county mayoral elections to avoid affecting these elections. Later, Lien Chan accepted the suggestions of members of KMT's localist faction and campaign consultants Wu Tun-I, Sisy Chen, and others, and mapped out a "three-step plan toward political reform." No baseline was set for the Referendum Law Implemented into the Constitution. The draft of the Referendum Law Implemented into the Constitution prepared by the KMT and the PFP was unveiled on November 21, 2003. According to this draft, six articles of the Amendment of the Constitution needed modification. The Amendment of the Constitution prior to the modifications stipulated that after the bills of the Amendment of the Constitution, territorial changes, and impeachment of the president and vice president were passed by the Legislative Yuan, they must go through the reviewing and approval procedures by the *ad hoc* (Special-Project) National Assembly. These would be amended as follows: Apart from turning over "the methods for impeaching the president and vice president" to the Constitutional Court of the Judicial Yuan for deliberation, the bills of the Amendment of the Constitution and territorial changes should be decided by referendum as the final confirmation.

When Lien Chan raised two warnings about the new Constitution and referendum related topics at an evening campaign rally held in Feng-shan in South Taiwan on November 21, 2003, he emphasized that the New Referendum Law pushed together by the KMT and the PFP represented the Taiwan people's basic human rights. He first warned that Beijing authorities must respect the Taiwan people's choice. In other words, Taiwan's referenda do not involve reunification or independence issues. Instead, they are about how to connect with the nation's constitutional system to implement direct democracy. After this warning, he immediately turned the subject to Chen Shui-bian. Lien Chan began by saying that Chen Shui-bian could not face the New Referendum Law proposed by the KMT and the PFP in the DPP's Central Standing Committee. Did Chen Shui-bian mean to abandon the Four Noes and One Without promise? Did he imply a rectification of the national title? Did he mean to initiate a cross-strait war by provoking clashes on both sides? Did he say all this just to be elected? Chen Shui-bian should make his intentions clear (*China Times Daily News*, 11/22/2003).

On November 26, 2003, the day before the Alliance of the KMT and the PFP put the draft of the Referendum Law to a vote, it had a heated internal debate due to "emerging U.S. pressure." Finally, the Alliance returned to the "safe, stable" baseline (*China Times Daily News*, 11/28/2003). On November

27, the Legislative Yuan passed the Referendum Law revised by the Alliance of the KMT and the PFP. The Defense Referendum was also passed.

Lien Chan Proposed the Express One China Respectively Viewpoint (10/21/2003–10/28/2003)

On October 21, 2003, Lien Chan was invited by the U.S.-China Policy Foundation and Washington's Regional Reporters Association in Washington, D.C., to give a speech at a luncheon meeting and answer on-the-spot questions from the audience. A reporter asked, "If the two sides resume talks on the basis of the 1992 Consensus, what do you think will be the future development of the 'one China' subject?" Lien Chan stated that the 1992 Consensus had already been put on the shelf. The KMT has always advocated "one China with respective interpretations by the two sides," but now as soon as "one China" is mentioned, the DPP immediately accuses you of selling out Taiwan!

Lien Chan emphasized that when people talk about this question, they should adjust the meaning of "one China with respective interpretations by the two sides." For Taiwan, this "one China" means the Republic of China; but for mainland China, "one China" means the People's Republic of China. Hence, though we all talk about "one China," the prerequisite is "different interpretations."

Later, during a Kaohsiung evening campaign rally on November 21, Lien Chan explained the so-called "express one China respectively" viewpoint, of which the most important matter is about shelving the sovereignty dispute, namely, "I respect your sovereignty, and you also respect my sovereignty" (*China Times Daily News*, 11/22/2003).

Conclusion

During Lee Teng-hui's 12 years as Chairman, KMT's mainland policies went through several changes. It is a fact that what he said in public and in private were often contradictory. After the KMT's defeat in the March 2000 presidential election, Lee Teng-hui resigned from the Chairman post and Lien Chan took his place, and the KMT's mainland policy changed again. Lien Chan had repeatedly shown his support for the confederation system and his interest in incorporating it into the KMT's charter. He gave up on this because of the many different opinions inside the party. Lien Chan and James Soong finally succeeded as joint candidates in the 2004 presidential election. The Chen Shui-bian camp also began to increasingly make a big issue out of ideologies like moving towards independence, and he often labeled Lien and Soong as pro-China. Lien and Soong counterattacked Chen Shui-bian by questioning his competence as a ruler, and they proposed their own economic and governing concepts. On the ideological side, Lien Chan did not respond at first. Later, when Chen Shui-bian's poll rose and the KMT's localist faction and campaign staff made persuasions and exerted pressures on Lien Chan, he began to talk a lot about expressing one China separately and that he would not push for reunification during his term. The draft bill Referendum Law Implemented into the Constitution proposed by the KMT and the PFP was also modified in that territorial changes could be decided by referendum. Clearly, in order to win an election the KMT and Lien Chan were willing to pay any price.

Lien and Soong believed that "without being elected, everything is false" and that those who support reunification certainly would not vote for Chen Shui-bian. Lien and Soong thought that if they stayed on middle ground and slightly leaned towards independence they could get votes from the middle and maybe even from the Pan-Green camp. Let's not discuss whether this strategy was effective or not. It was a known fact (Lien and Soong were more aware than others) that the green and blue camps were accusing each other daily as being pro-reunification. As time went on, people would think pro-reunification was incorrect, and independence became the mainstream opinion. Some Pan-Blue scholars and media believed that Lien and Soong would turn back on their promises after being elected. But this would not be possible. Even if Lien and Soong wanted to turn around, the Taiwanese people might not be able to turn around. Besides, the DPP and the more pro-independence TSU would not let the ruling Pan-Blue camp do what it wanted. In order to rule smoothly and strive for reelection, it would be hard not to continue moving ahead until all the people become pro-independent. Perhaps, the KMT's localist faction already foresaw such a result; consequently, there were suggestions to change the party name to Taiwan Kuomintang in anticipation of a complete segregation from mainland China.

SECTION 2
THE DEMOCRATIC PROGRESSIVE PARTY

On September 28, 1986, the Recommendation Assembly of the Outside the Party Supporting Association was held at the Grand Hotel in Taipei. The 135 participants initiated the formation of a party through their signatures.

The Democratic Progressive Party announced its formal establishment. It was the first political party formed after the ban on party formation was lifted. Most of its founding members had advocated Taiwan independence since the outside-the-party era; therefore, the establishment of the new party was viewed as an important breakthrough for the Taiwan independence movement.

The outside-the-party personalities always opposed the KMT's excuse of protecting the Republic legitimacy of the ROC in order to realistically exercise one-party autocratic governance. They also opposed the KMT slogan "Counterattack the mainland to recover mainland China" to impose martial law and maintain a system of general mobilization for the suppression of the Communist rebellion. They demanded that a democratic political system be implemented. In order to fight against the KMT and strive for the right to form a new party, the outside-the-party personalities attacked the KMT as a foreign regime that suppressed the Taiwanese from getting power and persecuted the Taiwanese intellectual elite in the 2/28 Incident. These pleas not only enabled the outside-the-party movement to develop the native (Taiwanese) ideology, but they also gradually gave way to statements about the nation's recognition and Taiwan's sovereignty. Although in the outside-the-party era many mainlanders and liberal personalities participated, their voices weakened after the establishment of the party. On November 10, 1987, the 2nd National DPP Party Congress included, "The people of Taiwan have the right to advocate Taiwan independence" in its resolution.

From the formation of the DPP until now, it has had ten party chairmen. Although their viewpoints on reunification and cross-strait relations were not entirely the same and there are also many factions in the party, on the whole the DPP's position on reunification and independence leans towards pro-independence. On other subjects related to cross-strait relations, there have been different positions; for example, when Hsu Hsin-liang was the party chairman, the Formosa faction led by him opposed Lee Teng-hui's "go slowly and exercise patience" policy. After Chen Shui-bian won the 2000 presidential election, the DPP's New Trend faction members took power one after another and strongly supported Chen Shui-bian as the party chairman in July 2001. The strengths of DPP's factions that did not hold real powers became weaker and weaker. This has led to greater agreement among the high-ranking DPP officials on their pro-independence positions.

The DPP Passed the Sovereignty Resolution and Stated That Taiwan's Sovereignty Does Not Extend to Mainland China and Outer Mongolia (10/07/1990)

The 4th DPP Party Congress passed Resolution No. 1007, which states, "Taiwan's real sovereignty does not extend to mainland China and Outer Mongolia." Later, after the KMT strongly rebutted and declared the illegitimacy of such a resolution, the DPP modified the resolution, "Confirm: Taiwan's real sovereignty does not extend to mainland China and Outer Mongolia." There are other positions in the resolution, including "Taiwan's future constitutional system, domestic policies, and diplomatic policies should be built upon the real territory" (*Central Daily News*, 10/08/1990).

The 5th DPP Party Congress Passed the Taiwan Independence Party Charter (10/13/1991)

After heated debates, the 5th DPP Party Congress overwhelmingly passed a resolution to include a Taiwan Independence Article in the party charter. However, to avoid arousing a dispute over reunification and pro-independence and to prevent an intense reaction, the Congress defined the resolution as only a "viewpoint."

The bill initiated by the New Trend faction to include the words "construct a Republic of Taiwan that has an independent sovereignty" in the party charter made the ruling and the opposition parties nervous. After heated debates among the party representatives, the DPP Party Congress passed the amendment proposed by Chen Shui-bian. The amendment modified the conclusion of the original bill to, "Based on the principle of the national people's sovereignty, the position of constructing a sovereign Republic of Taiwan and formulating a new Constitution has to be turned over to all the Taiwanese residents and decided by means of a referendum" (*United Evening News*, 10/13/1991).

The DPP Held a Forum on Mainland Policies (02/13/1998–02/14/1998)

When Hsu Hsin-liang was the DPP chairman, the party's New Trend faction had different opinions from the Formosa faction also led by Hsu Hsin-liang. In February 1998, the DPP convened a Forum on Mainland Policies. After two days of debates among the party staff and public officials from various factions, the DPP reached four agreements:

1. The cross-strait negotiations should be dealt with seriously in order to keep good exchanges.

2. The Taiwan and mainland China negotiations should shelve the sovereignty dispute.

3. The Taiwan and mainland China negotiations should be diversified in style and subject to ensure comprehensive exchange.

4. Replace the words "go slowly and exercise patience" with the words "strengthen the base and move west."

These four agreements were never practiced within the DPP, and they disappeared totally after Hsu Hsin-liang stepped down.

DPP's Seminar on the 1998 Cross-Strait Report (03/27/1999)

The DPP held a seminar to publicize the reports on 1998 cross-strait relations. Five reports on the cross-strait political, diplomatic, military, social, and economic development were released at the seminar. The important viewpoints of the report include not accepting "one country, two systems," continuing the support of "go slowly and exercise patience," and consideration about joining in the regional missile defense system, all similar to government mainland policies at the time.

In the area of political development, the report demands that the government should not accept "one country, two systems" and that the mainland should give up the idea of using military force in order to ensure the peace of the Taiwan Strait. In the area of diplomacy, the government should enthusiastically reorganize the consensus of Taiwan's different parties and people to increase exchanges with the U.S. government and enthusiastically strive for participation in functional, non-governmental, international organizations. In the area of the military situation, the current concept of "lasting war plan, quick war tactics" should be strengthened. Apart from increasing the "patriotic missile" bases, Taiwan should also consider joining the U.S.-led TMD system. In the area of economic development, the mainland's recent economic trend and the future of the cross-strait economic interchange indicate that Taiwan should continue the "go slowly and exercise patience" policy in cross-strait economic and trade exchanges (*China Times Daily News*, 03/28/1999).

DPP's National Party Congress Passed the Resolution Regarding Taiwan's Future (05/08/1999)

The DPP Party Congress (8th term, 2nd meeting) passed the Resolution Regarding Taiwan's Future. The resolution pointed out in its Explanation portion that "Taiwan is a sovereign nation. In accordance with international laws, Taiwan's jurisdiction covers Taiwan, Penghu, Kinmen, Matsu, its affiliated islands and territorial waters. 'Taiwan, although named the Republic of China under its current Constitution, is not subject to the jurisdiction of the People's Republic of China.'"

The resolution also proposed the following proclamations: 1) "Taiwan is a sovereign country. Any change in Taiwan's independent status must be decided by all the residents of Taiwan through referenda;" 2) "Taiwan is not a part of the People's Republic of China. Mainland China's unilateral advocacy of the One-China Principle and 'one country, two systems' is fundamentally inappropriate for Taiwan;" 3) "Taiwan should expand its role in the international community, seek international recognition, and pursue the goal of membership in the United Nations and other international organizations;" 4) "Taiwan should renounce the 'one China' position to avoid international confusion and to prevent China from using the principle as a pretext for forceful annexation;" 5) "Taiwan should promptly complete the task of incorporating the referendum into law in order to realize the people's rights. In time of need, a referendum can be used to establish consensus of purpose and allow the people to express their will;" and 6) "Taiwan's government and opposition parties must establish a bi-partisan consensus on foreign policy, integrating limited resources to face China's aggression and ambition."

DPP's Presidential Candidate Proposed a New Middle Way (Late 1999)

The DPP presidential candidate Chen Shui-bian, inspired by British Prime Minister Tony Blair's New Middle Way concept, used the Third Way as a model and proposed a Taiwanese version of the New Middle Way as the main theme of his campaign. His six main pleas included national security, economic policy, public policy, cultural Taiwan, knowledge-based Taiwan, and a "volunteer Taiwan." The content included the important topics of globalization, new individualism's responsibilities and obligations, government and non-government relationships, enterprise business partnership, environmental protection, and others. Chen Shui-bian said that he would like to start from a practical angle by "solving problems" and taking the non-dogmatic upper-level meanings of these topics for political operations. Unlike the traditional left wing that must define everything, he wanted to keep more flexibility in dealing with matters. This was also the main idea of the New Middle Way concept.

DPP's Party Chairman Hsieh Chang-ting Pointed Out the "One China" Structure of Taiwan's Constitution (09/11/2000)

The DPP Party Chairman Hsieh Chang-ting agreed to be interviewed by reporters on September 6, 2000. He stated that his party already recognized Taiwan independence through its acceptance of the Resolution regarding Taiwan's Future. Although the country's name is the Republic of China, its aim is to keep the current status quo. He held a more cautious attitude concerning whether Taiwan will move towards reunification, but at the same time he did not exclude reunification. On September 11, Hsieh Chang-ting accepted a radio station interview and stated that the DPP definitely was in favor of Taiwan independence. He stressed that "not excluding reunification" was only slightly moving towards the middle and that his final goal was to facilitate peaceful cross-strait negotiations. On September 13, the DPP Central Standing Committee convened a meeting to discuss Hsieh Chang-ting's "not excluding reunification" proposal. However, the committee reiterated its position of the Resolution regarding Taiwan's Future.

Hsieh Chang-ting was invited to attend a party organized by Cross-Party Task Force Chairman Lee Yuan-tseh on November 18, 2000. He pointed out that the ROC's Constitution was built on a "one China" structure. Within this structure, "one China" could have many interpretations. Since the DPP had participated in amending the Constitution, it should accept this Constitution. As a ruling party, further, it dares not to disobey or negate this Constitution.

Chen Shui-bian Became Chairman of the DPP and Pushed for Cross-Strait Party-Level Exchange Visits (07/21/2002)

After Chen Shui-bian was sworn in as the new party chairman during the DPP Party Congress (10th term, 1st meeting), he emphasized that the party would continue to enthusiastically push for cross-strait, party-level exchange visits in order to make a historical step forward in the development of cross-strait relations.

Chen Shui-bian pointed out that the Resolution regarding Taiwan's Future is an important milestone of the DPP party charter as well as the highest principle for dealing with the DPP's current cross-strait issues. He also claimed that the DPP has always kept the principle of "kind reconciliation, enthusiastic collaboration, and permanent peace." Whether it was the policy to "strengthen the base, move west" or to "enthusiastically open, effectively manage," this party had always had a practical, enthusiastic, and flexible attitude toward the cross-strait interchanges.

Party Chairman Chen Shui-bian Explained "One Country on Each Side" (08/06/2002)

When Chen Shui-bian presided over his party's Central Standing Committee meeting, he furthered his talk on "one country on each side." He argued that the "one country on each side" policy was oversimplified and could possibly create misunderstandings; "sovereign reciprocity" would better conform to the complete intended meaning. Since Taiwan is a sovereign country, its name is the Republic of China, it is not part of another country, it is not a local government, and it cannot be another country's special administrative region. He pointed out how Taiwan has gone through colonization, an authoritarian system, and finally walks on its own path. He called this path "a democratic path, a freedom path, a human rights path, and a peaceful path." Unless mainland authorities openly renounce the use of force, any talk was only a pretext for annexing Taiwan. Taiwan could not accept it.

DPP Chairman Chen Shui-bian Proposed a Referendum on Joining the WHO (5 - 9/2003)

On May 20, 2003, Chen Shui-bian proposed holding a referendum on joining the WHO on the 2004 presidential election day. The DPP held a press conference on May 21 and stated that a referendum would serve to show the international community Taiwan's determination to enter into this world body. Furthermore, being a member of WHO would have incalculable benefits in combating SARS.

Since the U.S. paid close attention to the referendum, the DPP changed its positions several times. At first, the DPP guaranteed that the referendum had nothing to do with reunification or independence. Then, the date for holding the referendum became uncertain. Next, the DPP decided to first push for the enactment of the Referendum Law. Although the Legislative Yuan held an additional temporary meeting to deliberate the draft Referendum Law, it was not passed due to the passivity of the DPP. As the campaign struggle drew closer, Lee Teng-hui initiated a rally for rectifying the ROC's name. Chen Shui-bian and the DPP then made a big issue of the referendum and pronounced that the Constitution had long furnished Taiwanese people the right of exercising direct civil rights.

Party Chairman Chen Shui-bian Called
for a New Constitution (09/10/2003)

At an evening celebration for the seventh anniversary of the founding of the DPP on September 28, 2003, Chen Shui-bian declared that the party would promote the birth of a new Constitution for Taiwan by 2006. Later, he proposed 11 concrete amendments to the Constitution. On October 1, Secretary-General Chang Chun-hsiung held a press conference and further elaborated Chen's proposal. He said that Chen Shui-bian was the nation's leader and that he wanted to have a long-term, well-established constitutional system. The contents of the proposed 11 amendments are all basic issues that have been disputed in Taiwan for a very long time.

On October 28, when Chen Shui-bian was presiding over the DPP Central Standing Committee, he stated that the big rally for the Referendum by All People, Pushing for a New Constitution in Kaohsiung on October 25 was a historic landmark for Taiwan's democratic movement. The grand crowd of the rally and various poll data indicated that the "referendum by all people, pushing for a new Constitution" advocacy received the majority of Taiwan people's support and recognition. This gave him firm confidence, and he used it as his main campaign theme for an all-out push for a referendum and the formulation of a new Constitution. Chen Shui-bian also stated that a referendum and the formulation of a new Constitution do not violate Four Noes and One Without.

Conclusion

According to the analysis ("The Change of DPP's China Policy and Its Effect on Cross-Strait Relations," 08/29/1998) of Yen Wan-chin, Director of the DPP Department of Chinese Affairs, the DPP mainland policies have gone through several stages. Prior to the DPP's formation, in order to compete with the KMT, the party initiators adopted an enthusiastic and open policy. Until the 1990s, in order to advocate independence, the policy became gradually more conservative. However, the Formosa faction led by Hsu Hsin-liang and Chang Chun-hsiung held a conflicting position. Both leaders visited the mainland and invited mainland China leaders to engage in party-to-party talks. The DPP's mainland policy opened again during the period when Hsu Hsin-liang was the party chairman after he convened the China Policy Seminar.

Perhaps the analysis of Yen Wan-chin then made some sense. However, today when we review the DPP history, we know that the advocacy for an open policy has never been the DPP's mainstream opinion. Even after the aforementioned seminar, when the DPP stated that it no longer wanted to avoid contacts with mainland China and would be glad to see both sides resume talks, the DPP's basic nature of pro-independence never changed. Perhaps Hsu Hsin-liang had different opinions from other DPP members on the cross-strait issues; yet at the end of 1997, during the time when the National Assembly was revising the Constitution, he supported Lee Teng-hui. Hsu Hsin-liang reached agreement with Lee Teng-hui on discarding the concept of a Taiwan province, adopting dual leaders (president and premier), and supporting a presidential election requiring no absolute majority. These later had a detrimental impact on the political turmoil, the power shift in 2000, and on Taiwan's stepping further toward independence.

In Chen Shui-bian's campaign white paper, he advocated that the two sides should engage in multilevel, multifaceted dialogues—including on official levels—to initiate comprehensive negotiations on the three direct links. However, since he took power, there had never been any dialogue on the three links. In 2003, for the sake of the campaign strategy, he announced, "Three links is a necessary road to take." But his position on the three links has changed repeatedly. The evaluation report on direct transportation promulgated by the MAC in August 2003 was full of concerns about direct transportation between Taiwan and the mainland, yet there was no concrete matching plan.

Although the New Middle Way has provided an adjustment for the DPP's transition from an opposition party to a ruling party, it lacked the structure for further planning and coordination. Hence, the cross-strait policy could not be put into action. Following the approach of the 2004 presidential election, in order to divert the attention focused on his governing incompetence, Chen Shui-bian proposed a referendum and made "one country on each side" and "enact a new Constitution" the central slogans of his campaign. Judging from this, the DPP's pro-independence actions are irreversible.

SECTION 3
THE PEOPLE FIRST PARTY

Soon after his election defeat, the supporters of the 2000 presidential candidate James Soong convened the party founders' first meeting. On May 31, during the PFP founders' meeting Soong was nominated as the interim Party Chairman and Chang Chao-hsiung was nominated the Vice

Chairman. On the same day, the party formally registered its establishment at the Interior Department.

Most of the PFP members and supporters are people who voted for Soong in the 2000 presidential election. Soong became a giant rival of Lee Teng-hui. Soong supports are against Lee Teng-hui, oppose Taiwan independence, accept themselves as Chinese, and believe that the two sides will eventually be reunified. Many of them used to be New Party supporters and voters. They supported Soong because they saw that he was against Lee Teng-hui's plan of discarding the Taiwan provincial framework. However, their reasoning was faulty. First of all, after the death of President Chiang Ching-kuo, Soong immediately showed his support of Lee Teng-hui and continued to do so for the next ten years. It did not take a lot of intelligence to determine if Lee Teng-hui was pro-independence. Yet, Soong also supported Lee Teng-hui's suppression of the KMT's non-mainstream faction. When Lee Teng-hui discarded the Taiwan provincial framework and disfavored Soong (Soong was the governor of the Taiwan province then), Soong began to fight against Lee Teng-hui. This behavior made people wonder about his motivation for opposing Lee Teng-hui. Furthermore, although Soong did not support independence, his attitude towards rejecting reunification was quite obvious. Prior to the 2000 presidential election, Soong proposed defining the cross-strait relations as "not subordinate to each other, being a sovereign state-to-state relation." He also advocated that both sides sign a peace agreement witnessed by the international community. These two positions actually are similar to Lee Teng-hui's "two-state theory" and Chen Shui-bian's "both sides set a mutually trusted military mechanism." Perhaps Soong thought that all the mainlanders, the people against Lee Teng-hui, and those who supported reunification would vote for him in order to prevent Chen Shui-bian from being elected. To win the election he needed to win votes from the localist groups, and as a result he did not hesitate to rid himself of the label "mainland Chinese spokesman."

In the 2004 presidential election, Soong made a compromise by finally agreeing to become Lien Chan's second hand. The KMT and the PFP also formed an alliance, which was discussed in Section 1 of this chapter.

The PFP's Cross-Strait Policies and Positions

The PFP's positions on cross-strait policies are to stabilize the cross-strait situation and use the Three-Phase Integration theory to push for the development of relations:

1. The PFP will adhere to the Republic of China's Constitution to define cross-strait relations, engage in cross-strait dialogues, and insist on the Taiwan people's consent for any change of Taiwan's status quo.

2. The PFP will adhere to the Three-Phase Integration theory to initiate cross-strait relations and shelve the reunification versus independence dispute. The first phase is to pursue "economic and functional exchange" in an effort to develop mutual benefit and collaboration of the cross-strait economy and trade. The second phase is to initiate cross-strait "social exchange," and the third phase is to step forward toward "political integration."

3. Mainland China should clearly renounce the use of force against Taiwan and initiate a mutually beneficial cross-strait dialogue to ensure Taiwan's living space in the international community.

4. The PFP will push for comprehensive three links using the policies of "laying out worldwide plans" and "be proactive and progressive" to develop the cross-strait economic and trade relations. The policies about stabilizing the cross-strait situations are:

    a) Adherence to the NUG: Adhere to the related principles of the National Unification Guidelines and start from the 1992 Consensus idea of "one China with respective interpretations by the two sides" to engage in cross-strait negotiations. However, any change to Taiwan's status quo requires the consent of the entire Taiwan population.

    b) Push for step-by-step integration: Use the Three-Phase Integration theory to push for the development of the cross-strait relations. Both sides should shelve the reunification versus independence dispute before reaching a consensus about cross-strait relations. Also, use the "economic and functional integration" idea to conduct a cross-strait economic and trade collaboration that is of mutual benefit. The "social integration" and the "political integration" plans will be put into place in the future (www.pfp.org.tw).

PFP Chairman James Soong Proposed Six Viewpoints on "One China" (05/05/2000)

PFP Chairman James Soong met the former Washington Chairman of the American Institute in Taiwan, Natale H. Bellocchi, and proposed six viewpoints on "one China." First, the important cross-strait political issues should not be dictated by any single side; instead, the two sides should reach consensus under the condition of mutual respect; second, both sides are part of "the whole China" and both sides should respect the current cross-strait reality; third, the ROC is a sovereign country and the existing two political entities are the result of history that cannot be denied; fourth, the

163

two sides should quickly begin negotiations on an equal footing to discuss "loosening up the cross-strait tension" and building a framework for future relations; fifth, the two sides should sign a peace agreement as early as possible; and sixth, the "final solution" of the cross-strait issue must respect the free will of the entire Taiwan population (*China Times Daily News*, 05/06/2000).

The PFP Acknowledged the 1992 Consensus (08/26/2000)

PFP Chairman James Soong acknowledged that during the 1992 cross-strait negotiation there was indeed a consensus about the One-China Principle. Both sides should respect history and accept the current situation, and use this as a base and foundation to restart dialogues.

The PFP pointed out that "in 1992 the SEF and the ARATS made an oral statement" and emphasized that in 1992 the consensus was "in the process of striving together for the country's reunification, both sides insist on the One-China Principle. But in acknowledging the meaning of one China, each has a different definition" (*China Times Daily News*, 08/26/2000).

A Delegation of PFP Legislators Visited Beijing and Shanghai (09/11/2000)

The ex-president of the Legislative Yuan Liu Sung-pan led a delegation of PFP legislators and visited Beijing and Shanghai in September 2000. The delegation reached three points of consensus with the mainland ARATS, including an acknowledgement of the consensus "both sides of the strait insist on the One-China Principle" reached by the SEF and the ARATS.

Liu Sung-pan clearly stated that the stalemate of the cross-strait relations was the biggest problem Taiwan had at the present time. He emphasized that if the cross-strait relations could not be changed, then it would be difficult for Taiwan's current economy and investment confidence to improve. He expressed his concerns about the cross-strait situation and emphasized that the risks should be reduced before the situation became dangerous (*Da Gong Bao*, 09/11/2000).

A Delegation of PFP Legislators Visited the Mainland for the Second Time (04/01/2001–04/04/2001)

Liu Sung-pan led a delegation of PFP legislators and visited Beijing on April 1, 2001. On April 3, they met with mainland China Vice Premier Qian Qishen. After the meeting, legislator Shen Chih-hui reported that

Qian Qishen agreed to follow the Hong Kong and Macao models of negotiating transport rights to conduct the three links negotiations and avoid the present One-China Principle dispute. Although this kind of negotiation would be taken in the non-government form, government officials could negotiate with the status of civilians. On April 3, the *Xinhua News Agency* reported this matter and categorized the cross-strait three links as "domestic affairs under one China."

PFP Director of the Policy Center Chang Hsien-yao pointed out that his party advocated a step-by-step, three-phase economic interchange, social exchange, and political integration to proceed with cross-strait relations. It also took a "confederated Euro-continental model" and a "roof theory" to prepare a larger space for discussing the future cross-strait relations. The "roof theory" emphasizes that both sides hold sovereignty: "In one China, there are you (mainland) and I (Taiwan)," which seems conceptually closer to the "both sides are part of China" idea mentioned by Qian Qishen not very long ago (*Da Gong Bao*, 04/01/2001–04/04/2001).

PFP Chairman James Soong Proposed
a New Taiwanese Nationalism (03/31/2001)

During PFP's one-year anniversary celebration party, Soong proposed the "New Taiwanese Nationalism" and "Save Taiwan Nationalism" slogans and proclaimed that when facing the international reality, firmly adhering to mainstream democracy was the strongest guarantee of Taiwan's survival. The political situation had to be stabilized, there should be no domestic ethnic discrimination or external cross-strait hostility, and the two sides should not engage in a long-term confrontation and arms race. The PFP and the KMT have similar viewpoints about insisting on protecting the existence of the ROC and on the cross-strait issues. In the past the DPP has made contributions in striving for Taiwan's democracy, but its downward degeneration has been too rapid. The success of the DPP was built on top of the KMT's split. The PFP would not build its success on top of the KMT's split and compete for degeneration. Instead, the PFP would walk the middle line and remain rational so that it will become the Taiwan people's future hope.

James Soong Spoke at the Tenth Anniversary of the Issuance
of the National Unification Guidelines (02/23/2001)

At the tenth anniversary of the issuance of the NUG, PFP Chairman James Soong made a speech in which he pointed out that the technical problem of the Cross-Party Task Force and the MAC lay not in integration but in returning to the fundamentals of the guidelines. The NUG was the line of demarcation and a historical document that was never meant to serve merely as a matter of form. The establishment of the SEF and the ARATS and the important cross-strait developments are all pushed forward by these guidelines.

The PFP Had Reservations on KMT's Confederation Idea and Emphasized Taking the Three-Phase Integration Theory (06/29/2001)

Directed at KMT's proposal of including the cross-strait confederation idea into its political platform at its 16th Party Congress, PFP's Director of Policy Center Chang Hsien-yao said that the KMT and the PFP agreed on the current cross-strait situation, including "one China with respective interpretations by the two sides" and the 1992 Consensus. However, their ideas about the directions of future development were somewhat different. The PFP preferred the three-phase model of beginning with economic interchange, and then going through social intermingling, and eventually ending with political negotiation. The decision on future direction would depend on the contact condition and adaptability of both sides. Chang Hsien-yao also offered the analysis that the confederation formula, from a theoretical point, would completely rule out the possibility of a political reunification. Stressing the framework of a loosely held, politically united "one China" as the final solution for the cross-strait issue also might not be accepted by mainland China (*Central News Agency*, 06/29/2001).

The PFP Expressed Opinions Directed at the Formulation of a Constitution in 2006 (09/29/2003)

Chang Hsien-yao pointed out that, in political theory, formulating a new Constitution meant forming a new country. Even though France went through its revolution, the original French Constitution was still operative; no new Constitution was enacted. Hence, he thought that Chen Shui-bian wanted to be distinguished from the Pan-Blue camp by formulating a new Constitution and forming a new country with an intent to use the ROC versus the Republic of Taiwan and maintaining the status quo versus destroying the status quo as the main themes for the next year's campaign.

Chang Hsien-yao pointed out that since the DPP had conducted a series of "de-Sinicization" policies, rumors began circulating in the outside world about Chen Shui-bian pushing for a new Taiwan nation as well as continuing for two more presidential terms. Chang Hsien-yao hence hoped that Chen Shui-bian would clearly explain whether the referendum was used for gathering support to build a new nation for Taiwan independence (*China Times Daily News*, 09/29/2003).

PFP Chairman James Soong Demanded the U.S. Define Its Position (11/21/2003)

The U.S. has repeatedly sent serious warnings to Taiwan on the DPP's referendum and actions aimed at writing a new Constitution. Directed at the U.S. dissatisfactions, James Soong pointed out that the American position was "creative ambiguity," which could easily mislead Taiwanese people toward inaccurate and erroneous judgments. Hence, the U.S. should express clearly whether America would stand by Taiwan if mainland China took military actions against it. Also, what would be the position of the U.S. if Taiwan unilaterally changed the status quo of the Taiwan Strait?

Soong emphasized that the KMT and the PFP had long insisted on Taiwan's people not accepting mainland China's military suppression, absolutely refusing "one country, two systems," and that they never would provoke military confrontations to make cross-strait relations unstable and insecure. Soong believed that for some time the DPP government had given much erroneous information to the Taiwanese people. It was really necessary for the U.S. to have a clear and accurate understanding about the Taiwan Strait situation when making statements. The U.S. should also state clearly whether it would stand by Taiwan to protect the Taiwan people's freedom and democratic position, if mainland China unilaterally changed the Taiwan status quo by using force. The U.S. should also indicate what it would do if Taiwan itself, through the wishes of the people, wanted to change the Taiwan status quo (*China Times Daily News*, 11/22/2003).

Conclusion

The PFP has been using the Three-Phase Integration theory to push forward the cross-strait relations and has acknowledged the 1992 Consensus since the establishment of the party. During the 2004 presidential election, James Soong chose to be Lien Chan's partner. The partnership made an immediate impact within the PFP. No matter the outcome of the election, the PFP would face the question of what course to take. For Soong, as Lien Chan's partner, facing his pro-independence opponent

Chen Shui-bian, perhaps it is still permissible to be vague on cross-strait topics. But, if he has the good fortune to become the vice president, he eventually will have to show his own position!

SECTION 4
THE NEW PARTY

The New Party, formerly the Chinese New Party, was formed in August 1993. The seven founders all walked out of the KMT, committed in their opposition to Lee Teng-hui and the Taiwan independence course. As soon as the New Party was formed, it gathered many "clean, highly educated" people from all social circles that were against Taiwan independence to be the candidates for public office. Based on the mottos "Protecting the Republic of China," "Against Taiwan independence," "Free of money politics," and "Against Lee Teng-hui," the New Party gained a high degree of support from ordinary citizens by not bribing the voters, not entertaining people, and by conducting clean elections. In 1996, during the third National Assembly election, the party gained 1.5 million (13 percent) votes and became a miracle in Taiwan's political platform.

From the beginning of its establishment, the New Party defined itself as a pacifist party. Its organization was more loosely held than other parties. Most of the New Party's supporters were senior KMT members. They were influenced by the education of the Presidents Chiang, they accepted themselves as Chinese, and they believe that the ROC is China. Although they knew that to counterattack mainland China and reunify China by the Three Principles of the People were not conceivable, they hoped that the two sides would eventually reunify. These people could not accept Lee Teng-hui's "false reunification, real independence." As soon as they saw the New Party's formation and its position "against independence, against Lee," they immediately rose and gathered more people to the party to protect justice. However, this type of voter easily changed his mind as soon a stronger and more powerful political figure that was "against independence, against Lee" showed up (such as Soong during the 2000 presidential election). This was precisely the main reason for the New Party's extinction.

The New Party Declaration and Policy White Paper

During the early stage of the New Party's establishment, its declaration agreed with Dr. Sun Yat-sen's idealism: to seek the reunification of the nationalities and "to strengthen the ROC and protect the safety of the Taiwan Strait as the highest standard." Its policy white paper states the basic viewpoints directed at cross-strait relations and mainland policies:

1. Both Taiwan and the mainland are Chinese territories. All Chinese sons and daughters should acknowledge this. The twenty-first century is the Chinese century, and China's reunification will certainly come to be. However, this reunification will require wisdom as well as opportunity. Hence, although the New Party is for the reunification, it absolutely is not for a hasty reunification. The reunification can be gradually achieved through increasing cross-strait exchange, enhancing mutual trust, proper adjustment of the systems, and later stepwise attempts by peaceful methods. If necessary, it could be achieved by the next generation.

2. The New Party advocates maintaining the current status quo to protect stability and peace, increase cross-strait exchange, and enthusiastically catalyze the democracy and prosperity of the mainland. If mainland China is willing to abandon the communist totalitarian system, under the prerequisite of having majority people's support in Taiwan, both sides could engage in democratic negotiation.

3. The 1.2 billion people in the mainland are also Taiwanese people's brothers and sisters. The New Party is not against them. When the New Party has excess capacities, it will use Taiwan's experience to assist the development of the mainland to raise the living standard of the mainland compatriots.

4. There are different opinions as to exactly what format the two sides should use to reunite. This requires long-term discussions. However, the New Party believes that according to the long-term goal, both sides shelving the sovereignty dispute and using the confederated system as a transition form to gradually move towards the federated system is a proposal worthy of consideration.

5. The New Party believes that both sides should work hard together to protect the stability and peace of the high seas. It opposes any action or viewpoints that would make the high seas unsafe or that would endanger the well-being of the people in Taiwan, Penghu, Kinmen, and Matsu. It proposes to eliminate the National Unification Guidelines since the guidelines are neither Constitution nor law. The NUG is not legally binding. Its content is neither practical nor appropriate and therefore should not become a stumbling block in the development of cross-strait relations.

6. The New Party advocates formulating active and progressive policies for Hong Kong and Macao to truthfully protect the rights and benefits of the Taiwan compatriots in Hong Kong and Macao. It supports the Hong Kong people's demand for democracy and human rights in order to guarantee the democratic development of Hong Kong.

7. Both sides (mainland China and Taiwan) should sign a peaceful agreement.

The New Party's Positions on Cross-Strait Relations and Mainland Policies

The New Party revised its party charter and policy white paper in 2000. Included are the following cross-strait relations and mainland policies:

1. The New Party believes that the mainland position toward Taiwan is:

   a) One China includes the mainland and Taiwan. Both sides can negotiate on an equal footing and afterwards follow a political relationship (in agreement with the National Unification Guidelines).

   b) The People's Republic of China does not have to come to Taiwan; the Republic of China cannot go to the mainland (see the consensus of the SEF and the ARATS).

   c) If Taiwan advocates "one China" in the international community, it will have diplomatic "space" (to be solved in negotiations).

2. The New Party predicts the future cross-strait political relations based on the following principles and reasoning:

   a) When Koo Chen-fu last visited the mainland, the mainland side only mentioned "one China," not "the People's Republic of China." Now, we should only mention "our one China" instead of "the Republic of China." When further explanations are needed, we can say, "Our one-China policy acknowledges that you are under separate governance."

   b) The New Party references U.S. President Clinton's two ways of dealing with the One-China Principle. First, Clinton stated the U.S. policy verbally instead of in writing; in fact, there have been previous examples that both sides could follow. Second, he used "ours," meaning "Washington's one China," to be differentiated from "Beijing's one China." The characteristic of the second point could be copied by Taipei; namely, agree verbally that the cross-strait administrative negotiations are "conducted under our One-China Principle."

3. The New Party's concrete actions on the mainland policies are as follows:

   a) Propose cross-strait exchanges and collaborations, which include choosing one place each in the North, Middle, and South Taiwan and Penghu for establishing "a special economic and trade zone" to engage in three links with the mainland to push forward the cross-strait economic and trade relations. After the two sides reach a consensus, the establishment of free trade zones can be planned for Guangdong, Fujian, Hainan Island, Hong Kong, and Taiwan.

b) Propose that the government authorities and the non-government societies on both sides set up a "fireproof wall" to discuss the content of laws related to criminal punishment, pollution regulations, and traffic management within the Taiwan Strait region. Both sides should reach unanimity through exchanges to develop the capacity for maintaining good order. Both sides should engage in talks to establish a committee for consultation by inviting Chinese participants from around the world, including those from the four places on the two sides of the strait (Taiwan, Hong Kong, Macao, and the Chinese mainland), and overseas. The New Party will push forward the globalization of the cross-strait exchange channels.

c) Propose to set up a cross-strait military agreement, which includes the obligation of giving advance notice to the authorities on the other side about related military exercises. The two sides should create opportunities to negotiate the exchange and research of military personnel, military affairs, military strategy and tactics and, most importantly, the missiles on both sides should not be targeted at each other.

d) Propose to prevent the Taiwanese people from attacking mainland people's human rights, thereby diminishing them. This would include pushing forward the legal system and setting up a framework for mainland labor coming to Taiwan with a provision of rights and obligations; mainland labors such as high-level research talents and family helpers should be given top priority to work in Taiwan, and the legalization of mainland fishermen should not be delayed.

e) Propose several plans to moderate cross-strait political relationships, including showing initiative by signing two agreements without further discussion about repatriating illegal aliens and hijackers; setting up interaction channels for the local council meetings of the county, city, country, and town on both sides; seriously gathering information related to the "one country, two systems" principle and investigating the corresponding proposal; inviting various political parties and scholars from both sides to hold consecutive debates about "one country, two systems;" exploring various forms of other alternatives, searching broad or creative policies directed at the execution of mainland policies, and proposing corresponding policies to balance the policy blind spot; and leading mainland authorities to continue expressing the position, "One China does not have to be the People's Republic of China" (the Policy Guidelines of the New Party in Year 2000, www.np.org.tw).

The New Party's Mainland Affairs Council Delegation Visited the Mainland (07/10/2001–07/12/2001)

The New Party's Mainland Affairs Council Delegation led by Hsu Li-nung, Wang Chien-hsuan, Yu Mu-ming, Lee Ping-nan, and Fei Hung-tai went to the mainland on July 10, 2001. The delegation met with Wang Zaixi, Vice Minister of the Taiwan Affairs Office on July 11 and had a dialogue that reached a six-point consensus:

1) The two sides jointly recognize and advocate "one China, peaceful reunification" in order to seek the improvement of cross-strait relations and the well-being of compatriots on both sides of the strait. The two sides will strive to push the restoration of cross-strait contacts and dialogues on the basis of the 1992 Consensus, and promote cross-strait economic and trade relations, contacts between personnel and various exchanges, and an early realization of the direct three links.

2) It is the view of both sides that compatriots on both sides of the straits are all Chinese. The 23 million Taiwanese people, whether they are natives of Taiwan province or of other provinces, are brothers and sisters of the same flesh and blood. They should care for one another and live together in peace and jointly boost Taiwan's social stability and economic development.

3) After both sides join the WTO, they will both face challenges in agricultural development. Hence, both sides should strengthen mutual exchanges and collaborations, and encourage Taiwan farmers to invest in and develop the mainland to seek profit.

4) The New Party hopes that the Chinese authorities will provide encouragement and assistance to Taiwan groups and individuals who go to the mainland to build schools and promote education. The Taiwan Affairs Office will forward these suggestions to the department in charge and push for their approval if policy permits.

5) Both sides agree on the basis of the spirit of mutual respect and equal negotiation to engage in opinion exchanges on cross-strait relations and the nation's reunification issues on an irregular schedule to gradually establish an ordinary frequent dialogue mechanism.

6) The New Party delegation indicated that its Mainland Affairs Council will establish a special agency to keep mutual contacts with the related bodies of the Taiwan Affairs Office to assist in dealing with matters that involve the rights and benefits of compatriots on both sides.

On July 12, the delegation met Qian Qichen, who indicated that in developing cross-strait relations, the Chinese mainland advocated upholding the "one, two, three" principle (i.e., "one China, negotiations between the two sides of the Taiwan Strait, and starting the three links as soon as possible"). He also explained the concrete contents of the "one country, two systems" principle and listed seven measures to illustrate the matter:

1) Taiwan continues to use the Taiwanese currency.
2) Taiwan continues to retain its armed forces.
3) Taiwan is an independent tariff zone.
4) Taiwan continues to keep its frame of government.
5) Mainland China will neither take any of Taiwan's money nor transfer any of Taiwan's funds.
6) Taiwanese people and entrepreneurs will retain their original properties.
7) Mainland China will not send any officials to Taiwan (i.e., Taiwan will have autonomy over personnel affairs).

Wang Chien-hsuan stated at a press conference held by the New Party delegation that the "one China" mentioned by the New Party was the "one China" of the future. At the present time, the two sides of China had their own interpretations; if someday China were to be reunified, both sides could sit down and talk about the country's name, content, and other issues. This was the one China acknowledged by the New Party.

New Party Chairman Yu Mu-ming Opposed the Viewpoint of "One Country on Each Side" (08/06/2002)

After Chen Shui-bian proposed "one country on each side" in 2002, New Party Chairman Yu Mu-ming sent an article to the *United Daily News*. Yu Mu-ming accused Chen Shui-bian of retreating from the middle road and said that Chen Shui-bian's referendum talk undoubtedly meant a move towards Taiwan independence.

Yu Mu-ming stated that recognition of Taiwan did not mean recognition of the Republic of Taiwan. The people who lived in Taiwan all recognized Taiwan. But by recognizing Taiwan, we must think about the well-being of the next generation and let them have a future and hope, and live a life of democracy and freedom. These were the Taiwan priorities. This was what was meant by "loving Taiwan." The recognition of a Taiwan nation being pushed by Chen Shui-bian could only bring disaster to Taiwan. Yu Mu-ming thought that the legally construed authority of the ROC Constitution sought the country's reunification and that the ROC was the concrete result of inheriting the political idealism of "keep peace, strive hard, and save China" of Dr. Sun Yat-sen, the Father of Modern China. This is an easily understandable theory. But today, except for the New Party, not a single party dares to clearly express this position. If the New Party disappears, then there will be no one who dares to stand up for the good conscience of the people and the parties of the ROC.

Finally, Yu Mu-ming said that he was Chinese. This was common sense. But, in the land of the ROC, this admission would make you a traitor to Taiwan, one who did not love Taiwan, and every political figure of all parties and political factions would avoid you. The existence of the New Party was a symbol that the people of the ROC treasure their country's past and honor their Chinese forefathers. This heritage should last forever and these values were the raison d'être of the New Party (*United Daily News*, the Public Opinion Forum, 08/06/2002).

The New Party Appealed to Mainland China and the U.S. Not to Get Involved in the Taiwan 2004 Presidential Election (11/30/2003)

The New Party held a press conference directed at the competition of the Pan-Blue and Pan-Green camps in regard to advocating a referendum and formulating a new Constitution. The New Party expressed its worry about Taiwan's presidential election campaign development and unveiled the Four Noes and One Without position. The party demanded the following from both the Pan-Blue and Pan-Green camps: "Do not use a referendum to push for Taiwan independence," "Do not let a foreign power seize a chance to step in," "Do not let oneself degenerate to a shameful position for the sake of the election campaign," and "Do not attack your opponents using judicial power." The New Party also demanded that both camps must guarantee that "both sides of the Taiwan Strait would be free from the threat of war" and take the opportunity in the final four months before the election to present concrete policies. New Party Chairman Yu Mu-ming stated that if Lien Chan and James Soong won the presidential election, the New Party would take a "small but beautiful" supervisory role and continue to protect people's rights and benefits. In the case that the DPP's candidates were reelected, the New Party would consider a plan of combining the KMT, the PFP, and the New Party to reform a Pan-Blue camp.

The New Party also presented an open letter to the mainland leaders. The letter pleaded with the mainland authorities to understand the determination of the Taiwanese people in their choice for a rational and practical leader—instead of a radical one—in seeking peace, stability, and prosperity. The letter stated the New Party's determination through concrete actions in response to the Taiwan people's wish for peace, stability, and prosperity. The New Party also announced an open letter to the U.S. emphasizing the following: "Lien Chan is amending the Constitution of the Republic of China within the current framework of the Constitution. However, Chen Shui-bian is advocating going beyond the current framework to enact a new Constitution aiming at Taiwan independence as an ultimate goal. We think the latter will provoke mainland China and get this region and America into an unnecessary war. The cross-strait relations are very complicated and delicate. The New Party thinks that the U.S. should insist on a non-intervention policy" (*China Times Daily News*, 11/21/2003).

Conclusion

The New Party was regarded from the beginning as a reunification faction due to its opposition to Lee Teng-hui's Taiwan independence line. Some people even labeled the New Party as Communist China's Fellow Traveler. In fact, inside the party, the viewpoints on reunification were not unanimous. Some senior members and elected officials were against Taiwan independence due to their backgrounds. They also were against mainland China. Some supported the ROC more than reunification.

In recalling the New Party's history over the past ten years, if the New Party had not engaged in wishful thinking about winning the native Taiwanese votes, it would have developed a better strategy against the Taiwan independence movement. Over the past several years, a group of New Party elected officials and voters began to realize the speed of "de-Sinicization" pushed forward by Lee Teng-hui and Chen Shui-bian, and became concerned that Taiwan was moving away from reunification. The New Party, hence, must have a clear position on reunification. However, the leaders of the New Party still hoped that the New Party could regain more than five percent of the seats in the 2004 legislative elections and were not willing to abandon the center-of-the-road voters. If the New Party could not break through this blind spot, it would be fairly difficult to gain five percent of the seats under the attack of both the KMT and the PFP. As for the possibility that the three Pan-Blue parties would combine after the legislative elections, it would also be difficult for the New Party to assume a key role.

SECTION 5
THE TAIWAN SOLIDARITY UNION

In 2000, after Lee Teng-hui resigned from the KMT Chairmanship, he joined the people who supported Taiwan independence and the so-called localist faction of the KMT, and formed the Taiwan Solidarity Union. In preparation for the 2002 year-end legislative elections, the TSU was formally established in August 2001. The Party Chairman at the time was Huang Chu-wen and the party spiritual leader was Lee Teng-hui. The result of the legislative elections showed that the TSU exceeded the five percent support level for its first election, and it became Taiwan's fourth largest party.

Although few TSU members are elected officials, they do share the same Taiwan independence ideology and strong fighting power, and often go in hot pursuit against the Pan-Blue legislators in the Legislative Yuan. Sometimes, they are even able to block Chen Shui-bian and the DPP from having their way. The TSU has become the most resolute and powerful pro-Taiwan independence party on the island.

The TSU Inherited Lee Teng-hui's Line (08/12/2001)

In its policy position on cross-strait relations, the TSU's party charter stresses the following points:

- The separate existence of the Republic of China and the People's Republic of China is an objective fact that no one can deny. Any change of the current status will have to be made by the people as a whole acting without any outside interference. All public affairs must be conducted in accordance with the "Taiwan first" principle.

- In regards to cross-strait political relations, the TSU will keep to the line pursued by Lee Teng-hui during his presidency, support the concept of a "special state-to-state relationship," oppose relaxation of the "go slowly and exercise patience" policy, and oppose the idea that the future of Taiwan's economy depends solely upon mainland China.

- In the area of cross-strait economic and trade relations, the TSU will oppose the relaxation of the "go slowly and exercise patience" policy, reject the practice of some Taiwan businesses of "investing in the mainland while leaving nothing but debt back in Taiwan," and propose to push for passage of "a law to protect Taiwanese businessmen doing business on the mainland" (TSU Party Charter, www.tsu.org.tw).

The TSU Held a One-Year Anniversary Celebration; Chen Shui-bian and Lee Teng-hui Were on the Same Platform (08/11/2002)

Chen Shui-bian and Lee Teng-hui made speeches on the same platform during TSU's anniversary celebration ceremony. Chen Shui-bian pointed out that ever since he became president he had to face mainland China's military threat and international suppression. He stressed that the people should not have illusions and downgrade themselves; instead, they must "insist on the right faith, never give up, walk on the right path, never stop" and "not be scared by other people's threats."

Lee Teng-hui stated that he very much supported Chen Shui-bian's cross-strait "one nation on each side" policy. This was the reality and would not create a threat. "What are we afraid of?" Lee Teng-hui asked. "China is not saying anything yet and the U.S. is not showing any worry either. But, inside Taiwan, people argued much more negatively than outside Taiwan. People threatened each other horribly!" (*Liberty Times*, 08/12/2002)

Lee Teng-hui Made Clear That the Republic of China Does Not Exist and Initiated the Movement for the Rectification of Taiwan's Name (08/09/2003)

Around TSU's second anniversary, Lee Teng-hui made the following announcements: "The Republic of China does not exist," "The Republic of China is only a name, absolutely not a country," and "Taiwan should change its name and enact a new Constitution." He and the TSU initiated the Rally for Rectification of Taiwan's Name on September 6, 2003. Afterwards, Lee Teng-hui told Japanese reporters that he would like to realize the dream of establishing Taiwan as a sovereign country within five years. He planned to hold a gathering of a half-million people on the whole Taiwan island before the 2004 presidential election (*China Times Daily News*, 09/12/2003).

Lee Teng-hui's statement on the nonexistence of the ROC and his movement to rectify Taiwan's name produced another climax for the Taiwan independence movement. It also made Chen Shui-bian more resolute about using the "one country on each side" and "the formulation of a new Constitution" policies as his main campaign themes. In order to avoid losing native votes and being labeled as pro-Communist, the Pan-Blue Coalition also began to move from the neutral to a pro-independence stance. As a former president, Lee Teng-hui surprisingly was able to organize the TSU and continue to play an important role on the path toward

Taiwan independence. The end of the struggle against Lee Teng-hui does not appear to be in sight yet.

Conclusion

In Taiwan's political spectrum concerning the dispute over reunification and independence, the establishment of the TSU caused the DPP to transform itself successfully into a centrist party with a tendency toward pro-independence, which was accepted by the ordinary centrist voters in the elections. The two parties' mutual promotions and competitions further increased the pro-independence arrogance.

In mid August 2003, the TSU's peripheral organization and Lee Teng-hui's mouthpiece, Taiwan Advocate, held a Hong Kong: Under One Country, Two Systems meeting. The meeting viciously attacked "one country, two systems." At the beginning of November, this committee held another very large conference on cross-strait relations. The pro-independence faction was very active. On one hand, this showed that in Taiwan there were really people longing for independence to build a new country. On the other hand, it also showed that the pro-independence people were actually waging a deathbed struggle. They knew very clearly that considering the international condition at the time, it was impossible for Taiwan to be independent, but they were not willing to concede defeat.

CHAPTER 9

TAIWAN AFTER THE
2004 PRESIDENTIAL ELECTION

Taiwan's people experienced more than six months of a painful, emotional, and chaotic campaign struggle. Just when it looked as though their struggle was over and things would improve, a shocking shooting incident took place on March 19 involving Chen Shui-bian and Annette Lu. The election results changed dramatically overnight, and after March 20, Taiwan fell into a morass of emotion and chaos. People took to the streets in blind anger and began a protest movement that lasted more than one month. Students initiated a sit-in hunger strike, making the Taiwan presidential election a focus of world attention. Much suspicion overshadowed the shooting incident. Many Taiwanese thought the shooting incident was directed by Chen Shui-bian, though the truth of its circumstances never emerged. The DPP's artificial ballot manipulations were proven through a judicial vote recount process. Regardless of the above, Lien and Soong's campaign strategies deserve criticism.

Chen Shui-bian was inaugurated on May 20, 2004. His inaugural speech was flowery, but the content was not accepted by mainland China. This is of great concern when one considers the possible outcome of the cross-strait policy that will lead Taiwan in the next four years. We should keep watch on how the Pan-Blue and Pan-Green Coalitions reshuffle their cards to organize themselves.

179

SECTION 1
THE PEOPLE'S MOVEMENT WAS THE LIGHT OF EARLY DAWN IN DEFEAT AND GAVE HOPE FOR THE FUTURE

When the results of the presidential election were published, several million Taiwanese expressed outrage. Many Pan-Blue voters in the preceding year who sympathized with Chinese nationality and thought themselves Chinese were heartbroken this time over Lien and Soong's policy statements. These voters were upset with Lien and Soong's trust of the localist faction and campaign consultants who used to be in the green camp. Irrespective of the cross-strait reality, Lien and Soong competed with Chen Shui-bian about pro-independence in the 2004 presidential election. But, in order to terminate the rule of the pro-independence green camp and stop the "de-Sinicization" policy, the Pan-Blue voters voted for Lien and Soong while they also tried hard to defend Lien and Soong. Some voters said that as long as Lien and Soong can be elected, they will restore their principle, and in the worst case, they would still recognize the 1992 Consensus and start the three links. Others said that perhaps scholars who had a national conscience and idealism would find opportunities to formulate cross-strait policies to repair the cross-strait relations. It was particularly difficult for these voters to accept the election results and they were overwhelmed with mixed feelings. Chen Shui-bian had such a poor record of political governance that even the DPP supporters had many complaints. Despite the favorable situation for the Pan-Blue, Lien and Soong still lost the election. This caused the thin thread of hope that their supporters held during the preceding four years to completely vanish. These supporters further worried that the DPP would govern for a long time and that it would be even more difficult to stay as Chinese in Taiwan due to the DPP's "de-Sinicization" policy. However, amid the emotions of defeat and loss of hope, the largest popular movement in recent Taiwan history took place on a grand and spectacular scale.

The Election Results and the People's Movement

On the night of March 20, 2004, after the election results were announced, a few tens of thousands of people protested at various places in North, Central, and South Taiwan. The crowd first gathered in Taipei at Lien and Soong's campaign headquarters, then moved to the front of the Presidential Palace in the middle of the night. The protest would last more than one month in the Po Ai Special District.

More than 10,000 people took turns in the wailing wind and weeping rain, demanding that the government conduct a comprehensive ballot recount and set up an investigation team for the shooting. The police forced the protestors to disperse in the early morning of March 28. Later, some of the crowd turned to the Chiang Kai-shek Memorial Hall to have a quiet sit-in. On April 3 and 10, again a few hundred thousand people regrouped and resolved not to retreat. This finally led to bloody clashes between the police and the crowds. A large group of students also embarked upon a hunger strike for as long as a month in front of the Chiang Kai-shek Memorial Hall, but they did not receive a goodwill response from Chen Shui-bian.

The often mild-mannered Pan-Blue voters finally stood up to protest the unfairness of the presidential election. Many were women and native Taiwanese youth. They acted on their own and encouraged one another, but they sought nothing for themselves. They were not like the self-centered politicians only concerned with their own advantage in the year-end legislative elections. Due to the bravery and self-sacrifice of these people, the world learned through the international media about the unfairness of Taiwan's election, the suspicious shooting incident, and the fact that Taiwan's "American-style democracy" was a farce. They should be heroes to all Chinese people.

The Meaning of the People's Protest Movement

Viewed from all points, the people's protest movement this time had a deep impact. First of all, Chen Shui-bian won only marginally in 2000, with fewer than 40 percent of the supporting votes, but he played the bully for four years. He was not a president of the people. He let his wife evade taxes, supported the public lies of high government officials, accepted bribes, and generally perverted the law. One year before the presidential election, he proposed a referendum and a new Constitution to solidify his own campaign stake. He did not care to sacrifice the cross-strait relations or the ethnic groups' split. If people did not take the responsibility to question the shooting incident and the ballot manipulation that seriously impugned his reputation and international image, no one would know how arrogant and high-handed he would be in the next four years. His true identity was camouflaged by his receiving 50 percent of the votes.

Two lawsuits aimed at nullifying the election and the question of whether the shooting investigation will bring the truth to light are of little concern for a moment. We will focus instead on the fact that the Taiwanese people believe the shooting incident was staged by either Chen Shui-bian or someone who wanted him reelected. There is a question of two bullets, and the suspicion that surrounds them followed Chen Shui-bian like a shadow for the four years after the election. In the meantime, the Pan-Blue voters also realized that after going through the protests, a people's movement is not the DPP's privilege. As long as people are united and insist on their principles in a peaceful and rational manner, they can be effective. Later on, if Chen Shui-bian goes too far, the Pan-Blue voters could take to the streets again at any time and strike against him.

Next, consider the improvement of the cross-strait relations. Chen Shui-bian has been playing with the ideology of Taiwan autonomy and the referendum card. After the failure of the referendum, at least one-half of the voters demanded that Chen Shui-bian's reelection be nullified. This made Taiwan, the U.S., and Japan realize that Taiwan independence was not the mainstream thinking. In particular, many protesters in front of the Presidential Square made it clear that they did not come in support of Lien and Soong. Instead, they were not willing to let Chen Shui-bian mess up the Taiwan situation to the point that the two sides of the Taiwan Strait would have no peace or no future. They held protest signs that read "We want peace, no war" and "I am Chinese" in order to broadcast their pleas around the world. These actions have sufficiently indicated that Taiwan independence is absolutely not Taiwan's mainstream thinking.

Section 2
The Examination of the Pan-Blue Campaign Strategies

Although Lien and Soong, and the KMT/PFP coalition still have a thin thread of hope in overturning the election results, the general public feel that it would be impossible for Chen Shui-bian to hand over his power to others. When protests and all other efforts can no longer alter the reality of Chen Shui-bian's reelection, people's passion and enthusiasms would eventually disappear. Those who opposed Chen and Lu might emigrate to the mainland or abroad. Those who could not leave must submit to humiliation in order to survive and live their lives in regret. In order to avoid rejection, some young people might just go along with the tide. Based on this, Lien and Soong, and the KMT/PFP coalition continue criticizing the unfairness and injustice of the election and Chen Shui-bian's uninspired victory. In order to bring home the lessons painfully learned for the sake of a better future, Lien and Soong, and the KMT/PFP coalition still should carefully examine their own performance during the campaign.

A Competition with Chen Shui-bian about Pro-Independence; More a Loss than a Gain

During the election, Lien and Soong did not care about the growth and decline of the relative strengths of the two sides. Taiwan's future depends on cross-strait stability and cooperation with the mainland. Lien and Soong's competition with Chen Shui-bian about pro-independence is difficult to understand.

Perhaps Lien and Soong felt dissatisfaction in the realization that although Chen Shui-bian's performance was so poor, he was still successful in using the Taiwanese conscience, the referendum and the formulation of a new Constitution to gain support. Lien and Soong accepted the suggestions made by the localist faction and the campaign consultants who had previously walked away from the DPP due to their personal or factional favors. Lien and Soong thought that if they followed these people's opinions and leaned toward "one country on each side," the voters would naturally focus on the difference in governance ability. The ROC title had a legally construed authority; one could use this name to either attack to make advance or retreat to maintain the base. The mainlanders and those who support reunification in any case would provide "solid votes." As long as Lien and Soong kept showing their Taiwanese localist ideology, their opportunity for success would continue to increase. Soon after this kind of strategy began to form, it escalated into a hopeless mess. In the end, Lien and Soong could only echo Chen Shui-bian, increased their Taiwanese localist ideology, and raced after Chen Shui-bian through the referendum and the formulation of a new Constitution. They generously let the defense referendum pass in a way that Chen Shui-bian was able to use this law on March 20 to tie the referendum to the presidential election. Even right before the election, Lien and Soong still did not want to give up using the DPP's thinking and campaign strategy to attack the DPP. Finally, this led the KMT's Wang Jin-pyng to propose "the theory of including Taiwan independence" and to suggest that "voting the referendum ballots is the people's right." The KMT's campaign consultants and favorite media stars Jaw Shaw-kang and Sisy Chen not only earned enough advertising fees and gained more than enough media exposure, they also surprisingly questioned the government representatives during the referendum debates. They said that if mainland China raised the One-China Principle subject, should we still continue the dialogue? Hence, the referendum debates became a succession of debates without an opponent. This really made Pan-Blue's enemies happy and their friends sad.

Did it ever occur to Lien and Soong that any pro-independence voter would certainly vote for the genuine pro-independence faction led by the prominent seniors Lee Teng-hui, Lin I-hsiung, and Peng Ming-min instead of the imitator Lien Chan and the mainlander James Soong? This was exactly the reason why these two failed in the seven southern cities and counties. Lien and Soong still failed, even after the KMT's localist faction, Wang Jin-pyng and others, claimed that they had campaigned full force and agreed in accepting the referendum ballots to please the voters in the south. Additionally, some Pan-Blue voters were not satisfied with Lien and Soong's lack of idealism and chose not to vote. Some voters in the political middle ground intentionally cast void ballots. Lien and Soong never expected that people would have these kinds of voting behaviors!

The Lien and Soong strategies described above not only hurt themselves, but also expanded the pro-independence faction's territory. In the year following the election, voters saw the Pan-Green Coalition attacking the Pan-Blue Coalition's pro-reunification stance, while the Pan-Blue Coalition tried very hard to clarify that they were not pro-China. All these debates only showed people that reunification was not correct, and that only independence would benefit the people. As a result of both sides trying to label the other side and remove its own label, "Taiwan (or the ROC) is a sovereign country" finally became the mainstream opinion. Perhaps Lien and Soong believed that winning was the only objective and that once they won they would have the opportunity to change everything. Since mainland China disfavored Chen Shui-bian so much, it was assumed that mainland China must be willing to cooperate with Lien and Soong to resume cross-strait relations no matter what. However, did Lien and Soong ever consider how difficult it would be to turn around the popular opinion after the election? As long as people's opinions do not change, even if Lien and Soong win, after they take office four years, perhaps they still have to give away their ruling power.

The "America Card" Did Not Work

The second card that Lien and Soong played was the "America card." Quite obviously it did not work. Lien and Soong were probably aware that the Taiwanese people were pro-America and would take instructions from the U.S. In order to gain support from the Taiwanese people, Lien and Soong had to gain support from the U.S. Moreover, both Lien and Soong earned their postdoctorate degrees from U.S. universities and speak English fluently. After they joined the campaign, indeed, the American media raced to interview them and made elaborate reports. In order to please America, Lien Chan also personally went to the U.S. and openly stated that after he was elected, he would approve the entire arms deal and the two sides of the Taiwan Strait would maintain their current status quo. After Chen Shui-bian unveiled his defensive referendum, Lien and Soong further publicized that Chen Shui-bian had offended the U.S. and worsened U.S.-Taiwan relations. They also hinted that the U.S. fully supported their being elected and that U.S.-Taiwan relations could be repaired only if they gained power.

Judging by the way that Lien and Soong frequently showed their goodwill and by the degree to which they were willing to take U.S. instructions, it was possible that the U.S. would not reject their election. As far as Chen Shui-bian was concerned, although on the surface he and the U.S. had clashes, secretly he sent many messengers to the U.S. to offer explanations. He said that the referendum and the new Constitution were just campaign language and that after the election he would still uphold Four Noes and One Without. He even used the referendum to guarantee the U.S. arms sale. Despite the fact that the ballots were manipulated and the shooting incident appeared questionable, candidates from both sides were obedient to the U.S. After all, Chen Shui-bian was reelected and the people's protest movements, though vigorous, ended. The U.S. did not have to support Lien and Soong and anger Chen Shui-bian. These results were difficult for Lien and Soong to accept, since they were playing the "America card" in earnest. What worsened the situation was that the Taiwanese people did not at all care for their playing the "America card."

After 16 years of brainwashing by Lee Teng-hui and Chen Shui-bian, the Taiwanese people generally believe that the U.S. would not want the two sides to be reunified and that mainland China would not dare attack Taiwan with force. Although the U.S. has called upon both sides to resume talks, in reality, it hopes that the leaders of Taiwan keep mainland China in check so as to avoid the threat resulting from "the rise of China" against the U.S. The American style of democracy pushed forward by Lee Teng-hui and Chen Shui-bian is mere window dressing for the U.S. to push democracy to the rest of the world. The Taiwan voters believe that the U.S. is inclined to support Chen Shui-bian, even though Lien and Soong tried to save the outcome as well as they could. Besides, even though the U.S. frequently warned Chen Shui-bian about the referendum, it did not oppose the referendum when it came right down to it. On one hand, this makes voters think that Chen Shui-bian was brave; on the other hand, people are firmly convinced that the U.S. is only posing for a show and that it does not really care about mainland China's response. In conclusion, Lien and Soong's "America card" not only did not work, but it strengthened the Taiwanese people's dependence on the U.S. This will weaken the future development of the two sides.

Other Factors

Apart from the two aforementioned unfavorable strategies, the following points were also factors in Lien and Soong's defeat:

- They made a mistake in making "being against Chen Shui-bian" the same as "supporting blue," and they lacked the spirit of a soldier who was determined to win. For more than half a year, Lien and Soong kept an upbeat, fighting spirit and attempted to visit the entire island. But many talented people and experts from the experienced think tanks were pushed aside by the KMT's localist faction and the consultants who defected from the DPP. These people could not offer their help or speak out, and they kept their anxious feelings to themselves. Inside the KMT and the PFP, there were continuous arguments and some people even began to fight for future positions. All of these attitudes reduced the strength of the Pan-Blue and became the target for the media and DPP's criticism. Hence, some voters who were dissatisfied with Chen Shui-bian's political performance and who did not want to vote for Chen did not want to vote for Lien and Soong either.

- Lien and Soong thought about taking chances but did not properly handle the pre-election night incident. The Lien/Soong campaign headquarters should have guessed that Chen Shui-bian would exhibit a dramatic performance immediately before the election. They claimed that they already made projections. Even if Lien and Soong didn't suspect the shooting incident, they should have held their last night campaign activities. They missed a crucial opportunity for the people to rally. What was more asinine was allowing Sisy Chen to hold a press conference to accuse Chen Shui-bian of setting up the shooting incident without providing any evidence. These two lethal determinations in fact exposed two basic problems of the Lien and Soong campaign strategies. First, Lien and Soong thought the shooting incident would take the originally solid winning situation to a marginal winning situation, unaware that the situation could change direction overnight. Second, Lien and Soong did not understand that those who trusted Sisy Chen were only solid Pan-Blue supporters; hiring her as a consultant in propaganda and overpaying her at this election did not help the Pan-Blue obtain any votes from the centrists. Instead, it made people wonder whether the Pan-Blue Coalition had any talented people. After the shooting incident, Pan-Blue voters knew the incident was suspicious. At that moment, anyone from campaign headquarters with a sincere attitude and some concrete proof would have been more appropriate than Sisy Chen to speak to the press. At least, no one else would have provoked those "light" green voters, who originally had no intention of voting, to actively vote for Chen Shui-bian.

- They did not exert every effort possible to prevent DPP's ballot manipulations. Many people expected from early on that the DPP would manipulate the ballots. The Lien/Soong campaign headquarters claimed that they already summoned tens of thousands of inspectors to supervise the ballot count. Nevertheless, on Election Day there were still several hundred unattended ballot boxes. Furthermore, Lien and Soong knew well that the void ballot standards had been changed the previous year. They also saw that the Void Ballot Alliance (VBA) inundated the citizenry with pre-election publicity to incite voters to cast void ballots. Under these circumstances, Lien and Soong should have reminded voters in advance not to cast void ballots and prevented the DPP from preparing void ballots on the spot, thus taking advantage of VBA's impetus.

SECTION 3
THE CROSS-STRAIT POLICY OF THE
CHEN SHUI-BIAN GOVERNMENT

In this section, I shall discuss Chen Shui-bian's positions before and after the election.

Chen Shui-bian's Positions before the Election

For two months before the election, Chen Shui-bian on one hand used the referendum to consolidate his stake and on the other hand spoke frequently to the U.S. and mainland China. He said that if he were elected, cross-strait relations would improve. He pretended that the cross-straight negotiations depended on him and that he intended to appoint Lee Yuan-tseh to convene the cross-strait initiating team. He went this far just to dupe people into thinking that he was sincere and had a method to improve cross-strait relations. Chen Shui-bian spoke and acted in a contradictory manner. Though he cheated successfully in gaining ballots, it would be impossible to improve cross-strait relations in this way.

The chapter "Peace across Taiwan Straits" from Chen Shui-bian's book *Trust Taiwan* published in January 2004 proposed that both sides designate representatives to engage in communications and set up mechanisms for dialogues. He also said that if the mainland China leaders were sincere about seeking peace across the Taiwan Strait, this would be a most concrete action. This was possibly a way to kill two birds with one stone. First, it would please the U.S., which had been for at least ten years repeatedly calling on the two sides to establish mechanisms for dialogues as early as possible. Second, it would deliver goodwill as well as put up a show of force to the mainland. The goodwill meant: "Please wait patiently for a little more time. After I am reelected, I will talk with you again." The show of force was to warn mainland China: "In the past, we have waited for four years. In the future, it would not be possible to wait for another four years. The two sides might as well sit down and have a good talk." Chen Shui-bian was telling the Taiwan voters that if he were reelected, Beijing would lose all hope and become more willing to sit down for a talk, thus giving him a good negotiating chip. Unfortunately Chen Shui-bian had lost all credibility. Not only did the U.S. not respond, but it also continued to oppose the referendum and even pleaded with the Taiwanese people not to trust Chen Shui-bian. The mainland scholars immediately stated that unless Chen Shui-bian recognized "one China," nothing could be talked about. The responses of the Taiwanese people were fairly consistent. It did not matter if sentiment was pro-independence or pro-reunification; it was viewed as a campaign trick and not worth discussion.

In the same chapter, Chen Shui-bian said that, according to the information Taiwan had access to "realizes that 'one country, two systems' and the 'One-China Principle' are inseparable and can be equated." Either Chen Shui-bian said this on purpose or he showed his ignorance about knowing that "one country, two systems" and the One-China Principle are inseparable. "One country, two systems" means clearly that there are two systems practiced in one country. Of course, its interpretation cannot depart from the One-China Principle. Could it be referring to one America or one Japan? Due to the complete information blockade by the DPP government, perhaps the Taiwanese people may not have understood the content of "one country, two systems." But Chen Shui-bian is the president; how could he make such non-professional remarks that would so totally confuse the people?

Besides, Chen Shui-bian emphasized repeatedly that only he was capable of striving for a "reciprocal and dignified negotiation position" for the Taiwanese people. But who would want to negotiate with a leader who has neither credibility nor integrity? Mainland China is a large and sincere country. It works hard to strive for a peaceful reunification and is unlikely to be threatened by Chen Shui-bian, a man who does not even acknowledge himself as Chinese.

Chen Shui-bian's Attitude after the Election

After the presidential election, Lee Yuan-tseh supported Chen Shui-bian again and said that Chen Shui-bian was going to deliver goodwill to mainland China in his May 20 inaugural speech by expressing hope that the three links would be brought about within two years. Soon afterwards, Secretary-General of the Presidential Office Chiu Yi-ren went to the U.S. for advice on the May 20 inaugural speech. There were also rumors about Chen Shui-bian sending secret messengers to the mainland in search of opinions from across the strait, but mainland China did not accept his proposal. As soon as Chiu Yi-ren returned from the U.S., Chen Shui-bian stated confidently that the contents of the May 20 inaugural speech received positive confirmation from the U.S., and that the Beijing authorities would not be able to find any pretext with it. However, judging from the experiences of the preceding four years, a mere inaugural speech did not appear to be sufficient to stabilize the bad cross-strait relations. Chen Shui-bian's words could not be trusted.

On May 20, 2004, Chen Shui-bian's inaugural speech indeed had gone through delicate revisions. He no longer openly and recklessly referred to "one country on each side." He vowed to keep the promise made in his 2000 inaugural speech. The 2006 reformulation of a new Constitution outside the current political system was also changed to amend the Constitution within the system. According to his "personal suggestion," the revisions of the Constitution would not involve topics related to changes in the country's name or territory. Concerning Taiwan's future course, Chen Shui-bian said that "as long as it is the choice of the 23 million people in Taiwan, any model is workable." This speech received "welcomed acceptance" and "confirmation" from the U.S. However, mainland China did not fall into Chen Shui-bian's trap. The PRC Taiwan Affairs Office stated at the May 24 press conference that although Chen Shui-bian tried his best to embellish his speech, he clearly did not change his pro-independence intention. The PRC Taiwan Affairs Office also believed that Chen Shui-bian's "personal suggestion" regarding revisions to the Constitution already provided a hint for the future Constitution reformulation (*China Times Daily News*, 05/25/2004). Apparently, mainland China's attitude towards Chen Shui-bian changed from "listen to his words, observe his acts" to the tougher "listen to our words, and observe your acts."

Apart from the inaugural speech, on May 6 Chen Shui-bian gathered Annette Lu, Koo Chen-fu, Lee Yuan-tseh, Tsai Ying-wen, and others for the first meeting of the Cross-Strait Interchange Framework Team. The team would be transformed into a Committee for Cross-Strait Peace and Development and later draft the Guidelines for Cross-Strait Peace and Development (*China Times Daily News*, 05/07/2004). Apart from a name difference, this team had a similar operational style and personnel to that of the Cross-Party Task Force. This made people wonder about the functional ability of the team. Besides, the essential aspect of the cross-strait relations is to have interchanges, not to draw up plans regardless of actual conditions. No matter how well written the guidelines, they would be useless if not carried out.

Some people said that the two bullets fired on March 19, 2004 would make Chen Shui-bian more humble. Others said that Chen Shui-bian no longer had the campaign pressure to deal with so he gave a free hand to repair the cross-strait relations. And still others said that in order to gain support from the Pan-Blue voters, Chen Shui-bian would have to work hard to enhance the cross-strait peace. But the reality was much different. The heavyweights Chen Tang-shan and Hsu Shih-kai of the Formosan Association for Public Affairs (FAPA) whom Chen Shui-bian hired had no diplomatic training to hold the Foreign Minister and Representative positions they were given in Japan. This was evidence that Chen Shui-bian's diplomatic policy would still be pro-independence. He also appointed Tu Cheng-sheng as the Minister of Education. Tu Cheng-sheng's merit was "de-Sinicization" and he had no background in education. Obviously he would make a comprehensive push for "de-Sinicization." Finally, the fact that Tu Cheng-sheng hired MAC Chairman Jaushieh Joseph Wu, a pro-independence hawk who knew nothing about the cross-strait issues, proved further that he did not want to make any progress in cross-strait affairs!

In fact, "one country on each side" had become the set goal of the Chen Shui-bian administration. Furthermore, in order to avoid DPP's votes being taken away by the TSU in the 2004 legislative election, it would be impossible to expect Chen Shui-bian—the DPP's Chairman—to make any breakthrough on the cross-strait relations. In the long run, perhaps Chen Shui-bian would make some superficial modifications to his pro-independence stance under both internal and external pressures, but his intention was certainly to push forward Taiwan independence by dismantling opposition forces segment by segment, like cutting sausages. In particular, there are still many Constitution reform variations. During his inaugural speech, Chen Shui-bian only made that "personal suggestion" about the inappropriateness of changing the country's name and territory. But whether he would change course in the future under the persuasions of Lee Teng-hui and the pro-Taiwan independence fundamentalists is yet to be seen.

SECTION 4

THE DIRECTIONS OF THE VARIOUS
POLITICAL PARTIES AFTER THE ELECTION

After Chen Shui-bian won his reelection with the help of the two bullets, the political parties in Taiwan faced a new situation and were forced to change their strategies. The Pan-Blue and Pan-Green camps had to compete again at the 2004 year-end legislative election. The tightness of the campaign struggle was unprecedented. In general, the Pan-Blue voters hoped that the KMT and the PFP could combine into one party or at least jointly nominate legislative candidates in order to maintain more than a 50-percent majority in the Legislative Yuan and to perform checks and balances on the Chen Shui-bian administration. However, judging from the objections about forming a united party to have a joint nomination, and the distrust between the two parties, the Pan-Blue's seats at the year-end legislative election might still be less than 50 percent even if a successful party integration or joint nomination were borne out.

The DPP

After the 2004 presidential election results were announced, the DPP's and its supporters' morale was high. They not only kept their governing power, but they also gained more than 50 percent of the votes. This was the first time since the establishment of the DPP that such a display of support was evidenced. The general explanation was that the results were due to the successful publicity surrounding the ideology of Taiwan autonomy. Hence, the people had no reason not to leap towards pro-independence. Some of the DPP's middle-aged generation even stated that within 20 to 30 years, there would be no need to change the nation's title or territory; but there was no follow-up to that statement.

This was an extraordinary victory in that the DPP defeated the Pan-Blue and had no more enemies to confront. Although prior to the election the mainstream media and academic circles predicted that Lien and Soong would win the election, the general tendency was for people to vote for the favored Pan-Blue candidates. Once that election prediction proved incorrect, Chen

191

Shui-bian's government and the DPP became a powerful force to be reckoned with.

The DPP's first campaign after the presidential election was the 2004 year-end legislative election. Secretary-General of the Presidential Office Chiu Yi-ren announced a "throat-cutting war" and wanted to make the Pan-Green win majority seats. If the DPP could succeed by pleading the "with a Pan-Green majority, the parliament would be stable," it would be possible to have a majority by combining with the TSU seats. By that time, the Chen Shui-bian administration would become fearless and intensify its push for Taiwan independence. However, based on the preceding four years, if the DPP took the governing power, there would be no benefit for either cross-strait relations or the U.S.-Taiwan relations. Since economic and political forces had shown obvious growth on the mainland and decline in Taiwan, it would be impossible for Taiwan's economy to grow without mainland China. If and when the people in Taiwan could not make a living or when the cross-strait relations became more tense, the general public would be politically awakened and the DPP would definitely have to step down. But the people of Taiwan should never be duped by the DPP. It would be better for them to take note of the thunder and take cover from the storm.

The KMT

The defeat of Lien and Soong apparently hit the KMT hard. After the defeat, there was a lot of internal discord in the KMT. Everyone from the campaign staff and consultants all the way to Lien Chan was criticized. Everyone, including the localist faction, the new generation, and Taipei Mayor Ma Ying-jeou, wanted power. These acts of internal discord within the KMT made their comrades sad and their enemies happy.

The defeat of Lien and Soong indeed was pitiful and so was the fact that the KMT did not know the reasons for the defeat. To make matters worse, some people blamed the KMT for not being clearer regarding the issues of pro-independence and nativization. When the mainstream media criticized the KMT or Lien/Soong, they claimed that since the ideology of Taiwan autonomy was already established, the KMT should have "given up the unrealistic 'one China' to accept the current status quo of having two Chinas." Some people even suggested that the KMT should take the policy of "two Chinas" and return to the middle road of the political spectrum. As noted, Lien Chan's defeat had something to do with his fear of accepting "one China," and the KMT from start to finish did not develop its own theory on the Taiwan issue. If the KMT could not see this reality clearly and change its habit of falling in line with the DPP—sticking to nativization and New Democratic Principle, and competing with the DPP on who loves Taiwan more—then its future would be in jeopardy.

Before May 20, in order to resist Lee Teng-hui taking back the KMT party power through the localist faction, Lien Chan insisted on combining the KMT with the PFP and so invited James Soong back to the KMT. As soon as the topic of a united party arose, the localist faction within the KMT showed great discontent. But Lien Chan was resolute, and with Soong he formed a task force to push for the united party. However, the outcry inside the KMT never ceased and the unification work went slowly. The KMT originally decided to convene a Provisional Party Congress in July to pass a motion to amend the party articles for combining the KMT, the PFP, and the New Party. That plan was quickly cancelled so the parties could only try to control the total number of candidates of the three parties for the year-end legislator election.

Perhaps the KMT still has a great deal of assets and that is why none of the localist faction has walked away. However, those who won't be nominated by the KMT at the end of 2004 will definitely break off from the party in order to turn to the TSU for nomination. Apart from this, the fight for the KMT party chairman and the 2008 presidential candidates has already begun. By watching both the Legislative Yuan President Wang Jin-pyng and Taipei Mayor Ma Ying-jeou calculating their own political futures and totally ignoring the entire party's social image, the people have become anxious about KMT's future.

The PFP

The PFP is a party solely dependent on James Soong. After the election failure, the PFP's elected officials tried to take the opportunity to lead the crowds into street protests. They established the New Democratic Movement Alliance, which aimed at grabbing the support of the Pan-Blue voters at the end of 2004. If this strategy works, perhaps the party will win some legislator seats currently belonging to the KMT. But in the long run, this party lacks a central ideology. Although the party depends on votes from the anti-Taiwan independence, anti-Chen Shui-bian camps, and mainlanders, it is not willing to define its position on the cross-strait relations. It simply wants to stay non-committal.

Whether the PFP was trying to meet the expectations of the Pan-Blue voters, or hiding from the face of the DPP's "throat-cutting war," or hoping to share KMT's party assets, Soong accepted Lien Chan's invitation and agreed on combining the KMT and the PFP. Since the merger proposal came up suddenly, PFP's elected officials had momentary doubts. But later they showed their support of the merger and indicated once again that the PFP members customarily follow Soong's lead. After seeing the KMT's internal objections on the merger case, the PFP members continued the taunting.

The TSU

The TSU relies on supporting Lee Teng-hui and his ideology of establishing an independent country. The TSU still has room to grow. If the KMT's localist faction seizes the power or if they encounter difficulties with the nomination process, then very likely these KMT people will also join the TSU. In any case, their ballots come either from bribes or from the faction's support group, both of which could easily transfer with them. With the KMT members joining in, the TSU's force will become even stronger and its power to constrain the DPP will also increase.

The New Party

The New Party completely failed in the legislative election of 2001. Apart from nominating too many candidates, its supporters overlapped too much with those of the PFP. The New Party could not compete with Soong, who also depended on anti-Lee Teng-hui people to gain votes. The New Party gained a few seats in the 2002 Taipei City Council election and regained confidence. The party hoped to regain more than five percent support in the 2004 legislative election.

During the 2004 presidential election, the New Party gave full support to Lien and Soong's campaign and performed acceptably. But when Lien and Soong began to lean toward pro-independence, the New Party kept quiet and gave away a good opportunity for dividing the votes. After Lien and Soong lost the election, there were many KMT and PFP legislators and other interested candidates who took consecutive actions to warm up for the year-end legislative election, but the New Party members did not have much chance to perform. On May 19, the KMT passed the merger motion for combining the KMT, the PFP, and the New Party. The New Party members were not notified beforehand and were puzzled. They stated that they would consider joining after the merger of the KMT and the PFP. The New Party members still wanted to walk their own road and change the party name to the Chinese New Party (*United Daily News*, 05/20/2004). After some communication, the New Party agreed to nominate the legislator candidates jointly with the KMT and the PFP. But up until the first half of June 2004, there was still no agreement with the other two parties about the number of nominated candidates.

The Non-Party Members

In the Legislative Yuan, there are always legislators who have no party affiliation. The number of such legislators varies from time to time, but the number is always sufficient to stalemate some bills between the ruling and the opposition parties. They claim to be the critical minorities, but in fact they often gain huge benefits by dealing with the ruling party.

In order to be adaptable to situations, ten incumbent lawmakers formed the Independent Solidarity Alliance (ISA) and established a preparatory committee on June 7, 2004, to form a party with former Interior Minister Chang Po-ya as its head. The new party was to be formed before the registration date set for the legislative election. The new alliance planned to nominate one candidate from each of the 26 constituencies. This large number of nominations would again add more uncertainties to the year-end legislative election.

The Interior Department did not approve of the use of the word Independent because the word and reality do not tally. In the future, party name disputes will be resolved through communications. No matter what the party name is to be, the word "Independent" probably will not be heard again. There are also ex-DPP members like Cheng Li-wen who were unable to get nominated by the KMT, the PFP, or the New Party, and who do not care about joining the ISA either. Cheng Li-wen is very likely to follow Sisy Chen's example and run as a non-party candidate to take away some of the Pan-Blue votes. Although these people are against Chen Shui-bian, once elected they would also probably act like Sisy Chen and attack Chen Shui-bian harshly. But as soon as they encounter the issue of reunification or pro-independence, they will probably act the same way as the DPP. When will the Pan-Blue voters ever be able to avoid being cheated?

Conclusion

The Pan-Green Coalition led by Chen Shui-bian claimed that it would walk the middle road and regard improving the cross-strait relations as its top priority. But deep in the hearts of Pan-Green members is the goal to realize Taiwan independence. Although the Pan-Blue Coalition, led by Lien and Soong, recognized itself as Chinese, it has never made reunification its goal. Hence, to rely on these ruling and opposition parties to lead Taiwan to peaceful reunification is an exercise in futility. Though the 2004 year-end legislative election would determine Taiwan's future political territory, it will not necessarily be a key indicator to watch in regard to Taiwan's direction for reunification or independence.

PART IV

"One Country, Two Systems" in Taiwan

Whenever "one country, two systems" is mentioned in Taiwan, the people say that it is unacceptable. In order to achieve the goal of reunification, perhaps mainland China needs to do some new thinking, change the way it does things, and create a system that is more easily accepted by the general public. Or, perhaps it needs to propose some appealing reasons for the Taiwanese people to accept the idea. Is "one country, two systems" really unacceptable to the Taiwanese people? From the several polling results obtained in 2001, we know that this was not so.

According to several public polls run from March to June 2001, the people's support of "one country, two systems" increased rapidly. The polling results were as shown on the following page.

There are many reasons for the huge changes in the Taiwanese people's attitudes:

1) Since the opening of the mainland, the number of Taiwanese people who went to the mainland to visit family, do business, travel, and make visits reached 20 to 30 million, which corresponds to the total Taiwan population. They have personally witnessed quality improvements and rising standards of living in the mainland. This has completely destroyed their anti-communism thinking and the Taiwan government's propaganda of defacing China.

Taiwanese People's Support of "One Country, Two Systems"

Poller	Date of Poll	Those in Favor (%)
Taiwan MAC	March 2001	16.5
China Times Daily News	June 2001	29
TVBS TV Station	June 27, 2001	31
United Daily News	June 27, 2001	32

Other Results

Taiwanese people who believe that "one country, two systems" adheres to people's interests on both sides	35
Taiwanese people willing to work in the mainland	34
Taiwanese people willing to move to the mainland to live	24
Taiwanese people who believe the cross-strait problems can be resolved peacefully	Up to 58

(*United Daily News*, page 4, 07/01/2001)

2) Since the mainland began a reform and open policy, its economy developed rapidly, the general national strength increased continuously, and its international status rose. These changes have influenced the attitudes of Chinese around the world.

3) In less than one year after the DPP gained power, dramatic changes occurred in the Taiwan situation. For example, Taiwan's economy declined, production suffered setbacks, stock prices shrank, real estate prices dropped, the unemployment rate increased, living standards lowered, political parties fought perniciously, and the political situation destabilized. The cross-strait economic developments have been showing growth in mainland China but degeneration in Taiwan. Hence, people's attitudes about "one country, two systems" changed.

In the spring of 2003, the SARS epidemic spread across the entire Taiwan Island. Chen Shui-bian blamed the mainland as the source of the epidemic while simultaneously and actively trying to burst into the WHO. He pushed the responsibility of Taiwan not being able to join the WHO to mainland China and even proposed referendum advocacy. Chen Shui-bian also took advantage of the July 1 parade in Hong Kong to once again publicly defame "one country, two systems." In order to win the localist votes and to get rid of labels such as "Communist China's fellow travelers" or "reunification faction," the opposition parties lied and voiced the opposition to the "one country, two systems" policy frequently. They also said that "one China is the ROC" and that they would "not announce reunification as long as they are the president and vice president." Under the environment of anti-reunification propaganda by the ruling and opposing parties, people's attitudes about reunification and "one country, two systems" might have changed. However, the relative strengths of the two sides showed a rise in the mainland and a fall in Taiwan, and created a certain expectation about reunification in the Taiwanese people. Reunification was the big trend, leaving the people with no choice. Proof of this can be found in the recent research results by the News Broadcasting Department of the Chinese Culture University in Taiwan. The University Students' Recognition on Taiwan research (11/21/2003) uncovered that up to 30 percent of the university students in North Taiwan wished to study in the mainland and that more than 60 percent of university students wished to work in the mainland after graduation (among them 61.9 percent were from the leading National Taiwan University).

While the presidential candidates were heatedly arguing about referendum, a new Constitution, and the nation's recognition, Taiwan's young people used their actions to express their desires by going to the mainland. Unfortunately, on the island, there were very few political parties, scholars, and organizations doing research or having discussions on "one country, two systems" that would enable more people at the grassroots level to totally understand its contents.

After stating the origin and development of "one country, two systems," the Taiwan government's and its political parties' attitudes toward it, as well as the U.S. position concerning it, we finally come to the last part of this book, *"One Country, Two Systems" in Taiwan.*

Certainly in order to discuss "one country, two systems" one must consider the prerequisite of having a future vision towards reunification. But reunification alone is not enough. It is the premise of this book that China be reunified peacefully as early as possible. A peaceful reunification is beneficial to the 1.3 billion people in mainland China and, more so, for the welfare of the Taiwanese people. Chapter 10 will list the benefits of reunification to the Taiwanese people from their viewpoint.

In order to carry out "one country, two systems" in Taiwan, two breakthroughs need to be made: the acceptance of "one China" and the acceptance of "two systems." Chapter 11 will discuss the disputes regarding "one China." This chapter covers the ideologies of defining Taiwan's status and the national recognition, which has been disputed for too long. Exactly how they should be resolved is perhaps a question in the hearts of all people who care about the country's reunification.

Chapter 12 will discuss the contents of "two systems." In the past, when the Taiwan academic circle discussed "one country, two systems," the scholars tended to focus on "one China." Few discussed "two systems." Some viewed the "two systems" as simply a way to maintain the current situation. Since Taiwan now has a different system, as long as "one China" can be properly addressed, everything is legitimate and the two sides can formally enter "one country, two systems." When the two sides of the strait really become "one country," the people of Taiwan will be protected under the banner of being Chinese and its "situation" should also become better than the current one.

The realization of a peaceful reunification and "one country, two systems" must be achieved through negotiations. In the past, the two sides had never conducted political negotiations, and now negotiations for practical matters have also ceased. When the talks resume, what should be talked about and what sort of attitude should be held during the negotiations all impact the timetable for reunification. Chapter 13 includes the author's viewpoints on various subjects that might be discussed during cross-strait negotiations. The last chapter will talk about Taiwan's future.

CHAPTER 10

WHAT BENEFITS WILL THE TAIWANESE PEOPLE GET FROM REUNIFICATION?

What benefits will the reunification have? Professor Chen Kongli, Director of the Institute of Taiwan, Xiamen University, published an article in *Da Gong Bao* entitled "Peaceful Reunification: The Ten Benefits" in 2000. He systematically summarized the ten benefits of a peaceful reunification. Although these benefits are closely relevant to the Taiwanese people, they are actually based on the mutual benefits of the people on both sides of the strait. At the end of his article, Chen Kongli encouraged the Taiwanese people to propose the benefits that reunification would bring to their hearts on their own initiative. Unfortunately, he did not receive much response.

In Taiwan, the scholars who study the cross-strait issues have done much research on the reunification models. The mainland affairs department or cross-strait team of the various political parties, regardless of their positions, also made detailed investigations of the reunification problem. Very few of the people in Taiwan have seriously thought about the benefits of reunification, despite the fact that through reading newspapers and watching television programs they receive information from mainland China or hear about disputes on reunification or independence. This is due to the long-time influence of the Taiwan government and the media's defamation of "one country, two systems."

SECTION 1
IS REUNIFICATION BENEFICIAL FOR ALL TAIWANESE PEOPLE?

When reunification is mentioned, the Taiwanese political figures and the general public ask the same question: What benefit can reunification bring to the Taiwanese people? Quite a number of Taiwan scholars and even some U.S. officials and scholars believe that the Taiwanese people's rejection of "one country, two systems" is simply due to a lack of appealing reasons to accept it. As such, unless the reunification has very concrete and practical benefits, it may not be accepted.

Taiwan's economic dependence on the mainland is becoming more and more obvious every day. Even though the two sides are not reunified, every year the mainland has a trade deficit from Taiwan of approximately 20 to 30 billion U.S. dollars. This amount will certainly increase after reunification. The opinion is that there will naturally be three links after reunification and that the Taiwanese merchants will travel between the two sides via direct routes. Just the savings on traveling expenses and shipping costs alone will yield a few hundred million dollars versus the current level. Indeed, facing the economic deterioration in Taiwan, the economic consideration is the most serious concern of the Taiwanese people when they think about reunification. After a bit more consideration, though, we can see that Taiwan is facing more than just economic problems. The economic deterioration and the government's improper measures have already caused serious effects: The unemployment rate continues to climb to new highs, personal income declines year by year, the gap between the rich and the poor enlarges, and more and more people are falling into depression. Suicide rates are rising every year and family tragedies caused by stressful relationships and the corrupted social order have created constant tension. Interestingly, cross-strait marriages are common. But owing to the different laws between the two sides of the strait, there are no mutual constraints or protections; hence, many family problems result. In the cultural and educational areas, the government has been pushing for a "localization" policy that is confusing students about their national identity. The Taiwanese people are gradually losing their roots and social justice.

Taiwan's many problems have much to do with Lee Teng-hui's 12-year rule and Chen Shui-bian's more than three years in office; the "black and gold" (corrupted) politics, the erroneous economic policy of "go slowly and exercise patience," and the cultural/educational "de-Sinicization" process. Even if the political parties changed hands so that the Pan-Blue Coalition were in power, completely reversing the economic deterioration, social tur-moil, and the system's lack of order would still be quite a challenge. Equally difficult would be to eliminate the unfairness, the injustice, the rampant political corruption, and the policy of excluding those who think differently. During the 3rd Plenary Session of the 16th Central Commission of the KMT, Lien Chan presented his main presidential election advocacy, which included the following statistics: lower the unemployment rate to less than four percent, raise the economic growing rate to five percent, and balance the government budget in six years. He also called for the following by 2010: increase the research and development budget to three percent of the GDP, eliminate the double increase of health insurance premiums, examine edu-cation reform, and others. These are difficult goals to accomplish. Apart from these, in order to win the presidential election, the DPP has spent huge amounts of money on bribes. This has caused Taiwan's economy to lose the competitive edge and its financial deficit to increase. Even if Lien won and fulfilled his campaign promises, balancing Taiwan's economy would be a hopeless task.

Strictly speaking, reunification is not necessarily a benefit to everyone. It may be better for the Taiwanese people to understand clearly which cate-gory of people will benefit and which category will be hurt. First, let us dis-cuss the disadvantaged categories. They are the politicians, like Chen Shui-bian, who rely on Taiwan's independence ideology for reelection. They use the shell of the ROC but carry out the independence reality. The econ-omy deteriorated and politics fell into turmoil during the first three years when Chen Shui-bian was in office. With his current term over, he had no political merit to show to the voters, so he proposed "one country on each side," to heat up the topic of referendum, and hoped to win reelection by saying that Communist China wanted to attack Taiwan and that "one coun-try, two systems" would downgrade Taiwan. Chen Shui-bian and his newly rich and powerful Pan-Green followers are the ones who ask what benefit reunification can bring to Taiwan. Of course, reunification will give them no benefit; it will harm them instead. The point is that these people represent only a small privileged group and not the vast number of Taiwanese. They are the ones who won the power by expressing publicly, "I love Taiwan the most, and hence Taiwan should not be reunified." It would be wise to observe just how they have changed Taiwan.

The Taiwan unemployment rate increased rapidly. Those who were active in the Taiwan independence movement donated money to Taiwan independence organizations and the DPP. Those who stayed close or stood by Chen Shui-bian's side—regardless of their professional experience or credentials—became high officials and national policy consultants. The people in Taiwan all fear that their sons will be bullied into compulsory military service, while Chen Shui-bian's son did his military service at the Naval Commander Center as a military judge and drove a Jaguar to and from his office. All Taiwan taxi drivers fear daily police harassment, but the high officials and their children are escorted by the police in government cars. All Taiwanese people are terrified of being monitored on the phone, but the Minister of Justice Chen Ding-nan said that an overall interim monitor did not violate the Constitution! When the Control Yuan (one of five branches of the ROC government in Taipei and a watchdog agency that monitors ["controls"] the government; it may [retrospectively] be compared to a standing commission for administrative inquiry) corrected Chen Shih-meng, the General-Secretary to the President, he accused the member of the Control Yuan of being the Pan-Blue hatchet man! During his three years in office, Chen Shui-bian did not do much correctly but he blamed all of his liabilities on the previous government! Did he forget that the previous government was led by Lee Teng-hui—who also relied on publicly expressing loving Taiwan but privately preferring Japan?

At the present time, Taiwan is neither reunified nor independent, so who benefits? Certainly it is not most of the Taiwanese. Instead, the ones who benefit are the small number of politicians and the financial groups that conspire with Chen Shui-bian. Chen Shui-bian announced that he would not use "one China" to exchange for the three links. But which Pan-Green financial group would not steal Taiwan's money to make a big fortune in the mainland? Which financial group that supported Chen Shui-bian in the 2000 presidential election and those who turned green after the election do not invest heavily in the mainland? The Evergreen Group that has nurtured Chen Shui-bian openly expresses support of "one China" because it has too many investments in the mainland and has to be held accountable to the Chinese government. But the son-in-law of Evergreen Group's Chairman Chang Jung-fa is still supporting Chen Shui-bian in Taiwan. It seems that with Taiwan not reunified or independent, these financial groups can gain advantages from both sides and use the privileges and connections to their benefit. But, do they represent most of the Taiwanese people? No, they do not!

For the most part, the Taiwanese people only wish to live and work peacefully, and insure stability and a safe environment for themselves and their families. Taiwan has the most capable and diligent farmers, fishermen, and laborers, and the most active small- and medium-sized enterprises in the world. But it is facing an economic slump. Whether reunification can improve its current depression and resolve most of the problems should be investigated by each citizen of Taiwan.

SECTION 2
EXACTLY WHAT BENEFITS CAN REUNIFICATION GIVE TO THE TAIWANESE PEOPLE?

Taiwan can enjoy many benefits as a result of reunification. Hopefully by expressing these benefits, others will speak out about the benefits of reunification.

Share the National Defense and Save Military Expenditures

For more than 20 years, Taiwan's military procurement expenses amounted to about US$43 billion. From 1994 to 1999, Taiwan topped the world list with purchased armaments that amounted to US$13.3 billion. From 1990 to 1995, Taiwan's military purchases from the U.S. amounted to US$8.3 billion, second only to Saudi Arabia. Taiwan topped the list in per-million-population military expenditure in Asia by spending a figure of US$0.54 billion for arms. A prosperous and strong country like Japan, in comparison, only has a per-million-population military expenditure of US$0.37 billion.

The U.S. media reports that since the 1990s, mainland China has been involved in the development of military armaments and has increased its military expenditures. This is one of the theoretical bases of the "China threat" theory. But in reality, the mainland military expenditures are only about 1.5 percent of its domestic GDP, and the general international levels are about 3 percent. During the recent two years the increment of the mainland military expenditures did not increase, it decreased (*China Times Daily News*, 01/06/2003).

The national defense expenditure of the mainland every year is about US$20 billion. Taiwan's expenditure on troops every year is also about US$20 billion. However, the mainland total scale of industrial production far exceeds that of Taiwan. They both use the same amount of money to purchase armaments. The impact on Taiwan's economic construction and people's lives is much larger. Taiwan's economy is deteriorating on a daily basis because of the military procurement.

Within three years of Chen Shui-bian's rise to power, Taiwan's financial condition became more and more of a strain. Regardless of this, it still decided to purchase over US$6 billion in advanced weaponry. In June 2003, the U.S. agreed to sell 12 anti-submarine planes to Taiwan; the asking price was about US$4.1 billion. Vice Defense Minister Lin Chong-pin thought the price was too high. But in the middle of August 2003, the Office of the President suddenly demanded that the Ministry of Defense arrange and list about US$15.2 billion as a special budget beginning the next fiscal year to pay for the Patriot PAC-3 missile systems, the Long Range Radar Space Surveillance Systems, and the diesel-powered submarines. The relevant officials revealed that Secretary-General to the President Chiu Yi-ren visited the U.S. in July 2003. Taiwan's sincerity was questioned by the U.S. and in responding to the pressure, Chiu Yi-ren promised that Taiwan would get rid of financial difficulties and arrange for a special budget in advance. The Legislative Yuan also confessed that the main consideration for the approximately US$15.2 billion special budget was due to U.S. pressure and the 2004 presidential election. The Ministry of Defense told the legislators that the eight submarines Taiwan wanted might be varied. The U.S. also told the visiting legislators many times that Taiwan should sign the contract as early as possible; otherwise, the earlier agreed-upon military procurement items might not be accepted by the next U.S. president (*China Times Daily News*, 08/28/2003). According to the recent report, the U.S. demanded that Taiwan sign the military procurement contract before July 2004. Surprisingly enough, on November 1, 2003, at a luncheon in New York, Chen Shui-bian shared a table with the largest U.S. arms merchant (*China Times Daily News*, 11/02/2003). The importance of the U.S. arms sale to Taiwan proven repeatedly by such incidents. It was not relevant to Taiwan authorities that the Taiwanese people had to tighten their belts.

People will be disappointed if they believe that the situation will change when a different party comes into power. When Lien Chan visited the U.S. at the end of October 2003, he specifically mentioned to the American people that only when Taiwan had enough defense weapons could it protect the safety of the Taiwan Strait. Hence, if he were elected president, he would definitely increase military purchases from the U.S. (*China Times Daily News*, 10/22/2003). In view of this, we know that the military procurement will not stop even when political offices change hands. Only reunification can reduce military procurement substantially.

After reunification, the two sides will no longer face each other with hostility. Taiwan will keep its military and carry out its necessary defense of the strait without spending huge sums of money to purchase arms. As such, astronomical amounts of government funds can be used for social welfare, education, construction, and other programs to greatly benefit the people of Taiwan.

The Cross-Strait Economy and Trade as an Integral Whole, Orderly and Complementing Each Other

Taiwan has an economy that relies on export, which makes it strongly dependent on the external world and vulnerable to any changes or uncertainties. Without a peaceful and stable environment, it would be impossible for Taiwan's economy to keep continuity and development. After the reunification, Taiwan's industrial circles can use the mainland as a base and both sides can sign the CEPA. As such, Taiwan's economy can be brought back to life, and it will have the possibility of realizing an upgrade in industrial circles and structural reform.

When the mainland joined the WTO, it became a market for international investment capital. According to the published numbers of the United Nations Conference on Trade and Development in 2002, the foreign direct investments in the mainland exceeded US$50 billion. On the other hand, due to a lack of recovery strength and confidence, the U.S. attracted only US$44 billion (down from 2001's US$124 billion). This marked the first time that the mainland was able to absorb foreign investment money that exceeded the U.S.

The rapid economic growth of mainland China over the past ten years has made it the country with the greatest potential in the global economy. After the Asia economic crisis in the late 20th century, many countries suffered economic depression. But due to the special relationship with the mainland, Taiwan avoided such a crisis and became the envy of many countries. As long as Taiwan is willing to partner with mainland China to form an integral economic whole like Hong Kong and Macao, it is in a better position to recover from its economic slump. Many scholars knew this, but were hindered by their insistence on Taiwan sovereignty. While most of them suggested "economic corporation but political separation," the economic scholar Liu Chin-jing in Japan proposed that only when Taiwan accepted "peaceful reunification, one country, two systems" could the cross-strait economy and trade become an integral whole, orderly and complementing each other. In addition, the cross-strait industrial and economic mechanisms could make an overall, policy-wise adjustment. The most important aspect is that reunification not only can save Taiwan's economy, but it will also protect the benefits of Taiwanese peasants, workers, and fishermen.

The three links plan is considered the most important task for the cross-strait policy. But three links may not completely solve the Taiwan problem. Although the three links is not implemented now, entrepreneurs still take concrete actions in expressing their determination by walking out. Those who cannot move are the grassroots Taiwanese people. The unemployment rate is climbing and the people are faced with transferring capital, talent, and technology to the mainland, while the mainland products dominate the Taiwan market. At some point there will be suspicion if the three links benefit only the rich entrepreneurs who went to the mainland for development, while the laborers, peasants, and fishermen were denied benefits. The three links definitely will initiate a new wave of industrial circles and capital moving to the mainland, making Taiwan industrial circles more hollow and unemployment rates higher. Although the three links plan is necessary and important, only reunification can resolve the problems faced by Taiwan's entire society.

The Two Sides Come Together with Their Labor Forces and Complement Each Other to Create a "Chinese Miracle"

In the past few years, the government used various excuses and denied all responsibility for the economic depression. Among these excuses, the weekly working hours being reduced from 44 to 42 was cited as the main reason for the large-scale decline of Taiwan's competitiveness. But, according to statistics from the general accounting office, Taiwan's average hourly pay dropped to the level of five years earlier and Taiwan's laborers often had to work overtime to keep a basic living standard. The law has not been able to regulate Taiwan's average weekly working hours for quite some time. According to the statistics of the Institute of International Management at the University of Lausanne in Switzerland, Taiwan's annual working hour average is a total of 2,282—the highest in the world. According to the joint report by www.udnjob.com and the *Cheers* magazine on the subject of manpower and man-hours, 75 percent of those being interviewed thought they were overworked. Nearly 30 percent worked more than 62 hours a week, which far exceeded lawful working hours. These differences did not match the number promulgated by the Council of Labor Affairs.

To avoid layoff and salary reduction, laborers also overworked themselves. The government has repeatedly claimed that government-owned enterprises have been reformed successfully and have turned loss into profit. But the workers in government-owned enterprises saw only salary reduction, layoffs, and stock dumping. Hence, the unions of China Telecom, the railroad, and the Taiwan automobile industry initiated worker's demonstrations and protests. Even the laborers working for government-operated enterprises developed a sense of insecurity, making the situation even more serious.

During the last part of October 2003, Chairman of the Labor Party Wu Rong-yuan stated in *The New Democratic Forum* that since the 1990s, Taiwan has been under the challenge of system reconstruction of a global division of labor. Taiwan's industrial enterprises have long been forced to face the choice of either transformation or closing down the plants to move elsewhere. However, Taiwan's politics have intervened and limited the two-way exchanges of the cross-strait economy and trades, which caused industrial capitals to vacate, thus abandoning the industrial enterprises on the island. The related policies that would adjust the transformation of the whole economic structure were null and void. This kind of unemployment caused by structure transformations inevitably results in a continuous widening of the gap between the rich and poor. Unless the two sides reunify and together both governments plan a set of methods to combine and complement their labor forces, Taiwan's labor problems cannot be solved and will become more serious (see website of *The New Democratic Forum*, 10/26/2003).

If the mainland continues its development with the current speed, it will soon become the factory of the world. At the same time, because mainland China is open to foreign investments, every country has made money there and will obviously continue their investments. The mainland, by making products for other countries, can both solve its employment and economic problems and gain skills in advanced production, management, and marketing to insure its future progress. On the other hand, without reunification, Taiwan's situation will become more difficult as China's industrialization continues to rapidly progress. Although the three links and the relaxation of mainland investment policies can benefit Taiwan businessmen, they cannot recover Taiwan's industrial enterprises; instead, the unemployment rate will increase. Some people say that by transferring certain industrial enterprises to the mainland, Taiwan can transform its industrial enterprises to higher technology areas. It is good to have a successful transformation, but the newly established high-tech factories only hire young and trained workers. Where do the unemployed senior workers who know traditional techniques find jobs? According to statistics, the number of mainland laborers hired by the mainland factories established by Taiwan enterprises has exceeded the total number of laborers hired by Taiwan enterprises on the island. If this trend continues, Taiwan laborers will fall into a hopeless situation.

After the reunification, enterprises on both sides of the strait, through the help of related units and private associations, will be able to discuss how to create a win-win situation for the division of their work. The experienced laborers in Taiwan's industrial enterprises can take jobs at levels above foreman in the mainland because they are of the same culture and race. The mainland is just initiating the opening of the Great Northwest and the recovery of the Old Northeast. In order to train a large number of local people, China needs a huge number of foremen and seed laborers. If Taiwan does not grasp this opportunity, the Taiwanese laborers may face starvation. Considering these circumstances, the talented Taiwanese technicians should be the ones who support reunification the most. After the reunification, their employment problems will be solved and they will be able to construct a prosperous and strong new China together with the mainland laborers.

Economist Liu Chin-jing proposed a series of suggestions for the resolution of the employment problems. He suggested that:

1) The Taiwan government should demand that Taiwanese businessmen who invest in the mainland through the construction of factories pay certain ratios of taxes for professional training in Taiwan.

2) Mainland Chinese capitalists can invest in Taiwan by setting up factories and hiring Taiwanese local laborers.

3) The two sides should negotiate to have certain types of production stay in Taiwan. For example, the world largest auto manufacturers all build plants in the mainland. Taiwan could be in charge of the production of certain parts to provide Taiwan autoworkers with continued employment.

As Liu Chin-jing said, in order to draw up concrete steps, Taiwan must ask for advice from the grassroots laborers of various professions. The suggestions made by scholars will serve as stimulation for discussions and encourage others to come forward with valuable opinions (see Liu Chin-jing's speech draft on *The New Democratic Forum*, 10/26/2003).

In addition, Taiwan has an urgent demand for mainland laborers but has trouble recruiting them through proper channels, so it hires illegal aliens. These illegal aliens not only create social chaos, but they also subject Taiwan to discrimination and human rights violations. After the reunification, the quota, minimum wage, and benefits for mainland laborers can be reached through agreements. By working together in an organized manner, the shortage of the Taiwan labor force in not only construction, but also fishing and home care can be solved. Taiwan can also ask the mainland to arrest illegal aliens, which will reduce Taiwan's unilateral management costs. As long as the wages and attitudes are reasonable, the Taiwan employers will experience the benefits of hiring mainland laborers. This will allow better communications and management than can be attained through the hiring of foreign workers.

The Whole China as an Agriculture Base: Peasants on Both Sides Can Exchange Techniques

Due to the crowded conditions in Taiwan, after the land reform policy of Peasants Farm Their Own Land, the amount of land allotted to every peasant family was limited. Hence, they had to improve their crop strains and increase their planting density. For more than 50 years, Taiwanese peasants have achieved the top position in the world agricultural arena through the instructions of their agriculture research and development units. These include the use of fertilizers and the maintenance of farm equipment, the installation of automatic irrigation systems, the care of crops, and the nurturing of new crop strains. These Taiwanese peasants, who have less than a junior high school education, guarded their limited land, improved their crop strains, and produced an agriculture output of the best quality and the highest per unit area productivity. Although they may not know exactly how things worked, their actual experiences cannot be superseded by anyone.

Taiwanese peasants produce the world's best quality fruits and vegetables. Since they have a surplus, the best and most reasonable option is to export their products to the near coastal areas of the mainland—such as Shanghai, Beijing, and Guangzhou. In these places the average income is higher and many Taiwanese and foreign businessmen gather. These consumer markets deserve enthusiastic development because they are major consumers and the transportation is convenient. Lee Teng-hui as an agricultural and economic specialist must have known that the vast area of land and the 1.3 billion compatriots could be the main market base for the Taiwanese peasants. Yet he suggested "go slowly and exercise patience" as his agricultural policy. As a result, the Taiwan peasants could only sit idly by in distress.

Following the growth of the Taiwan economy, land prices and labor transportation costs increased and competitiveness decreased. The financial enterprises tried to solve these problems by moving to areas where land, labor, and shipping costs were lower for farming. The United Enterprise went to Xinjiang to grow tomatoes, turn them into by-products (tomato juice and sauce), and market them worldwide. In contrast, the Taiwanese peasants grow the same tomatoes and have a similar harvest, but can only use them to feed pigs. The Won-Won Food Company established a few dozen plants in the mainland more than ten years ago. They sell their products to every city in the mainland as well as to the entire world including Taiwan. Recently, Won-Won diversified its operations by opening restaurants in Shanghai and hospitals in Changsha. Meanwhile, the Taiwanese peasants were forced to stay on the island at a loss. The peasants who obey the rules and always do their duty had no choice but to protest on the street. Though the government tried to comfort them, they were not able to improve the difficult situation of the peasants.

Taiwan has belonged to the WTO for just over a year. Following the government's lowering of import tariffs, a large quantity of cheap foreign agriculture and fishing products came in, which put Taiwan's agriculture in peril. It is a waste of time for any individual peasant, and even for the agricultural associations, to fight against this situation because they cannot survive the international competition. The agricultural specialists suggest strengthening the functionality of the agricultural association and its production/sales, as well as increasing the push for strategic alliances to integrate the various agricultural resources to compensate for the production deficiency of the small farmers. However, these suggestions cannot stimulate the revival of Taiwan agriculture.

After the reunification, China—which has an abundance of land, a large population, and an enormous market—can serve as the heart of Taiwan's agriculture. The surplus can be sold to the rest of the world. Taiwan's peasants can go to the mainland farms, become agricultural technology instructors, lead the mainland peasants to work, and teach their experience and skills. In this way, not only can they solve their own problems, they can also make contributions to agriculture and consumers all over China.

With the Protection of the National Military, Fishermen No Longer Have to Fear

Taiwan's fishing boats often encounter accidents while fishing in the sea. In recent years, fishermen were often taken into custody by foreign governments in the East-South Asian water territory. Some of the fishermen were detained in the Philippines for a long time and could only escape during typhoon days or political insurrections. Fishing boat captains often were murdered for hiring Indonesian fishing workers. These incidents indicate that Taiwan's ocean fishing environment is very dangerous, and fishermen cannot be protected from trouble through self-discipline or private mediation. The fishermen need help from the government in order to survive.

Taiwan can get cheaper, non-violent, laborers who communicate well to work on the fishing boats. But due to government restrictions, Taiwan can only hire workers from Vietnam, Indonesia, and the Philippines. The Fishing Union repeatedly demanded that the governmental decision-making unit evaluate the risks, eliminate the suspicion of ideologies, and allow the captains to hire a manageable, quality labor force. However, the Union got no results.

The continued tragedies inflicted on the fishermen had angered the Taiwanese people. The media and scholars called on the government to pay attention to the fishing disputes. They said that even though Taiwan's diplomatic situation was rather difficult, the government should not leave the fishermen to themselves to solve their problems by paying ransoms or running away. If the government did not take any action to stop these kinds of incidents, the fishermen's families would be afraid that every time their husbands or sons or fathers go fishing, they will not be able to come back.

The fishing industry is an extension of the national strength. Chen Shuibian and Annette Lu often went abroad to strive for diplomatic relations, but because Taiwan does not have diplomatic relationships with most of the world's countries, Chen and Lu dared not complain about their fishermen's unfair treatment by these countries. Facing the anger of the general public, the Pan-Green politicians only said that the water territory issues were very complicated and that Taiwan could not afford to offend its neighbors. Under these circumstances, there seems to be no hope for relieving the difficulties of fishermen's lives.

When the ROC was still one of the permanent members of the UN Security Council, Taiwan's fishermen could fish freely from the Southern Pacific to the Indian Ocean and from Samoa to Cape Town, South Africa. These fishermen sailed their 200- or 300-ton small boats across the oceans, taking risks and challenging difficulties. Their fishing harvest topped the world, even superseding the Japanese and Korean boats.

In conclusion, after the reunification and with the strong back-up of China's tri-service military, what country's government or fishermen would dare to detain Taiwan fishermen's boats, penalize their profits, or invade Taiwan's economic water territory? Also, the Taiwan fishing boat owners would be able to legally hire mainland fishing workers with reasonable wages, which would reduce the disputes and tragedies between the Taiwanese fishermen and foreign fishermen.

When the Reunification-Independence Dispute Ceases,
Clean and Positive Politics Are Hopefully Possible

Lee Teng-hui did not govern Taiwan properly. He connected himself with the black and gold force, fought within the party, and eliminated opponents for the 12 years he was in office. During that time he also secretly helped the DPP so that it could become the ruling party after he finished his term. Lee Teng-hui used the pretext of amending the Constitution to discard the Taiwan province and to eliminate the veto power of the Legislative Yuan on the nomination of the Premier. This crippled the Legislative Yuan and gave the president all the power but no responsibility. Even his successor Chen Shui-bian said that the entire Constitution had been amended to the extent that it could not be amended anymore; hence, a new Constitution was needed.

The political mess extended far beyond these incidents. In order to win the direct general presidential election in 1996, Lee Teng-hui initiated the "Taiwanese finally rise" populist movement to hit his opponents. He used the pretexts of nativization and democratization to incite ethnic emotions that had gradually disappeared due to a large number of interethnic marriages. During the last four years of his term (1996–2000), he worked in consonance with the DPP by invoking the people's will to intensify more and more opposition between the pro-reunification and the pro-independence groups. In 2000, Chen Shui-bian again used the nationalistic enthusiasm for nativization, populism, and ethnicization to win the presidential election. This ethnic sentiment blurred the conflicts between pro-reunification and pro-independence and set the fate of the Taiwanese people. In 2003, the Pan-Blue and Pan-Green presidential candidates, in order to win the election, competed with each other over who loved Taiwan more, ignoring Taiwan's security and international realities and making the campaign strategies even more caustic. This strategy even created violence among the voters.

The fight for pro-reunification or pro-independence has also misplaced people's focal point when examining democracy in Taiwan. In the past ten years, the contrast between the mainland growth and Taiwan's decline has been visible to everyone. People have only paid attention to the obvious economic side, since numbers speak. In fact, though, the political side is the more serious aspect: Lee Teng-hui amended the Constitution to the point that it was unrecognizable; Chen Shui-bian did not even care about amending the Constitution again. Still, every one of Chen Shui-bian's administrative officials, from the President of the Executive Yuan to the Interior

Minister, thought that they could interpret the Constitution. As soon as any of them is blamed for something, they will declare that their behaviors are adhering to the Constitution and are, therefore, legal. If that were the case, what is the purpose of having the Grand Justices? Although both Chen Shui-bian and Annette Lu have studied law, when did they ever care about the law? During the past three years, the DPP violated the law numerous times, but every single violation against the law or against the Constitution was justified by them as legal and the discrepancies disappeared.

After reunification, Taiwan politicians would no longer be able to use the disputes on reunification/independence or ethnic sentiment to divide voters. Anyone who wants to be a politician must propose a set of blueprints for governing Taiwan to win the votes. This will show how he/she loves Taiwan. Aren't these the benefits of reunification to the Taiwanese people? After excluding the reunification independence disputes and the ethnic sentiment, the voters can fairly supervise their politicians' political performance, conduct, and morality. As a result, the financial enterprises will not be able to bribe politicians, and the corrupted politics will gradually disappear.

In addition, after the reunification, there will be more room for Taiwan politicians. Those politicians who are idealistic, ambitious, and have professional expertise can go to the mainland and make contributions to Greater China's modernization and legalization, instead of staying in Taiwan's crowded and deteriorating conditions to wage war on their brothers and sisters.

Collaboration on Science and Technologies, Be Complementary to Each Other

In recent years, Taiwan's investments in the mainland have reached 50 percent of its total foreign investments. In 2000 alone, the investments of Taiwan's leading high-tech electronic and electronic equipment industries in the mainland exceeded 50 percent of Taiwan's total investments there. This is indicative of a rapid emigration of Taiwan's high-tech industrial enterprises.

Using 2003 as an example, the estimated annual computer hardware industrial output in Taiwan was nearly US$50 billion. The local Taiwan production was 34.1 percent, but the output manufactured in the mainland surpassed the Taiwan local production for the first time to reach 51 percent (in 2002, 47.1 percent of the hardware was manufactured in the mainland versus 36.9 percent in Taiwan). In the areas of assembly-type production of items such as motherboards, monitors, notebook personal computers (notebook PCs), and LCD monitors, the emigration of production bases to the mainland has been a serious setback. During the first half of 2003, the production ratio of notebook PCs in the mainland increased from 5.2 percent in 2002 to 24 percent. The world's number one notebook PC producer, Quanta Computer Company, had 75 percent of its production in the mainland. In 2000, computer hardware production in the mainland exceeded Taiwan's local production. Using 2002 as an example, the mainland computer hardware production increased by 25 percent compared with the prior year, leaving Taiwan's production in a 13.8 percent decline.

Concerning Taiwan's investment law and its mainland investments, in August 2001, Taiwan's Economic and Development Conference terminated the "go slowly and exercise patience" policy and replaced it with the "active opening and effective management" policy. But since its execution, people have only seen effective management, no active opening. More than 70 percent of the people in industrial and business circles thought that "active opening and effective management" was another form of "go slowly and exercise patience." In addition, after both sides joined the WTO, the Taiwan government did not keep its promise to speed up the normalization process for cross-strait economic relations. Instead, it stepped up the speed of establishing a "precautionary system for cross-strait economic and trading safety" and a "long-term safety net" to continue imposing strict limitations on imported mainland products and investment capital.

After the reunification, the computer hardware industry may not return to Taiwan to set up plants because the mainland labor, land, and shipping costs are cheaper and the quality of labor increases annually. But the software industry may consider staying in Taiwan to continue its research and development by hiring high-tech mainland talents. For the past ten years, Taiwan has worked hard in the hopes of making a breakthrough in the software industry. But due to a lack of high-tech talent, it has not been successful. In the latter part of October 2003, Chen Shui-bian announced that in 2008 he would invest three percent of the national GDP in high-tech research and development. But the government sectors protested that this would not be at all workable and that the ratio of the mainland's investment in research and development has ranked number three in the world since 2003. If, instead, the mainland combines its high-tech talents with Taiwan's software experts, they could create new and competitive products.

Recently the mainland proposed a Scientific Education to Make the Country Prosperous policy. Taiwan also has the Science and Technology

Island plan. If both could develop together, there would be mutual benefits. Considering that basic science and technology talents are the strong points in the mainland, and the applied science and technologies, managerial skills, marketing abilities, and experience are the strong points in Taiwan, then their collaboration will definitely benefit both sides.

Reunification Will Rehabilitate Chinese Culture and Promote the Quality of Education

Lee Teng-hui and Chen Shui-bian have pushed "de-Sinicization" in Taiwan. This is perhaps the greatest sin they have committed and they will be condemned by history. Not long after Lee Teng-hui took power, he openly selected a new book *Understanding Taiwan* as a university teaching material, using "nativization," the "theory of self-determination," and the "theory of autonomy" to deny that Taiwan is part of China. When Chen Shui-bian took power he continued to promote the "culture Taiwan independence" idea enthusiastically. He announced that he would abandon Chinese pronunciation in favor of general pronunciation with Taiwanese dialect (Minnan dialect) as the official pronunciation system in Taiwan. He also advised the universities to set up a Taiwan Literature Department and to push aside Chinese Literature. He stipulated that junior high school and primary school students should choose one of the languages among the Hakka dialect, the Minnan dialect, or the Aborigines language in order to weaken the status of Mandarin in Taiwan. He ordered the destruction of any signs or slogans that had words supporting reunification or opposing Taiwan independence in an attempt to clear the long-existing reunification concept in Taiwan society. He also replaced the emblem of the Press Bureau since it contained a drawing of the Chinese territorial map. He added the word "Taiwan" on passports, changed the names of all the offices abroad to Taiwan Representative Offices, and forced companies, academic organizations, and private groups that had "China" in their titles to use "Taiwan" instead. In short, he tried "de-Sinicization" on everything so that Taiwan could achieve a gradual independence.

In August 2003, the DPP government decided to place Chinese history after the Min Dynasty into the world history curriculum designed for the high school course. The government also promoted various local dialects and minority nationality languages as national languages and used Minnan dialect to design test questions in the government employees' examinations to downgrade the status of Mandarin. These measures have gained great attention and strong opposition from various circles on the island. National

Taiwan University philosophy professor Wang Hsiao-po made a pointed remark; namely, that trying to extract Taiwan history from Chinese history and placing Chinese history after the Min Dynasty into world history was a typical "one country on each side" and even a "two-state" historical viewpoint (*China Times Daily News*, 08/25/2003). A high school student wrote an article that was published by the *United Daily News* and in it he questioned, "The authority repeatedly emphasizes separation from the mainland. Can it be said that we came out of nowhere? With this sort of self-abandonment, will it give us more of a worldview or make us disappear into the annals of history?" (*United Daily News*, 08/26/2003)

The "de-Sinicization" of culture and education in Taiwan has been practiced for many years. Its impacts on various sections are both deep and broad, and cannot be turned back by a change in a political regime. Only through reunification could we readjust Taiwan's present cultural and educational policies and make a fresh start by blending with the long history of Chinese tradition and culture. This would not only enable the Taiwanese people to correctly understand their own patriotic tradition, but also to understand clearly the sufferings of the Chinese people over the past 200 years. This would also arouse the Taiwan people's recognition of China and the patriotism of the Chinese people. Furthermore, the unimpeded cross-strait exchanges will establish the compatriot passions between the Taiwanese people and the mainland people. Sooner or later, the Taiwanese people will be proud of being Chinese and will be willing to work hard for China's future.

Regarding Taiwan's educational policies, apart from the confused amendment of its education reform plan, Taiwan's academic level declines annually. With respect to the issue that more and more students have gone to the mainland to study, the Taiwan government has not examined its own educational policies; instead, it refuses to acknowledge the mainland diploma. As a result, more than 10,000 students complain continuously and plan to protest on the street (*China Times Daily News*, 11/21/2003).

In the latter part of November 2003, former President of National Taiwan University Sun Chen and former Education Minister Wu Jing made urgent pleas at The First Cross-Strait Exchange Symposium on Economic and Entrepreneurial Development and Collaboration. They pleaded for the Taiwan government to accept mainland educational credentials as soon as possible and to work toward inviting mainland talents to Taiwan in order to raise its ability to compete. Sun said, "The longer the government delays an open policy, the more students will be pushed to choose sides. It is immoral for a government to force its people to choose sides." Professor Chen Zhangwu at the School of Economics and Management, Tsinghua University, pointed out that Taiwan's universities were very attractive to mainland students. Taiwan's open policy should speed up. Wu Jing said, "The issue of mainland educational credentials has lingered on for three generations. To this day, Taiwan is still talking about it. What is Taiwan afraid of?" He emphasized that the mainland was the largest talent pool in the world; Taiwan was the mainland's neighbor and had the same culture and race. Many students would like to attend universities, but good universities were scarce. It was time for Taiwan to acquire mainland talents, but if the Taiwan government did not recognize mainland educational credentials, this would be a loss to Taiwan (*China Times Daily News*, 11/22/2003).

After the reunification, these barriers can be cleared away. The young people of both sides can attend their favored universities by passing examinations. Each side will accept the other side's educational credentials. The universities will engage in exchanges, and positive competitions will serve to raise academic levels so that the two sides will become one in developing intelligence and talent.

Taiwan's International Status Will No Longer Be an International Orphan

In recent years, Taiwan has been most dissatisfied with mainland China's suppression of Taiwan's international living space. As a result, Taiwan actively started "practical diplomacy," "head of state diplomacy," "money diplomacy," and "transit diplomacy." The reasons for this are simple. Taiwan knows that diplomacy is the symbol of a nation's sovereignty. Keeping or even establishing diplomatic relations with more countries, and developing certain relations with the U.S. and other countries, would mean that Taiwan is a sovereign country. Despite the hard work, Taiwan's record in establishing diplomatic relations is not satisfactory. Among the 191 countries in the world, only 25 "mini-size states" have diplomatic relations with Taiwan. Taiwan cannot enter the WHO or become an observing member because it is not considered a sovereign country by the international community. In September 2003, the "return to the UN" action failed for the eleventh time. Even though Taiwan tried to hold on to the U.S. as well as it could, the U.S. State Department still excluded Taiwan as a "nation" from its 2003 list of world countries and categorized Taiwan as an "other." In order to enter the WHO, Chen Shui-bian suggested holding a referendum. But even the ordinary Taiwanese person knows that if the referendum result shows that all

Taiwanese people support entering the WHO, Taiwan still will not be able to become a member because it is not considered a sovereign country.

The Taiwan government always blames its diplomatic difficulties on suppression by mainland China. Quite a few Taiwanese scholars also suggest that mainland China should give Taiwan more diplomatic living space, show goodwill, or even help Taiwan enter organizations that do not require their members to be sovereign states. For example, Taiwan has already participated in the international organizations APEC, Asian Development Bank, and WTO. Why can't Taiwan be allowed to use this model to enter other non-political international organizations? The New Party's white paper indicated that the cross-strait diplomatic tug of war produced no practical benefit to either side; it only hurt their relationship. Before the cross-strait negotiations can have a positive result, the two sides should simply stop their disputes and freeze their diplomatic relations with other countries. On the subject of Taiwan's return to international society, some scholars and the New Party also suggested the principle of "one country with multiple seats." At the current stage, the emphasis would be for Taiwan to join international economic, trade, and financial organizations and to actively strive for participation in global meetings and various summits held by the UN and its related organizations as an observing member.

Although these suggestions are good, the international community only recognizes "one China" at the present time and the mainland is afraid that as soon as it compromises, Taiwan not only may not be grateful, but will also announce to the world that it is indeed a sovereign country. Before the two sides reach any agreement, the mainland perhaps will not make any major adjustments to its policy on Taiwan's foreign relations. But after the reunification, things will be different. Once Taiwan gets past insisting on being a sovereign country, it can begin to participate in China's foreign affairs—including with the UN, the WHO, and other similar organizations under the UN that only sovereign states can join—with great poise. At the end of August 2002, Tang Shubei, former Vice Chairman of the Beijing-based ARATS attended the annual meeting of the San Francisco Chinese for Peaceful Reunification organization. He mentioned that for the cross-strait negotiation, problems like Taiwan's participation in the UN could be discussed. He said, "Some people say that contemporary Russia has three votes in the UN. After the reunification, the question is whether Taiwan could send its representatives along with the People's Republic of China representatives. These questions can be discussed by the leaders on both sides of the strait. Just as Jiang Zemin once said, 'Under the One-China Principle, any thing can be discussed,'" Tang Shubei continued by saying, "We can also assume that after the reunification of China, the Head of the Chinese Delegation will be from Beijing and the Deputy Head of the Delegation will be from Taipei" (*The Strait Commentary*, v. 144, 12/01/2002).

After the reunification, those who benefit the most are still the Taiwanese people. Wherever they go, there will be embassies and consulates offering help. There is no need to set up Taiwan representative offices at various countries anymore; some are called Culture Centers; others are called Economic Centers or Traveling Offices. These offices can perhaps handle ordinary notarization matters without any problem. As soon as there are conflicts with the countries where the offices are located, these offices will no longer be able to offer help due to a lack of diplomatic relationship with the country. Years ago, when Iraq invaded Kuwait, Taiwan's foreign office retreated and the remaining Taiwanese engineers were unprotected. Hence, they sought help from the local Chinese Embassy, which provided a safe haven for them in Jordan until they could return to Taiwan.

In all fairness, diplomacy is an extension of domesticity as well as an exhibition of a nation's strength. Is it meaningful, if Taiwan has diplomatic relations with only a few small-sized countries after offering them financial assistance, while Taiwan's own economy continues to decline? Taiwan should avoid wasting its limited resources. Taiwan should further avoid subjecting itself to being used as a pawn by foreign countries for containing mainland China. Just by observing the international organizations joined by Hong Kong and Macao, and the numerous international conferences held in Asia at these two places, we know that Taiwan's international living space would be much larger after reunification than it is now.

A Sound Legal System That Protects the Rights and Benefits of the People on Both Sides

Since the people on both sides of the strait have more and more frequent exchanges, regardless of their status and profession, they all need the mainland's legal protection. Also, there are increasing numbers of cross-strait marriages and the resulting families' rights and benefits also need to be guaranteed by Taiwan laws.

Even if the Taiwanese people are facing fewer legal restrictions in the mainland, there are still differences in their status from the local mainlanders. For example, there is a limit on how long they can stay in the mainland, and the companies established by the Taiwanese people are different from the local mainland companies. The tuition for Taiwan merchants' children and young Taiwanese students is much higher than that for local students. All of these issues need to be resolved after the reunification. The current mainland laws, regulations, and ordinances that involve the Taiwanese people in the mainland can only be written unilaterally. They should be modified with the help of the Taiwanese people after reunification so that these laws can better protect the Taiwanese people's benefits in mainland China.

In the recent past there were frequent criminal cases involving Taiwanese merchants being kidnapped or murdered in the mainland. Some of these were caused by disputes between employers and employees, others were due to debts or breakups of their corporation, and there were even kidnap cases due to love affairs. Indeed, in the past ten years, those Taiwan merchants who did not bring their spouses with them sometimes had lovers, and these situations often ended in polygamous marriages. Hence, there were often emotional and family disputes. These cases were severely criticized by Taiwan's women's movement. There was much concern that the problems that were initiated in the mainland would spread to Taiwan when the Taiwanese merchants returned. As a result, there were extensive discussions concerning merchants bartering family values for money. Although these incredible statements do not deserve special attention, they clearly demonstrate that the Taiwan merchants in the mainland have created many social problems on the two sides. Advising the Taiwanese merchants to cease doing business in the mainland is clearly not a solution. Only reunification can gradually remove the estrangement between the people on both sides so that phrases such as "you are Taiwanese, I am Chinese" will no longer be used. Too, through reunification, the marriage law that covers both sides will apply to all Chinese and instances of polygamy and broken homes can be avoided and families would be more willing to move to the mainland.

The mainlanders in Taiwan are facing more problems. Cross-strait marriages are frequent, but the status of these mainland spouses in Taiwan is even worse than that of the foreign brides from other countries. They are discriminated against by law. For example, they have to wait for 11 years to get a personal ID in order to work legally. In addition, mainland spouses are unfamiliar with both the people and the place, and they speak a different dialect. The wives are subject to abandonment, abuse, violence, and prostitution. The effects of media exposure and government inspections are limited in protecting them. According to statistics, the adaptability and performance of children born by mainland spouses are worse than those of the local children, mainly due to discrimination and economic inferiority. Discrimination against mainlanders has damaged Taiwan's image of protecting human rights and resulted in the persecution of Taiwan's future generations.

Taiwan needs mainland workers for fishing and basic construction work, but due to government restrictions, the owners can only hire mainlanders who illegally enter Taiwan. This has created social problems. In addition, Taiwan's fishermen smuggle in mainland agricultural products and Taiwan's criminals often migrate to the mainland to avoid being sentenced and punished. This chaos is the direct result of the inequitable court systems of the two sides, which nullify effective prevention.

After the reunification, the laws on both sides can be further adjusted. People can get married freely and be protected by the fair laws of each side. The mainland will no longer be the hiding place for Taiwan's criminals, and smuggling agricultural products into Taiwan will no longer be necessary. The current chaos will be gradually reduced until it completely disappears.

The Senior Citizen's Problem Will Be Solved

In August 2003, the Directorate-General of Budget, Accounting and Statistics, Executive Yuan, promulgated a statistical report that showed that the gap between the rich and the poor widens and that the poor are becoming poorer.

According to these statistics, Taiwan's low-income households increased from 55,000 units at the end of 1998 to a historical high of 70,000 units at the end of 2002. The medium-low income household also hit at least 4,100,000 units (exceeding 60 percent of the total families) and a new high of 12,860,000 individuals. According to the definitions of the Interior Department, in 2002 the families that made an average monthly income of less than about US$250 per person were categorized as low-income units and those that made less than about US$620 monthly income per person were listed as medium-low income units. Using Taiwan's current living standard, those who earn only about US$600 will not have easy lives. Hence, more than 60 percent of the population is living on a very tight budget.

The number of Taiwanese people who realize a "sense of poverty" increases daily. About a decade or two ago, more than half of the Taiwanese people thought they belonged to the middle class. Society then had a general psychological expectation of "moving upward." The public had substantial confidence about their personal situations, social progress, and even the anticipation of "equalization of wealth." The scholars at that time thought that Taiwan's education was popularized, politics were moving towards democracy, and economic transformations were successful. All these were closely related to broad middle-class phenomena. Perhaps it can be said that the entire society then developed a tendency of being "turned into middle class." By comparison, the current Taiwan, theoretically speaking, has a more popularized education and an increased professional talent pool. But surprisingly, more than 60 percent of the population is listed as medium-low income units. Today, the Taiwanese people are afraid of losing their jobs. They dare not retire. The panic indexes are high and people are feeling insecure about the future. These are the signs of "poverty fear."

Following the trend of an upcoming aging society, the "poverty fear" of the middle-aged and senior people, who comprise a substantial percentage of the Taiwan population, is even worse. Considering the increasing budget deficits of the Taiwan government in recent years, it is impossible to increase the senior citizens' annual retirement income. If the children of these seniors are not able or not willing to support them, their old days will be fairly sad. Some economically capable families either hire foreign helpers to take care of their relatives or place them in senior citizens' homes. Oftentimes, ill treatment and death result in either case. Private enterprises see this as a kind of social phenomenon and treat the senior people's living problem as a money-making opportunity. They build and sell luxurious retirement homes everywhere. But the seniors who can afford to live in the better-equipped and better-cared-for senior centers are few. Adequate care for most of the elderly is a serious social problem in Taiwan.

After the reunification, retired and senior people in Taiwan can live in the mainland, and with the same amount of retirement income and savings they will have better living conditions and be better cared for. If a retired person can get about US$300 to US$600 retirement income and a senior person can get about US$300 from the government or their children, they can move to places where the commodity, housing, and labor costs are lower and where they will enjoy a better material life and receive better care.

The Peace Will Be Enjoyed Forever
and a New China Will Be Established

DPP Legislator Shen Fu-hsiung said during the tenth anniversary (February 2001) of the NUG that the Taiwanese people are "not willing to be reunified, and dare not to become independent" so they stay in the middle ground of no reunification and no independence.

Although it is not easy to accept Shen Fu-hsiung's statement, he accurately represents the true feelings of many Taiwanese people. While searching for the true causes, in addition to considering the 15 years of brainwashing by Lee Teng-hui and Chen Shui-bian, one should look at how the Pan-Blue's cross-strait policies bear some responsibilities. For a long period of time, when the Taiwan independence force was rampant, the Pan-Blue often warned that China would attack if Taiwan did not support "one China" or reunification and that in order to safeguard the Taiwan Strait, Taiwan should not support Taiwan independence. Such simple and easily understandable theories were somewhat effective in intimidating the Taiwan independence supporters and made the Taiwan people imperceptibly distance themselves from mainland China. During every election, in order to gain votes from the centrists, the Pan-Blue further pushed its cross-strait policies to the middle or pro-independence. The politicians may be able to turn around after the elections, but it would be difficult for the confused voters to change their opinions one formed.

The mainland has always propagandized the realization of a peaceful reunification and its benefits to the Taiwanese people. When the two sides live in harmony and safety, the whole nation can enjoy peace, and the Taiwanese people no longer have to worry about intimidating cross-strait situations or mainland China's military attack. Removing this constant fear will indeed be beneficial for stabilizing Taiwan society.

In the past ten years, the economic and political situations have shown growth in the mainland and decline in Taiwan. The mainland economy has developed prosperously, and its democracy and legal reform have been on the right track. Mainland China has proudly ascertained the diplomatic style of a big country, and it is now acting as a big country in diplomatic affairs. Why aren't the Chinese in Taiwan proud of being Chinese? Taiwan's economy can no longer survive without depending on mainland China. Why doesn't Taiwan take the key opportunity while mainland China is progressing to initiate the resumption of talks with the mainland? Both sides can discuss reunification affairs to prevent the Chinese from being controlled by foreign nations so all Chinese people can concentrate on development and construction to increase the general strength of the nation. With China's peaceful way of governing, it will achieve a realm of world harmony and the entire world will remember that the people of Taiwan were the ones who planted the seeds.

CHAPTER 11

WHEN WILL THE "ONE COUNTRY" DEBATE END?

The easiest understandable content of "one country, two systems" is simply one country that has two systems. Namely, after the reunification, the people in Taiwan can continue to keep their current lifestyle. If reunification has always been the goal and ideal of Taiwan, then "one country" should not be a big problem. Instead, defining the contents of the "two systems" and how to carry them out in a concrete manner should be the real focus of Taiwan's wielders of power as well as of the Taiwanese people. But the reality is quite different. During the past few decades, Taiwan leaders and political parties have had ongoing disputes about the meaning of "one country." Even scholars who support the reunification and agree with "two systems" have very different opinions and concerns about the "one China" prerequisite. Some scholars suggest using "whole China" or "China on both sides" to represent the mainland and Taiwan. Others suggest that after the reunification, the two sides should give up their own country names and establish a new name, or even call themselves China.

Based on the above facts, it is necessary to deal with "one country" and "two systems" separately in order to discuss the implementation of "one country, two systems" in Taiwan. This chapter will first review the cross-strait "one China" policy in earlier times, then the cross-strait "one China" policy after 1987. These summaries will include mainland China's newest interpretation of "one China," and Taiwan's various deviations from "one

China." Finally, a judgment on the controvercies and ways to resolve the cross-strait disputes are presented.

SECTION 1
THE CROSS-STRAIT "ONE CHINA" POLICY BEFORE 1987

In 1947, the Nationalist government promulgated and enforced the Constitution of the ROC, in which Article 4 stipulates: "The territory of the Republic of China within its existing national boundaries shall not be altered except by a resolution of the National Assembly. Here the territory of the Republic of China within its existing national boundaries includes mainland China, Taiwan Province, Hainan Island, and Pescadores Islands."

After the Nationalist Government moved to Taiwan in 1949, the two sides of the Taiwan Strait insisted on the existence of "one China" and their own government being the only legal government. But both sides regarded reunification as their ideal. Hence, no matter whether it was a military confrontation or a united front, the intention was always to achieve the reunification of the two sides via different methods.

In 1971, during the ROC's fight for the UN Chinese representative's seat and prior to the UN cancellation, both sides insisted on only one China seat but with their own government being the legal government. Neither side ever proposed to have two China seats in the UN. The foreign policies of the two sides also kept an absolute One-China Principle. When one nation recognized the Chinese government on either side, that nation had to denounce the legality of the other side in representing China. After 1971, the "one China" concept in the international community became stronger. After mainland China's legality in representing China took a superior position, the countries that had diplomatic relationships with mainland China increased rapidly, whereas the countries that had diplomatic relationships with Taiwan decreased dramatically. In 1976, the number of countries that had diplomatic relationships with Taiwan decreased from 56 in 1971 to 26, whereas the number of countries that had diplomatic relationships with mainland China increased from 74 to 118. It is clear that in the international community there has never been adherence to a diplomatic strategy of recognizing two Chinas. Up until the present time, Taiwan and mainland China are still separately recognized by world countries. In the past 20 years, fewer than 30 countries recognize Taiwan, but there has never been a dual recognition. It is apparent that the countries in the world all adhere to the "one China" policy.

When Will the "One Country" Debate End?

In 1979, the U.S. recognized mainland China as the only legal government representing China, and the 30-year battle for the legitimacy of "one China" finally ended. Earlier, in 1972, the U.S. declared in the Shanghai communiqué that "the United States acknowledges that all Chinese on either side of the Taiwan Strait maintain there is but one China and that Taiwan is part of China. The United States government does not challenge that position." But the communiqué does not specify China as the Republic of China or the People's Republic of China. The term China was still ambiguous. But such ambiguity was clarified in 1979 when China and the U.S. signed the joint communiqué on the Establishment of Diplomatic Relations. In the joint communiqué,"the U.S. recognizes the government of the People's Republic of China as the sole legal government of China." Regardless of the U.S. position on cross-strait relations or whether it supports "two Chinas" or "one China, one Taiwan" secretly, the U.S. official statements and policies have supported the One-China Principle since 1949, and mainland China as the sole legal government of China since China and the U.S. established a diplomatic relationship in 1979.

In December 1978, the 3rd Plenary Session of the 11th Central Commission of the Communist Party of China abandoned the military liberation of Taiwan and took a peaceful reunification guideline. Since then, mainland China has not changed its plan of using a peaceful method to reunify the two sides. In 1982, mainland China's NPC passed the Constitution of the PRC. In the preface, it declared that "Taiwan is part of the sacred territory of the People's Republic of China." In 1982, Deng Xiaoping formally proposed the concept of "one country, two systems" and summarized the model for solving the Taiwan issue as "one country, two systems." Specifically, the model describes one country based on its Constitution and laws and clearly stipulates that a portion of its region will carry out a different political, economic, and social system; but this portion of the region cannot exercise the nation's sovereignty. Afterwards, despite the fact that mainland China made the contents of "one country, two systems" more flexible and concrete, it has always kept a consistent stance about the "one country, two systems" policy. And furthermore, the "peaceful reunification, one country, two systems" guideline was established for the sake of ensuring the "one China" framework.

On the Taiwan side, before the U.S. and Taiwan terminated their diplomatic relationship in 1979, the main purpose for the ROC government's "one China" advocacy was to insist on ROC as China's legal government. After 1979, the "one China" policy suffered a serious impact on the island

and the opposition movement proposed to cut off relations with mainland China. But with President Chiang Ching-kuo's insistence, the "one China" policy continued. In October 1984, Chiang Ching-kuo declared, "One China is the Republic of China." From this we can see that Taiwan specified a very clear concept of "one China."

As a whole, from 1949 to 1987, although the two sides went through many diplomatic changes, their own "one China" policy did not change very much. After proposing "peaceful reunification, one country, two systems," mainland China has used the policy as the highest-level guidelines for resolving the Taiwan issue. And Taiwan's "one China" policy, even though it faced challenges in the 1980s, did not change under the strong leadership of the KMT.

SECTION 2
DISCUSSION OF TAIWAN AUTHORITIES'
"ONE CHINA" POLICY SINCE 1987

Chiang Ching-kuo passed away in 1988, soon after he opened the door to allow family visits to the mainland on November 2, 1987, and Lee Teng-hui became president. Despite the fact that Lee Teng-hui repeated more than 200 times that he "opposed Taiwan independence" during his 12-year term, the rhetoric of Taiwan's "one China" policy changed dramatically. First of all, the NUC's interpretation of "one China" and the "Relations across Taiwan Strait" published in 1994 both said that "one China, two political entities" was the framework that regulated the cross-strait relations. But exactly what "one China" was has never been clear. Besides, the "one China" interpreted by the NUC was what the ROC established in1911, with its sovereignty extending to the entirety of China. However, in "Relations across Taiwan Strait," China was replaced with a "traditional and conceptual China," connected to Taiwain by history, geography, culture, and blood lineage. Other contents of that paper—such as the reality of the split and separate governance, the two reciprocal political entities, the proclamation about not competing to represent China, and the temporary shelving of the sovereignty issue—also clearly indicated that Taiwan's One-China Principle went through large-scale adjustments in the mid 1990s.

Lee Teng-hui was also eager to push for practical diplomacy. Although, according to him, this would not affect the One-China Principle; any country that intended to establish a diplomatic relationship with Taiwan would have to deal first with its existing diplomatic relationship with mainland China. Taiwan's Foreign Ministry made several announcements that the diplomatic relations of a particular country with mainland China and Taiwan could be dealt with separately. In other words, even though mainland China continues to keep diplomatic relations with a country, it would not affect Taiwan's wish to also establish diplomatic relationship with that country. Because of this duality, there would have been several cases of "double recognition" (of both mainland China and Taiwan) if mainland China had not insisted on terminating diplomacies with those countries. This is proof of mainland China's criticisms against Taiwan that on the surface Lee Teng-hui talked about "practical diplomacy," he was actually pushing for the "Two Germany Model," seeking for "double recognition," and striving for independence in order to establish a new country.

Furthermore, concerning the issue of reentering the UN, Taiwan obviously knows that the UN always insists on a "one China" policy and has already confirmed that the People's Republic of China is the legal Chinese government making it impossible to accept the "two China" proposal. Even if Taiwan wants a new name, as long as the PRC or one of the members of the Security Council does not agree, the result will be the same. Anyone who has common sense can understand such a simple matter. Why did Lee Teng-hui still spend a huge amount of money every year from 1993 on to push for Taiwan to enter the UN? Perhaps Lee Teng-hui's main purpose was to internationalize the Taiwan issue instead of really trying to enter the UN. He wished to accumulate the self-recognition consciousness on the island to make the Taiwanese people blame their difficult diplomatic position on suppression by mainland China in preparation for future independence and the establishment of a new nation. Besides, after having these reasons for entering the UN, Lee Teng-hui could further be confident about abandoning the One-China Principle and implementing the "one China, one Taiwan" policy. He wanted to make the Taiwanese people believe that it would be possible for Taiwan to return to the UN and other international organizations using the name of Taiwan.

In all fairness, the policies that strove for diplomacy and increased international living space proposed by Lee Teng-hui incited many responses. Not only did the pro-independence people agree with him, but middle-of-the-road voters and scholars also complained about Taiwan's diplomatic plight. Some people suggested that when the cross-strait diplomatic war ends in the future, mainland China could at the same time guarantee that Taiwan could enter the UN under "one country, two seats." There were also people suggesting that Taiwan should continue to keep existing embassies with countries that had diplomatic ties with Taiwan, and reestablish the more than 100 consulates with the countries that had diplomatic ties with mainland China. At least Taiwan would not suffer more. In fact, for ordinary citizens, perhaps the meaning of being able to be accepted by the international community is not so complicated. The most they wish for is that their passports will allow them to travel freely throughout the world and that wherever they go there will be embassies and consulates to service them. Exactly how Taiwan will keep certain rights for foreign affairs and diplomacy can be researched and discussed. Concerning Taiwan's desire to join international organizations, Taiwan can use the title of China Taiwan or China Taipei.

Lee Teng-hui's viewpoint about "one China" is very questionable. Judging from the official documents and his speech drafts, whenever Lee Teng-hui mentioned the "one China" policy, he always confined it to the reunification topic. But when he answered reporters' questions and accepted foreign media's interviews, his viewpoint on "one China" was often different from his official version. For example, on April 14, 1995, Lee Teng-hui accepted a special interview by the *Liberty Times* and pointed out, "At this stage, it is the ROC in Taiwan and the PRC in the mainland. We should try our best to forget the words of one China, or two Chinas." Another example was the conversation with Shiba Ryotaro, in which Lee Teng-hui said, "Sovereignty is a vague term," and, "'China': This word is also ambiguous." These statements show that the China in his mind was at most only a goal and no longer existed. The ROC is one of the countries within the split China. He also emphasized that if "one China" was the PRC, then it should not include Taiwan. Lee Teng-hui very often told one story to one person and another story to someone else. Whenever people began to doubt his stories, he would cover himself by immediately announcing that the "one China" policy had not changed, causing these people to doubt their own interpretations.

Despite Lee Teng-hui's obvious changes and strong criticisms coming from the New Party and anti-independence supporters, the KMT high-level officials not only did not question Lee Teng-hui's position, but they also tried hard to defend him. The reason was that Lee Teng-hui controlled the KMT and the various government departments. Many scholars also attributed Lee Teng-hui's changes to China's suppression. In July 1999, Lee Teng-hui formally claimed that the two sides had "special state-to-state relations" and accomplished his desire of getting rid of "one China."

After Lee Teng-hui's term ended, he did not waste any effort in pushing for the Taiwan rectification movement. In August 2003, he announced that "the Republic of China does not exist." Later he admitted that from the time he took office in 1988, his behavior had been consistent. All of a sudden, Lee Teng-hui's mind was like Sima Zhao; even the street people understood him. (San Guo is one of the most interesting dynasties of China. The three strong leaders—Liu Bei, Cao Cao, and Sun Quan—each conquered a part of China to form the three kingdoms. The three kingdoms ended when Sima Zhao conquered the rest of China.) Lee Teng-hui and his jackals refuted Taiwan's "one China" policy down to the last point. The Taiwanese people should take lessons from Lee Teng-hui and disallow any leader to invent all sorts of names, use the pretext of democratization and nativization, and use the name of the ROC to carry out independence.

In the 2000 presidential election, Chen Shui-bian was elected by only 39 percent of the votes. In order to make clear that he would become a president for all the people, he announced the Four Noes and One Without. But a few days after his inauguration, through MAC Chairperson Tsai Yin-wen, he completely denied that in 1992 the two sides had any consensus. His intention of denying "one China" was obvious from that point on. On New Year's Day of the next year, he proposed the "integration theory" in his proclamation and received positive responses from the opposition parties and the general public. However, due to internal oppositions from the DPP, he immediately amended his statement to, "Integration theory can be used for either reunification or independence." Clearly Chen Shui-bian did not take the Taiwan people's rights into account. He only intended to become the representative of the DPP people or the independence supporters. In August 2002, Chen Shui-bian finally proposed "one country on each side." Hence the "one China" policy originally insisted on by Taiwan ended in reality as well as in name at that point.

After half a century's struggle, Taiwan should clearly realize that the One-China Principle is not only the prerequisite for cross-strait reunification, but also the requirement for maintaining the stability of the Taiwan Strait. Now mainland China has a more flexible meaning of the One-China Principle and a better understanding about the situation of the cross-strait separate governance. The Taiwan authorities should grasp the opportunity and implement the "one China" policy again, restart dialogues with the other side, improve cross-strait relations, and seek to create a favorable condition for Taiwan to be peacefully reunified with mainland China.

Section 3
Discussion of Chinese Authorities' "One China" Policy since 1987

Comparing the direction of Taiwan's "one China" policy with China's "one China" policy, it is clear that China's position has always been firm, but its attitude has become more and more flexible. In 1995, after the publication of Jiang's Eight-Point Proposals, many cross-strait scholars guessed and evaluated mainland China's interpretation of "one China" as serving as a principle while maintaining ambiguity. It was later shown that in order to respect Taiwan's position, mainland China indeed began to gradually make more flexible interpretations of "one China." In August 2000, Qian Qichen proposed a new three-sentence theory on "one China" that made China's "one China" policy appear to have incurred changes that it never had before. During the 16th People's Congress, Jiang Zemin furthered established the One-China Principle by saying, "There is only one China in the world, the mainland and Taiwan are all part of the same China, and China's sovereignty and territorial integrity must never be allowed to suffer a split."

To be fair, mainland China's land and population are more than ten times larger than Taiwan's, and recently China's total national strength and international status have risen to one of the strongest nations in the world. But it has been willing to lower its position by not insisting on China as the PRC and maintains that the two sides can abbreviate their country names to China. This is rare and it shows mainland China's respect and goodwill toward Taiwan. From the above discussion, we can see that mainland China has become more flexible on the "one China" policy since the mid 1990s. But, because Lee Teng-hui had changed his direction long before that, some people think that mainland China's change was too late. In 1998, Taiwan's scholar Shaw Chong-hai analyzed the mainland's "one China" policy and stated, "The policy is trying to circumvent or tie up Taiwan to avoid alienation ideology. However, the result shows unexpectedly that due to the rigidity of the policy after many years, the harder the push was, the further Taiwan walked away." (See *The Cross-Strait Relations: Consensus and Disparity* by Shaw Chong-hai for more information.) This kind of viewpoint might have made sense before Lee Teng-hui proposed the "two-state theory" and before he secretly helped the pro-independence DPP to attain power. But today, when recalling what happened in the past, one can't help but wonder how things might be different if mainland China had changed its attitude a few years earlier.

Some mainland scholars believed that mainland China should have properly seized the opportunity when the KMT and the CPC conducted peaceful talks during the Chiang Ching-kuo era. Others said that mainland China should have taken the opportunity to show support and immediately begun the cross-strait political negotiations when Hao Po-chun proposed "one country, two regions." But after careful thinking, one can see that ten or 20 years ago, conditions for the reunification were not yet mature. Perhaps due to the fact that Taiwan was colonized by Japan, governed by the KMT, and pushed around by the U.S. in the past, most Taiwanese people have become very practical. Hence, before mainland China's total national strength and average people's living standard rise appreciably, the Taiwanese people might not have found reunification beneficial. Namely, on a material basis the time was not ripe to consider reunification. Trying to bind up the Taiwanese people by using national assimilation would not have achieved a satisfactory result. Hence, mainland China need not be concerned about whether the two sides missed the right negotiation timing. It is presently vital to look ahead.

Although the present Taiwan wielders of power still have no good intentions, based on the growth of political and economic strengths in the mainland and the decline of the same in Taiwan, it is an undeniable fact that Taiwan's economy must depend on the mainland in order to survive. Regardless of who is elected in Taiwan's 2004 presidential election, this leader must face the reality and work hard to seek a resolution. Hence, as long as mainland China can keep a good relationship with the U.S. and make sure that the U.S. adheres firmly to the One-China Principle and resolutely opposes Taiwan independence, mainland China's flexible and practical measures regarding "one China" will become Taiwan's best choice.

SECTION 4
WHERE SHOULD TAIWAN GO?

At the end of August 2003, Lee Teng-hui openly said that the ROC didn't exist anymore. He initiated the Taiwan Rectification Movement on September 6. On September 12, he was interviewed by Japan's *Sankei Shimbun* reporters and he clearly stated that since he became president in 1988, his actions had been consistent. He also emphasized that, after his term, he planned to push for the rise of non-governmental force through the inherent conscience of the Taiwanese people in order to "establish a sovereign country and to have Taiwan recognized by the international community.

This is what I have worked for my entire life." Lee Teng-hui expressed that "the best time for establishing a sovereign country is between 2008 and 2010: This is in consideration of the 2008 Beijing Olympic Games and the 2010 Shanghai World Exhibition." He said that it was necessary for Taiwan to establish its international status before mainland China gained strong economic power and international recognition through the Olympic Games and the World Exhibition (*China Times Daily News*, 09/12/2003).

After the Taiwan rectification parade on September 6 and the anti-rectification parade on September 7, public opinion demanded a statement by political figures to explain their reasons for or against rectification. There was also a demand for politicians who supported rectification to explain the benefits of changing the country's name. What would be the internal impact of rectification and would there be a complete preparation so Taiwan could avoid falling into the white-hot split? Those who were against rectification should also answer the question of whether supporting the name of ROC would enable a bigger breakthrough to come out of a difficult situation. "Where should Taiwan go" became a hot political topic for a while, and it is also a topic that average Taiwan citizens should consider seriously.

Can Taiwan Keep Its Current Situation Forever?

The immediate response of the mainstream media was, "Between independence and reunification, there is a very huge area that is neither reunified nor independent, and the ROC Constitution, name, and national flag still have living space." They also called upon the "voters who are in the middle ground" not to be easily categorized by political figures as the "independent group" or the "reunification group" so that Taiwan's politics could walk a true "new middle road" (*China Times Daily News*, 09/08/2003). This kind of talk sounds reasonable, but it is in fact meaningless. What is the "new middle road"? Perhaps it means no reunification, no independence, keeping the status quo, or waiting for changes. After a six-month struggle, even Lee Teng-hui said that Taiwan's status quo could not be sustained and that Taiwan was walking the path of becoming alienated from mainland China forever. Why do most people in Taiwan still believe the status quo can be sustained forever?

Those who want to keep the status quo should think hard. Isn't Taiwan's current situation worse than it was five years ago? The problems Taiwan faces today include economic plight, corrupted politics, and the worsening of the social order. Most people do not feel secure and do not know what to do in the future. More frightening is the fact that the Chinese cultural tradition has been reduced to near nonexistence after the 15-year "de-Sinicization" pushed by Lee Teng-hui and Chen Shui-bian. Presently, even Chinese history is listed as part of the world history. Those who cannot speak the Taiwanese dialect will not be able to understand the test questions on the examination to become government employees. If this situation continues, will Taiwan's next generation recognize themselves as Chinese?

Take a further look. With political leaders like Lee Teng-hui and Chen Shui-bian, how long will Taiwan be able to keep its current situation? Some people place all their hopes on the Pan-Blue leading again in 2004. But even if Pan-Blue can win this time, will Taiwan become better? After seeing Lien and Soong's behavior of ignoring idealism in order to win, who will have confidence? The fact is that even if Pan-Blue can win again, won't there still be political party transformation in the future? To avoid the same mistakes made in 1966 and 2000, mainland China does not want to respond strongly to the continuous pro-independence statements by the Pan-Blue and Pan-Green camps. But will this temporary cautiousness suggest that both sides will live in peace from now on? Taiwan has elections almost every year. Can it be said that people are willing to let their relationships with relatives and friends be torn apart every year by the deliberate manipulations of the politicians with their reunification versus independence arguments, the ethnic hostility, and the provincial complexities? And every four years, due to the presidential election, will people be willing to stay on tenterhooks and be cautious everyday?

A detailed analysis shows that the main reason for Taiwan people's general belief in maintaining the status quo lies in their strong hope in the U.S. to keep the two sides "not reunified, not independent, and not in war." But, can the Taiwanese people decide U.S. policy? During the past half-century, China-U.S.-Taiwan triangular relations have changed many times and every time the U.S. changed direction, Taiwan suffered. Beginning in 2003, the U.S. diplomatic needs from mainland China have become more extensive and U.S. investments in the mainland have become increasingly appreciable. These trends have already created readjustments in China-U.S-Taiwan relations. Taiwan's politicians ignored the dangerous realistic environment and spoke out incessantly for the sake of winning. If the U.S. decides that because Taiwan does not care about its own safety that the U.S. will not protect Taiwan, what will Taiwan do? Moreover, in order to seek U.S. protection, will the Taiwanese people be willing to tighten their own belts in procuring a large number of armaments, which are claimed to be used for Taiwan's self-defense but in reality are used to protect the U.S.? Should Taiwan seek U.S. protection forever?

The dispute about "one China" in fact has never been a big problem for those who want to keep the status quo. The only problem is that government and political figures have never provided people with information on "one country, two systems" or helped them to understand that "one country, two systems" is actually the best guarantee for Taiwanese people to keep the status quo. Besides, people will have the opportunity to slightly modify Taiwan's current non-satisfactory regulations and systems during the process of planning the "two systems."

Is the Republic of China the Last Stand of Taiwan?

Among statements that appeared in September and October 2003 that refuted Lee Teng-hui was, "The Republic of China is the last backing of Taiwan." A *China Times Daily News* editorial stated: on the basis of an international entity, the national people's will, and the government framework, the existence of the ROC is real and has never disappeared. As for the title of the ROC at international occasions, it has had hard times in gaining international recognition. But this is not equivalent to a disappearance; we have to be clear that it was mainland China on the other side of the strait that has made the ROC's visibility diminish. This editorial also emphasized that "mainland China on the one hand demands that Taiwan must insist on the One-China Principle, but at the same time tries to suppress Taiwan's use of the name 'the Republic of China.' Hence, the Beijing authorities are the principle culprit in trying to get rid of the ROC. In the face of this dangerous situation, we should try our best to protect the ROC. How can we stand by and help the PRC extinguish the ROC?" (*China Times Daily News*, 09/12/2003)

The *United Daily News* published an editorial entitled "No Dispute on Reunification or Independence; Only Dispute on Independence and Anti-Independence." It claimed that the so-called "dispute on independence and anti-independence" was actually the dispute of the Republic of China versus the Republic of Taiwan (*United Daily News*, 09/12/2003). Perhaps, the *United Daily News* was trying to convince the voters who believed in keeping the status quo, anti-independence and anti-reunification, to vote for the Pan-Blue Coalition. But that statement not only deviated from the reality in Taiwan, it also obviously misled the Pan-Blue and the public, making them think that protecting the ROC was the last stand of Taiwan.

As expected, when the polls showed that Chen Shui-bian's support rate was nearing Lien and Soong's support rate, the localist factions and campaign staffs of the KMT and the PFP proposed to clarify their relations with mainland China and used a more definite way to show their disapproval of "one country, two systems." During the latter part of October, Lien Chan took the opportunity of his visit to the U.S. to publicly state, "One China has only one principle and that is the ROC. It is different from the China of mainland China, which is the People's Republic of China. The two are different," that only "'one China with respective interpretations by the two sides' can have space for ambiguity and can be used for the basis to resume the dialogues," and that "Taiwan will not accept China's 'one country, two systems.' The best way for the two sides now is 'parallel development.'" Lien Chan also proposed his guarantee to the U.S. that in order to ensure the safety of the Taiwan Strait, Taiwan needed ample defensive weapons. Hence, if he were elected, he would assuredly strengthen arms procurement from the U.S. (*China Times Daily News*, 10/22/2003).

Aiming at Lien's statement, Premier Yu Hsi-kun immediately stated in Taipei that he welcomed Lien's support of the "one country on each side" viewpoint. Later, Lien argued that the ROC had been around since 1912 and was completely different from mainland China's definition of "one China." He hoped that the DPP would not create rumors arbitrarily. But after November, the KMT and the PFP proposed "the three steps of a new Constitution" and stated that, apart from the nation's title and the national flag, there was no restriction on constitutional revisions. As expected, on November 21, the KMT and the PFP proposed a referendum to have a new Constitution bill, which even made territorial changes to be determined by referendum. On the day Lien proposed this bill, he blamed Chen Shui-bian's pro-independence while insisting upon "shelving the dispute on sovereignty" and demanding the Beijing government to "respect our sovereignty, if we respect your sovereignty." This left Taiwan's media and public unable to distinguish between the Pan-Blue and Pan-Green camps. How could the Taiwanese people still be fooled by Lien's tactic of using the ROC to play "one country on each side," which was exactly what Lee Teng-hui did for more than a decade?

As early as August 2003, the Pan-Blue had proposed to use "the ROC and the PRC, one country on each side" as its campaign strategy. SEF's former Secretary-General Chen Chang-wen published an article to support this strategy. Charng-wen expressed that Pan-Blue's "one China" was a "future China." This was a negation of "one country, two systems." The reasons for opposing "one country, two systems" were twofold. First, "one country, two systems" implied a kind of "principal and subordinate relationship," where the mainland was the principal and Taiwan was the subordinate. This was in violation of the basic demand of all the Taiwanese people (blue or green camp) for treating both sides as reciprocal entities. Second, "one country, two systems" meant the present realization of reunification, whereas the "future China" pointed to the future expectation of reunification. The premise of China's reunification in the future was the democratization of the mainland and an approximate equal economic level with Taiwan. Chen Chang-wen's interpretation truthfully expressed the Pan-Blue's and the KMT's position at the time and also solidly provided the proof that while the cross-strait policies of the Pan-Blue and Pan-Green groups differ somewhat in their mentalities, the results are not much different.

There is not much difference in the "principal and subordinate relationship" stated by Chen Chang-wen from the so-called "downgrade, localization, and marginalization" idea by Lee Teng-hui. Will Taiwan be "downgraded"? This can be discussed at two levels. First, what is being downgraded? Whether Taiwan makes rectification or not and regardless of the name used, Taiwan cannot enter the UN or any organization formed by governmental organizations (such as the WHO). Is this being downgraded by the UN? The U.S., which has always been regarded as looking out for Taiwan, excluded Taiwan from the 191 countries in the world. Can't this be considered being downgraded by the U.S.? After spending an astronomical amount of money to procure armaments from the U.S., Taiwan is still laughed at by the U.S. for being inadequate in defending itself, and is further threatened by the U.S. to make hasty purchases before it is too late. When people questioned this, Secretary General of the Presidential Office Chiu Yi-ren replied by saying that how could we possibly manage without hanging onto the U.S. apron strings? Isn't it shameful that Taiwan has already become a sub-colony? Isn't Taiwan cheapening itself, when its own former president says that the ROC no longer exists?

Second, exactly who is afraid of being downgraded? For many years, the Taiwan public has been brainwashed by politicians and the media to believe that Taiwan will be shortchanged if it accepts "one China" and "one country, two systems." Exactly what will change about the people's self-dignity and self-recognition? There have been very few comparisons and discussions about this. After the reunification, perhaps only a very few people will deny being Chinese, and those who want to be the subordinates of Japan or the U.S. will probably feel conflicted. In addition, from the prospect of practical benefits, those who really have reasons to worry about being demoted are the president, the government officials, and the elected representatives for the government. It would be hard for those in power to relinquish their mentality of "rather being a leader in a small country than nobody in a big nation." But for the future of 23 million Taiwanese people, what would it matter if those who claim to love Taiwan the most feel somewhat aggrieved?

It may not be easy to ask Taiwan's politicians to give up their insistence on being the ROC, but politics cannot deny reality. Mainland China has changed its rhetoric to "the mainland and Taiwan are all part of China" and some Taiwanese people have also seriously challenged the existence of the ROC. Under this situation, will the Pan-Blue Coalition be willing to lose its sense of integrity just for the sake of protecting the legitimacy of the ROC, or of winning an election, or of avoiding being labeled "pro-China"?

All politicians who think of themselves as Chinese should see clearly the political reality and the cross-strait trend. They should honestly let the Taiwanese people understand that only a peaceful reunification will be the true salvation of Taiwan. If the wielders of power can be open-minded under the principle of "one China" and work for the most favorable conditions for reunification, then this would show true love of Taiwan. Their sincere efforts to avoid war, a division of China, foreign domination, or a cross-strait war would make them heroes in the eyes of all Chinese nationals.

CHAPTER 12

WHAT ELEMENTS SHOULD BE IN "TWO SYSTEMS"?

Even though Taiwan's public agrees that reunification has many advantages, there are still great difficulties in getting the people to accept the mainland political and social system. In order to respect Taiwan's lifestyle and political system and to get rid of the barriers to reunification, mainland China proposed the "one country, two systems" concept in the 1970s and 1980s. "One country, two systems" has been carried out in Hong Kong and Macao since their handover to mainland China in 1997 and 1999, respectively.

Despite the examples of the successful implementation of "one country, two systems" in Hong Kong and Macao, due to huge differences in historical background and a public outcry in Taiwan, what "one country, two systems" should include when it is carried out in Taiwan has gained great attention. Over the past 20 to 30 years, the Chinese government has many times, and on many occasions, explained the concrete contents of "one country, two systems." But there was little response from Taiwan. Perhaps this was due to the unsettled "one country, two systems" interpretations of the two governments. In particular, the Taiwan scholars focused mostly on the disputes of "one China," but many of them did not have a problem with "two systems." Very few scholars (such as Liu Jin-qing) maintained that the contents of the "two systems" demanded immediate study and suggested that the results would determine whether the Taiwanese people would be willing to accept "one country, two systems."

History shows that the results of a political power in a country forcing a political power in another country to change its systems are always bad. Since entering the twenty-first century, many regions in the world have experienced wars, riots, and terrorist attacks. This means that either many countries have not learned from history or their interference based on different systems or religions was only pretext used for conquering other countries! Based on these lessons, mainland China proposed "one country, two systems" in order to respect Taiwan's capitalism, which is obviously different from the mainland's socialism. It is not only full of great wisdom, but it also contains great toleration and generosity.

Section 1
What Are the Elements of the "Two Systems" Now?

There are two main reasons why the Taiwanese people do not want to accept reunification: The systems are different on the two sides and the standard of living of the mainland is lower than that in Taiwan. The latter argument is not as persuasive as before due to economic growth in the mainland and decline in Taiwan. It is still true that the two sides have different systems, and this is an important factor in why the Taiwanese people are not willing to accept reunification. However, "one country, two systems" can alleviate this problem. After more than three decades of change and development, mainland China has given many meanings to the "two systems." Following is a discussion of the two principles of "two systems."

The Principles of the "Two Systems"

The Coexistence of the Two: Under the premise of "one China," the socialist system in the mainland and the capitalist system in Taiwan will coexist for a long time and develop together. No one side will annex the other. After the reunification, Taiwan's present socio-economic system, lifestyle, and economic and cultural relations with foreign countries will not change. Things like private property, houses, land, business ownership, legal inheritance rights, and investments of overseas Chinese and foreigners will be protected by specific laws.

The High Degree of Autonomy: After the reunification, Taiwan will enjoy a high degree of autonomy. It will have its own administrative rights, legislative rights, independent judicial rights, and the right of final appeal. Taiwan's party, politics, military, and economic and financial matters will be self-governed. Neither the various departments in the central government nor the local governments in China can intervene with the Taiwan government in autonomous areas: Taiwan can enter into business and cultural agreements with foreign countries and enjoy specified rights for handling foreign affairs. Taiwan can have its own military and the mainland will not send troops or administrative personnel to stay in Taiwan.

The Specific Contents of the "Two Systems"

Following the return of Hong Kong and Macao, and the changes in their cross-strait situations, mainland China developed a more flexible interpretation of "one China" and made further applicable statements about the "two systems." According to Chinese officials' past statements, the "two systems" has at least two specific contents:

1. After the reunification, Taiwan not only will enjoy all of the rights owned by Hong Kong and Macao, but it will also enjoy certain rights that are not owned by Hong Kong and Macao. These include keeping its own military with no mainland China troops stationed in Taiwan and keeping its frame of government without replacement of its highest level officials. In Hong Kong and Macao, the administrative officials have to report to, and some of them are appointed by, the Chinese central government.

2. When Qian Qishen met with the New Party's Mainland Affairs Council, he proposed seven specifics of "one country, two systems." These include:

   a) Taiwan's continued use of Taiwanese currency

   b) Taiwan's retention of its armed forces

   c) Taiwan remains an independent tariff zone

   d) Taiwan maintains its frame of government

   e) The mainland will not take a single cent of Taiwan money or transfer Taiwan's fund

   f) Taiwanese people and entrepreneurs keep their original properties

   g) The mainland will not send any officials to Taiwan (Taiwan will have autonomy over its personnel affairs).

Clearly the "two systems" policy is specific. After the reunification, Taiwan should be able to keep its current systems and maintain a high degree of autonomy and self-government. Based on this, Qian Qishen said that "'one country, two systems' is the best method to maintain the current status." After Hong Kong and Macao returned to mainland China, Tang Shubei, Head of the Research Center of the Cross-Strait Relations, also described that for Taiwan, "one country, two systems" was "maintaining the status quo." However, the Taiwanese people found this questionable. Apart from the "one China" dispute, it is worthwhile to analyze why the people still oppose "one country, two systems."

SECTION 2
WHY DO PEOPLE OPPOSE THE "TWO SYSTEMS"?

Since the "two systems" was established to respect Taiwan's current system and to guarantee the coexistence of the two systems with a high degree of autonomy, why don't most Taiwanese people accept it? The reasons are as follows.

Some Questioned: Are the Contents of the "Two Systems" Determined by the Taiwanese People Themselves?

The Taiwanese people generally think that "one country, two systems" is determined strictly by mainland China and with no participation by the Taiwanese. Some scholars who support reunification also think that "one country, two systems" will make Taiwan a special administrative region, per Article 31 of the Constitution of the PRC. But since the Taiwanese people have never approved the PRC Constitution, they have no obligation to obey it. These scholars suggest that there should be a new name for the reunified China that is derived from mutual discussions and a new Constitution in which Taiwan is listed in a special chapter and "one country, two systems" is specifically defined. Moreover, in order to guarantee the Taiwan people's rights, the special chapter on Taiwan should be first approved by the Taiwanese people or the council representing them, and then be passed by the entire Chinese population or the People's Assembly.

It is undeniable that the lack of support for "one country, two systems" by the Taiwanese people is closely related to the fact that Taiwan has never participated in the planning of "one country, two systems." The principles of keeping a high degree of autonomy guaranteed by "one country, two systems" must first be broadly discussed by various Taiwanese professional circles. After a consensus is formed, the political parties, factions, specialists, scholars, and organization members should draft a plan to be presented for public discussions. After most Taiwanese people agree with the plan, it should be sent to the relevant mainland unit for final discussions.

Mainland China is aware of this issue and has made numerous public requests to the various Taiwanese circles to actively propose specific contents. So far there has been no response. Perhaps the people who care about this issue in Taiwan think that the time is not ripe, the disputes on "one China" are not yet over, and the rashly proposed contents of "two systems" would not be meaningful or would promote antipathy. The contents of the "two systems" will be relevant to every Taiwanese person's daily life after the reunification. Only when the Taiwanese people are exposed to the correct spirit and contents of the "two systems" and directly participate in the planning process can they make a wise decision about reunification. Undoubtedly there will be countless debates, drafts, modifications, and re-modifications to create a "two systems" proposal that is acceptable to the majority. Hence, instead of waiting for the complete resolution of the "one China" dispute, it is better to begin planning for the "two systems."

Some Questioned: Since the Purpose Is to Keep the Status Quo, Why Is "One Country, Two Systems" Necessary?

From Taiwan's public survey results over the years, we know that most people in Taiwan support keeping the status quo. Because of this, Qian Qishen and Tang Shubei each made well-intended remarks that "one country, two systems" was intended to keep the status quo, though not many Taiwanese people accepted their viewpoint. People might have asked themselves, "The current lifestyle in Taiwan is already good enough. Why do we need 'one country, two systems' to guarantee the Taiwan people's right to 'keep the status quo'?" Others might have said, "The Taiwanese people really do not have to walk a big circle to come back to the starting point." So, many people support keeping the status quo and believe that the status quo excludes reunification and independence. In recent years Lee Teng-hui and Chen Shui-bian unveiled the "two-state theory," "one country on each side," "Taiwan's rectification," and "Taiwan enacts a new Constitution." Will there ever be reunification for Taiwan? Even if the Pan-Blue Coalition can take back the governing power in 2004, who can guarantee that the DDP would not win the presidential election later on? And, who can guarantee there would not be another Lee Teng-hui? The reason the Taiwanese people want to keep the status quo or become independent is because they believe the U.S. will protect Taiwan no matter what. Hence, the Taiwan government has been pro-America, and it continues to purchase the astronomically high-priced armaments from the U.S. even when it can no longer afford to do so. Many people in Taiwan believe that the U.S. is willing to sell more advanced weapons to Taiwan to show a solid alliance between the U.S.

and Taiwan. Will it never change? Clearly U.S.-Taiwan relations over the past 30 years have gone through many changes.

Next, what is the status quo? If we investigate deeply, we find that various changes in the Taiwan environment have left the people with a different understanding of the term "status quo." Who would have guessed that so many people with undergraduate and graduate degrees would be unable to find jobs, many middle-aged workers would be laid off, and real estate values would drop by more than 30 percent? Who would have guessed that the status quo included Taiwanese people taking jobs, attending schools, emigrating to, and purchasing houses in the mainland? Who would have guessed that Chinese history would become a part of world history and a person who does not speak the Taiwanese dialect could not pass the government tests and find jobs?

The status quo changes all the time—and not always in the right direction. As long as Taiwan does not reunify the possibility remains that Taiwan will be brought to independence by the wielders of power and will not be able to remain Chinese. Taiwan must spend huge amounts of money to buy arms from the U.S. and still face the possibility of being abandoned by the U.S. again. The possibility of the Taiwanese people suffering brutal military attacks in pursuit of independence certainly exists. Simply stated, to keep the status quo, Taiwan must accept "one country, two systems."

Some Questioned: Will "One Country, Two Systems" Actually Be Implemented?

Some people do not believe that mainland China will keep its promise to let Taiwan keep the status quo under "one country, two systems." After such a long-term separation, it is understandable that the two sides do not trust each other. Still, it is generally believed that the claim that "one country, two systems" is mainland China's conspiracy to use "keeping the status quo" as a ruse to actually walk towards "one country, one system" is a childish idea that lacks common sense.

The most important reason for mainland China to implement "one country, two systems" in Taiwan, Hong Kong, and Macao is to show respect for the capitalist systems their people are accustomed to, and to lower the barrier for reunification. An equally important reason is that mainland China does not want capitalism implemented in Taiwan, Hong Kong, and Macao to disturb their socialism with Chinese characteristics, which has been practiced for more than half a century, nor to create numerous troubles for the mainland. Mainland China has its own timetable for reformation, legalization, and democratization. It does not want Taiwan to push for its American-style democracy in the mainland. Furthermore, Taiwan has encountered many problems since its implementation of capitalism and democracy. If Taiwan implemented "one country, one system," its bubble economy and dirty money politics would come to the mainland and create even more problems. Lastly, it is clear to mainland China that even if the two sides reunify, the U.S. will not completely abandon its control of Taiwan due to America's interest in the Asia-Pacific region.

Second, mainland China, as a large country and a permanent member of the UN Security Council, has its reputation to consider. China is affected by how it keeps its promises. Since mainland China's establishment in 1949, China has never broken an agreement or treaty and has accepted—with subtle anger—some of the agreements signed by the KMT during the KMT era. Taiwan has always actively promoted its intention to return to the UN and international organizations so that the concerns about cross-strait relations and the security of the Taiwan Strait are known worldwide. When the two sides agree to terminate the hostility and enter into an agreement regarding "peaceful reunification, one country, two systems," it will be a world event. It would be impossible for mainland China to ill-treat Taiwan and lose the trust of the entire world.

Hong Kong's and Macao's implementations of "one country, two systems" are good examples that mainland China has kept its promises. Only the Lee Teng-hui and the Chen Shui-bian administrations have tried to cover up the positive responses about "one country, two systems" from the Hong Kong and Macao residents and the international communities. They also deliberately blamed "one country, two systems" for causing the Asian financial crisis and its impact on Hong Kong. On July 1, 2003, the big demonstration in Hong Kong gave Lee Teng-hui and Chen Shui-bian the opportunity to bitterly criticize "one country, two systems." But the criticisms also revealed that either the demonstrators lacked an understanding of "one country, two systems" and the contents of Hong Kong's Basic Law, or they were simply opposing it for the sake of opposition. The target for the Hong Kong residents' complaints was mainly the Tung Chee-hwa governance. This also meant that the system in Hong Kong had problems. Mainland China proclaimed during the entire process that it hoped the Hong Kong government could improve its system. As a whole, the Hong Kong people still had hope about the implementation of "one country, two systems." They believed that "one country, two systems" was the best and only road for Hong Kong's return. The U.S. and Britain took advantage of the big demonstration and pointed a finger at mainland China and Hong Kong's governments, but they could not find any signs to prove that the mainland did not adhere to "one country, two systems."

Taiwan believes that Hong Kong and Macao have not been able to select their administrators and legislators through universal suffrage; therefore, their systems are not completely democratic. But this is not due to the poor implementation of "one country, two systems." Also, there should be no concern that after reunification Taiwan will lose the right of universal suffrage. Hong Kong's and Macao's political systems differed from Taiwan's before the handover; hence, during the process of drafting the Basic Law, it was decided to have elections in a gradual and progressive manner. If keeping universal suffrage is so important to the Taiwanese, it should certainly be included in the planning of "two systems."

SECTION 3
WHAT SHOULD BE INCLUDED IN THE CONTENTS OF "TWO SYSTEMS"?

The director of the Shanghai Institute of East Asian Studies, Zhang Nianchi, wrote an article for the monthly *China Review* in November 1999. There he suggested that mainland China's central authorities should establish a national reunification commission. Additionally, he suggested that one of the important cross-strait issues in the middle of a new century was that both sides agreed to terminate the situation of hostility and jointly drafted a Taiwan Basic Law. Unfortunately, this has remained only a suggestion.

Despite the disagreements about the interpretations of "one China," the Taiwanese people should begin the planning process of "two systems." After all, "two systems" is closely related to the lives and rights of the Taiwanese people and should be the most important topic to them. If "two systems" is planned satisfactorily, it would promote people's confidence in "one country, two systems" and leave the disputes about "one country" without merit. On the contrary, if the "one country" disputes are resolved but a consensus on "two systems" cannot be reached, "one country, two systems" is still all talk and no action. Judging by this, instead of waiting for the political negotiations to resolve the "one country" disputes, the determined Taiwanese should consider what "two systems" should look like in order to enable a betterment of the status quo and their current quality of life. Taiwan scholar Shih Chih-yu suggested many years ago, "We may face bigger risks, if we give up on explaining 'one country, two systems' by no action," and, "If you do not trust Beijing, why don't you interpret 'one country, two systems' yourselves?" (See *Turn the Tables against Great Odds* by Shih Chih-yu for more information.)

The Taiwanese People Have the Right to Understand "One Country, Two Systems"

In order to carry out a high degree of autonomy and to protect the Taiwan people's rights, the contents of "two systems" should first be decided by the Taiwanese. Before making the draft, however, the Taiwanese people should agree on the basic framework of "two systems." This will not be an easy task.

In order to make the Taiwanese people reach a consensus on "two systems," the greatest challenge is to make the Taiwanese people understand the "one country, two systems" advocacy and its contents. They believe that "one country, two systems" is designed to downgrade Taiwan, make Taiwan like Hong Kong, to turn a central government to a local government, or to allow mainland China to annex Taiwan. To be sure, these ideas are related to propaganda from Taiwan leaders. Taiwan's cross-strait policies over the past few decades have separated the two sides. The NUG are the equivalent of the No NUG. Especially during the last few years of Lee Teng-hui's governance and the three years of Chen Shui-bian's governance, no opportunity was missed to attack or defame "one country, two systems." Working under this kind of leadership, it was a small wonder that the officials in charge of the cross-strait affairs, including the MAC and the SEF, made no effort to engage in cross-strait dialogues and denied doing so afterwards. No one had the guts to take the matter as it stood and to speak the truth about Taiwan's future. After the political power changed hands, some former officials made a clean break from their past errors. We can be sympathetic towards these people who regret what they did, but would there be any sympathy towards the Taiwanese people who have been repeatedly cheated?

It is urgent that the Taiwanese people begin broad and in-depth discussions about "two systems" in order to reach a consensus. Then the government should give them the knowledge of what has really been proposed to them. Ideally, the new leaders elected as a result of the Taiwan 2004 election will clearly understand the international reality and take the nation's reunification as a great historical responsibility, and will be broadminded enough to stop defaming "one country, two systems." These leaders should provide people with complete information related to "one country, two systems" and analyze the international and cross-strait situations, allowing the Taiwanese people to make wise decisions about their future.

The Taiwanese people should not waive their right to knowledge and should actively seek information about "one country, two systems." Taiwan has very few books on "one country, two systems," but the mainland and Hong Kong have recently published books on the subject. The Internet also provides updated information that is beneficial to anyone willing to open their minds and let go of their prejudices.

The Taiwanese People Should Agree on "Two Systems"

In order for the Taiwanese people to have a consensus on "two systems," a mechanism must be established to assist the public in expressing their opinions and reaching that consensus. The government should establish this mechanism under the premise that Taiwan's leaders must recognize that "one country, two systems" is the most important choice for Taiwan's future and that the Taiwan government has the obligation to begin planning for the "two systems." Before the government realizes the importance of this work, Taiwan's various political parties, scholars, specialists, and private organizations can begin the planning and initiating work.

Since the contents of "two systems" affect every level and every field of society, in order to gain society's biggest consensus, each profession, field, and stratum must send representatives to participate in the research work right from the beginning. In order to stimulate and initiate discussions, scholars in various fields should form small teams and conduct research work, prepare several proposals, and submit them to the related representatives for discussion. After listening to the opinions of the representatives, the teams should sort out their opinions and modify the proposed drafts. They should hold public hearings to gather opinions from the people of that profession/stratum until the representatives are completely satisfied with the proposal. Ideally, this method will result in a consensus.

In the areas where sensitivities and conflicts of interests among the classes are involved, consensus will be more difficult to reach. Concerning these areas, the teams should invite neutral third parties to be the arbitrators. They should use fair and impartial attitudes to mediate the opinions of the two sides and to try to find proposals that take care of the interests of both sides. If this is still not workable, all relevant parties must remember to give the interests of Taiwan the greatest consideration.

Suggestions for the Contents of "Two Systems"

The spirit of "one country, two systems" is to keep Taiwan's current systems. But, if some of the existing systems are not satisfactory or have problems—and the ruling party, opposition parties, and the public hope to make changes—the system can also be modified during the discussions and planning of "two systems." In short, no matter whether the contents of the "two systems" keep the current system or make adjustments to it, the system should conform to the principle of "one country, two systems"—the coexistence of the two systems and a high degree of Taiwan's autonomy—as long as the Taiwan system is supported by the Taiwanese people.

As stated above, in order to draft the "two systems" contents to satisfy everyone, we must first develop a mechanism for seeking consensus. Following are suggestions for encouraging others to come forward with their valuable opinions.

POLITICS: In late September 2003, Chen Shui-bian proposed the writing of a new Constitution in 2006. Lien and Soong followed and also proposed three steps for a new Constitution. Taiwan's political system indeed has had problems since Lee Teng-hui carelessly amended the Constitution.

The Taiwanese people have gone through numerous elections over the past 20 years. They regard voting as part of their lives. Some people even believe that voting is proof of Taiwanese people being their own bosses and making them get out of the strait. Accordingly, after the reunification, Taiwan should continue to keep its universal suffrage system. The only concern is that the number of elections is costly; therefore, the election system should be further adjusted and regulated. For the candidates to attract votes using rational political viewpoints and performances, elections should be made in a single district or small districts. In order to stabilize Taiwan's political situation after the reunification, the administrator should have clear rights and responsibilities, and a cabinet system should be adopted. The cabinet system improves the efficiency of the legislative organizations, and avoids deliberate incitement of radical voters by the political candidates so that the painstakingly established "one country, two systems" will not fall into the swamp again.

In the area of legislation, Taiwan should enjoy sufficient and complete legislative rights while adhering to the "one country, two systems" principle. The number of legislators should be reduced to improve the efficiency of legislation. In the judicial area, Taiwan should enjoy independent judicial rights and the right of final appeal. The current family, marriage, inheritance, and investment laws of the two sides should be adjusted to eliminate any incompatibility or inapplicability of the cross-strait laws.

NATIONAL DEFENSE: After the reunification, the navy's main duties should be the protection of fishermen, the patrol of the sea territory (e.g., cruising the Bashi Channel), the buildup and defense of bases at the Macclesfield Bank and Spratly Islands, and the patrol of the Ryukyu Islands sea territory. This patrol can be carried out after the cross-strait stalemate is over. The army's main duty is to protect the sea and the mountains. The original mainland army plan to protect against enemy landing and defend against deep penetration can be removed because the penetration depth in Taiwan will no longer be a narrow 60–120 miles. Instead, it will be the whole of China. The air force's focus should be redirected to the south, east, and north directions. Taiwan's air force will also have the capacity to support the navy in protecting the fishermen.

After the reunification, the current equipment of Taiwan's tri-service military should be more than adequate to carry out defense duties in the Taiwan area. Hence, during the initial period, Taiwan should opt to not renew outdated equipment. As for the number of militaries, Taiwan should consider using the mercenary system. Those who decide to retire early from the military should receive assistance in making career changes. From a long-term point of view, depending on Taiwan's need for renewing the military equipment, it can invite bids from countries all over the world to buy goods and less expensive equipment under fair competition. Taiwan can also enjoy technical exchanges with the mainland to manufacture its own products.

Problems are very possible if Taiwan continues to keep its military. If Taiwan's election system cannot be reformed, the politicians are likely to incite voters' emotions or take radical actions to gain voters' attention. At the present time, Taiwan's international status is low. If after the reunification Taiwan keeps its military power and if by chance an unscrupulous leader is elected, the whole world could be endangered. Also after reunification, if Taiwan has a military conflict with another country, then mainland China would take up the fight. In order to prevent this kind of tragedy from happening, the scholars who plan for the "two systems" should pay special attention to this subject.

THE RELATIONS TO THE EXTERNAL WORLD: After the reunification, Taiwan can set up offices to service the overseas Taiwanese people at more than 100 countries in the world. Taiwan can also strive for the most favorable visa status or visa waiver status for Taiwanese people from the global community. Taiwan can participate in mainland China's foreign affairs, which include the status of being a permanent member of the UN Security Council and the participation in the UN's work. (As Tang Shubei once said in regards to mainland China's UN delegation, the leader is from Beijing so the vice leader can be from Taiwan.) Taiwan can also join organizations established by the UN for the participation of only sovereign states, such as the WHO. Apart from keeping the business and cultural agreements signed with other countries, Taiwan can actively strive for more agreements on bilateral business and cultural exchanges, as well as endeavor to hold large-scale international financial, economic, and cultural conferences to broaden people's vision.

In addition, when the international community eliminates its concerns about "two Chinas" and "one China, one Taiwan," visits to Taiwan by world leaders and officials will greatly increase. By then, Taiwan's international living space will have increased substantially.

THE POLICIES FOR LABORERS, PEASANTS, AND FISHERMEN: After the reunification, various enterprises and labor unions on the two sides can discuss with the related units and private associations how to create a win-win situation for both enterprise and laborers to carry out the division of labor. The experienced workers of certain Taiwan manufacturing industries can go to the mainland to take jobs at a level above foreman. The mainland is now pushing for the development of the Great Northwest and the recovery of the Old Northeast. Taiwan's skilled workers can become the foremen who can train large number of mainland local people.

As to employment for most of the laborers who must remain on the island, the economics scholar Liu Jinqing suggested a series of concrete proposals. Whether they are workable still awaits the advice from the laborers at the basic level of the various professions and fields. In addition, Taiwan has already engaged in software research and development. If the two sides can work out a division of labor between the software and hardware industries, keep the software research and development in Taiwan, and invite mainland's software talents to reinforce the work in Taiwan, breakthroughs are sure to occur within a short time.

Concerning the peasants, apart from treating the whole of China as the heart of production, Taiwan's peasants can go to various cities and counties in the mainland to become agriculture technology advisers and teach mainland peasants planting techniques. They can also develop new products to extend the agricultural export market. After the reunification, Taiwan's fishermen will be protected and fishermen on both sides of the strait will enjoy the freedom of fishing in any waters of the world.

THE POLICIES FOR SOCIAL WELFARE: After the reunification, Taiwan should keep its social welfare plans, such as its healthcare plans for all people and its senior citizens' monthly subsidiary, and make any necessary improvements. Apart from using the budget saved from the huge military expenditure on social welfare programs, the government should raise the upper limit of the healthcare benefits and increase the efficiency of the Bureau of Health Care. If necessary, the current healthcare law for all people should be revised to avoid bankruptcy. In the case of senior people's monthly subsidiary, the government should modify the laws to exclude wealthy people in order to avoid the continued deficit of the government budget and to reduce the gap between the rich and the poor.

THE ECONOMIC POLICIES: After the reunification, the two sides should implement the economy as a whole and sign the CEPA to orderly integrate the mechanisms for cooperation and division of labor on the two sides. This will help upgrade the level of Taiwan's manufacturing industries, solve its economic difficulties, and maintain the living standard of the Taiwanese people.

Concerning financial and money matters, Taiwan's finances should be completely independent and financial income should be used for the needs of the island. No tax should be collected from Taiwan. Taiwan will use its own currency and maintain its own financial policies to protect the operational freedom of financial enterprises and markets.

In the area of the shipping industry, the experienced shipping companies of the two sides may form a strategic alliance to make mainland China and Taiwan the world's largest and most competitive shipping groups.

EDUCATION, SCIENCE, AND CULTURE: After the reunification, Taiwan's educational and cultural policies should strengthen the advocacy of Chinese history and culture, reestablish the recognition of mainland China, and enhance the feeling of respect for the people of the two sides. The two sides should increase academic and cultural exchanges, together nurture and bring in professional talents, recognize each other's curriculum backgrounds, and assist those students who intend to study on the other side. The two sides should also assist those educators who hope to teach or research on the other side to find suitable positions so the two sides can complement each other in the areas of education and nurturing talents.

In the area of science, the mainland could use its achievements in basic sciences and high technology to upgrade Taiwan's manufacturing industries. The two sides should jointly share their achievements in technological research and development to bring about further progress in high-tech industries.

CHAPTER 13

IS THERE URGENCY FOR THE TWO SIDES TO RESUME TALKS?

The reunification of the two sides must be accomplished through direct cross-strait negotiations. Even though Taiwan believes that negotiations will be unfavorable to the Taiwanese people, both sides realize that they must engage in dialogue as soon as possible. This is irrespective of Taiwan's considerations of the Taiwan Strait safety, U.S. pressure, or mainland China's intention of achieving reunification. This chapter reflects the author's personal viewpoints on this topic.

SECTION 1
REVIEW OF CROSS-STRAIT NEGOTIATIONS

Ever since mainland China changed its Taiwan strategy in the 1970s to peaceful reunification, it has repeatedly called for speedy party-to-party negotiations between the KMT and the CPC. For example, mainland China's SCNPC took the opportunity on January 1, 1979 (when the U.S. established a diplomatic relationship with mainland China), to publish a "Message to Compatriots in Taiwan." The message suggested that the two sides end the condition of military confrontation. This peaceful offensive came to a climax after Deng Xiaoping proposed "one country, two systems." Later, one of Jiang's Eight-Point Proposals suggested cross-strait peaceful reunification negotiations. In 2000, the second white paper also suggested that the two sides peacefully resolve the cross-strait reunification issue through negotiation. Hence, we can understand mainland China's insistence on cross-strait dialogues.

Taiwan responded by first condemning mainland China's suggestion as a united front conspiracy, then took a "no contact, no negotiation, no compromise" stance (the Three Noes Policy). In November 1987, Taiwan permitted people to pay family visits to the mainland though the officials still kept the Three Noes stance. In order to solve the problems created by the private sectors of the cross-strait exchanges and interactions, the SEF and the ARATS held the first chairman-to-chairman level talk in Singapore (April 1993). After that, the SEF and the ARATS held many negotiations, but Taiwan refused to engage in any negotiations about political matters. Later, due to Lee Teng-hui's "two-state theory," the negotiations on practical matters also stopped.

In 2000, the DPP became the ruling party and refused to accept the One-China Principle. It also completely denied the 1992 Consensus. As a result, cross-strait relations were stagnant for three years. Although Taiwan's MAC maintained that apart from practical matters it was willing to extend the negotiation level to political topics, and mainland China repeatedly called for Taiwan to enter political negotiations, the two sides did not begin political talks. The negotiations for practical matters did not resume either. In fact, in March 2003, Jiang Zemin clearly stated that "no matter who has the power in Taiwan, we all welcome him to talk to the mainland. At the same time, we can also go to Taiwan. But there needs to be a basis for these talks and negotiations, and that is that the One-China Principle must be recognized. Under this premise, anything can be talked about." Before the 2000 presidential election, the DPP advocated that the two sides engage in official multilevel, multiphase dialogues and negotiations on any topic as well as begin the three link negotiations. After Chen Shui-bian promised the Four Noes and One Without on his inauguration day, mainland China immediately promulgated an announcement. It pointed out once more that as long as Taiwan clearly promised not to promote the "two-state theory" and agreed with the 1992 Consensus, China was willing to authorize the ARATS to have dialogues with authorized Taiwan organizations. But for the next three years, the tense cross-strait relations did not improve. On the contrary, the relations suffered serious setbacks due to Chen Shui-bian's gradual Taiwan independence policy in foreign relations, cultural, educational, and military areas. The poor cross-strait relations were aggravated when Chen Shui-bian proposed the "one country on each side" theory in August 2000. In the spring of 2003—when the SARS epidemic attacked the mainland, Hong Kong, and Taiwan—Chen Shui-bian and the pro-independence groups incited anti-China emotions. They later used the excuse of not being a member of the WHO to create a referendum to push Taiwan into entering the WHO. Even though the DPP government repeatedly guaranteed the U.S. that the referendum had nothing to do with reunification or independence, the U.S. was concerned. Once held, the referendum would be equivalent to the opening of a breakthrough hole for the Taiwan independence referendum with the possibility of developing it into an unmanageable situation. As the 2004 presidential election drew nearer, Chen Shui-bian again advocated writing a new Constitution and cross-strait relations suffered a serious setback. From all these signs, it was impossible for the two sides to have further contact. Everything had to wait until after the March 2004 presidential election.

SECTION 2
ANALYSIS OF CROSS-STRAIT NEGOTIATIONS BASED ON THE NEGOTIATION THEORIES

In this section, I shall discuss cross-strait negotiations in detail.

The Negotiation Theories

Political negotiations are usually regarded as the most difficult type of negotiations. The western political scholars have done extensive research on this. If we categorize the negotiations according to their natures and results, the types are zero-sum, non-zero sum, and win-win negotiations. If we differentiate them by the negotiation chips used, we see symmetry negotiation and asymmetry negotiation. The former indicates that the negotiators' chips more or less match while the latter means the negotiators' chips do not match. As for negotiation strategies, there are two categories: the reconciliatory strategy and the confrontational strategy. The former means that the negotiators are sincere about reaching an agreement. They take cooperative, compromising, and sincere strategies with the hope of finding solutions that would achieve the greatest benefit for both sides. The latter means that in an attempt to win the greatest victory the negotiators use competitive, threatening, and non-compromising strategies. Concerning the negotiating stages, there is the pre-negotiation stage and post-negotiation stage.

*Analysis of Cross-Strait Negotiations
    Based on the Negotiation Theories*

Using these theories to evaluate cross-strait negotiations, if the two sides carry out national reunification negotiations and if one side will likely lose its so-called sovereignty, this would conform to the zero-sum negotiation case. To achieve the goal of reunification, mainland China will not take a confrontational strategy. On the other hand, it is quite possible that during the negotiation Taiwan will use delay tactics. According to the overall national strengths of the two sides, the cross-strait negotiations would be an asymmetrical negotiation; namely, small Taiwan will fight against big mainland China. Besides, owing to the internal reunification/independence disputes, the ruling and the opposition parties have very different opinions. Negotiations that will reach consensus between these parties will be just as difficult as negotiations between Taiwan and mainland China. Taiwan's main interest during negotiations should be on terminating the state of hostility. Even the suggestion of mutual visits by leaders on each side was made to ease the Taiwan Strait situation. Apart from this, there is no strong enticement for Taiwan to engage in political negotiations. If Taiwan agrees to proceed with negotiation, it perhaps will employ a near-confrontational or competitive negotiation strategy.

Using the pre-defined stages of negotiation, it can be said that cross-strait political negotiations are still in the pre-negotiation stage. According to Feng Chi-jen, overseas scholar in the U.S. (see his book *The U.S.-China Policy and the Taiwan Relations*), Taiwan has used all kinds of excuses to delay the negotiations in recent years. Taiwan often proposed principles that are difficult for the other party to accept, just to avoid the negotiations.

The attitude taken by the Taiwan authorities is roughly as follows:

1. Using all kinds of pretexts to delay negotiations: Two particular situations have caused Taiwan to use delay tactics to avoid entering into political negotiations with the mainland. One is its inferior total national strength and the other is its lack of internal consensus on mainland policies. At the same time, Taiwan gradually loosens up exchanges with the private sectors in the hope that the mainland's internal political structure will eventually be favorably changed enough so Taiwan can conduct negotiations. The NUG stipulates that the two sides must reach short-term exchanges and mutual benefits and go through the mid-term mutual trust and cooperation stage before the two sides can enter the stage of long-term negotiation for reunification. However, the mainland has great difficulty in accepting some of the matters Taiwan has stipulated for the short-term stage; for example, "on the subject of mutual bene-

fits, both will not deny that the other side is a real political entity," and "respect each other, not exclude each other in the international community." So, the NUG is partly responsible for the delay in negotiations.

Taiwan has repeatedly emphasized that the two sides should first conduct negotiations for practical matters to establish a mutual trust in preparation for political negotiations. In May 1996, Lee Teng-hui was interviewed by *Newsweek* and stated, "If Jiang Zemin's power becomes stable, it will be a very suitable moment for a cross-strait talk. Before that, it would be very difficult to talk." At the end of 2002, Chen Shui-bian claimed that he wanted to observe the results of the 16th Communist Party Congress and the performance of Hu Jintao to decide whether or not to resume negotiations with mainland China. All of these talks are Taiwan's delay tactics.

2. To avoid being blamed for not resuming cross-strait talks, Taiwan proposed principles that mainland China found difficult to accept: In order to respond to calls by the international community to ease up the situation of the Taiwan Strait, Taiwan expressed its willingness to enter political negotiations. On the other hand, it proposed principles that obviously could not be accepted by mainland China. For example, on August 1, 1995, Lee Teng-hui stated during the National Assembly's Interim Meeting that as long as mainland China formally renounces the use of force against Taiwan, Penghu, Kinmen, and Matsu, the two sides could immediately begin negotiations on how to end the hostility situation and hold preparatory consultation meetings. The MAC also claimed that the two sides must proceed with negotiations under the principle of "a free, democratic, and equitable-prosperity mainland China." On April 8, 1995, Lee Teng-hui made six proposals at the 1st Meeting of the 3rd Session of the National Unification Council. Among these, the fourth proposal demands that the "two sides equally participate in international organizations and leaders from both sides should meet naturally through their participation." Taiwan obviously knew that mainland China would not accept this. The purpose of proposing this idea was to divert attention from the responsibility of resuming the cross-strait talks.

    Chen Shui-bian's administration might have thought that the two sides not carrying out political negotiations was not in conflict with Taiwan's interests. After the 2004 presidential election, Taiwan could not avoid the problem of resuming cross-strait talks, particularly when it faced pressure from mainland China and the U.S.

3. Taiwan resolutely opposes negotiations before being guaranteed negotiations on equal footing: Taiwan maintains that it would be impossible for mainland China to negotiate with Taiwan on an equal footing. Hence, as soon as Taiwan begins the cross-strait negotiations, it is already downgraded by mainland China. As early as 1995, however, Jiang's Eight-Point Proposals emphasized that

"consultations on an equal footing can be held at an early date." In 1998, Qian Qichen said that the two sides could make arrangements about the procedures on political negotiations. Through discussions on the procedures, the topics of the political negotiations, the names of the representatives, and the manner of negotiation, the two sides can reach agreements that are acceptable to both. In May 2000, Qian Qichen further stated, "The cross-strait negotiations will not use the name of the central or local government; instead, it is under the One-China Principle that the two sides equally carry out discussions." In 2003, during the 16th Communist Party Congress, Jiang Zemin emphasized again that certain political disputes could be shelved temporarily in order to resume cross-strait dialogues and negotiations as early as possible.

Instead of guessing and questioning whether Taiwan can get a negotiation status on an equal footing, the consultations should begin before the negotiations and as soon as possible. By then, Taiwan would be able to discover firsthand whether mainland China will carry out its promise of consultations on an equal footing.

SECTION 3
THE U.S. ATTITUDES TOWARD THE TWO SIDES RESUMING THE CROSS-STRAIT TALKS

Facing the more complicated and sensitive cross-strait relations on a daily basis, from the eras of President George H.W. Bush (1988–1992) to President Clinton (1992–2000), those U.S. officials who were involved with the cross-strait affairs all thought that keeping a strategic ambiguity policy best conformed to U.S. interests. Beijing would not be able to figure out Washington's intention and Taipei would not make trouble; hence the U.S. will be able to use the "Taiwan card" to harass mainland China with less danger. This kind of policy apparently encouraged the separatists in Taiwan, and during the second half of 1995 it provoked a tense situation that led to the Taiwan Strait crisis in the spring of 1996. In 1997, Clinton proposed the concept of "strategic partners," and he voiced approval of the Three Noes policy in 1998. These were all revisions to the U.S.'s strategic ambiguity policy. In July 1999, Lee Teng-hui proposed the "two-state theory" and the Taiwan Strait was again in a tense situation. The U.S. government felt the need to replace the strategic ambiguity policy with strategic clarity. During the later part of his presidency, George W. Bush's (2000–present) important campaign advisors like Paul Wolfowitz and Richard Armitage expressed the necessity of taking a strategic clarity policy. Namely, if Taiwan declares independence unilaterally, it should not expect U.S. assistance and if mainland China invades Taiwan for no good reason, the U.S. will retaliate. This kind of policy is not far from the interim agreement that Washington scholars suggested that both sides should sign.

The "Interim Agreement"

The "interim agreement" initially came from U.S. scholar Kenneth G. Lieberthal. In February 1998, Lieberthal proposed his "interim agreement" during a forum in Taipei. He advocated that the two sides establish a comprehensive political framework and slow down the sovereignty talks. However, under the One-China Principle, Taiwan would not seek legal independence and mainland China would not use force against Taiwan. There would be a 50-year period for developing the relationship between the two sides to ensure the stability of the strait. The concept was a "single" agreement and it comprehensively regulated cross-strait relations. Its nature was close to a treaty. In March 1993, U.S. Deputy Assistant Secretary of State of East Asian and Pacific Affairs Stanley Roth also proposed an "interim agreement," but this one had no time limit and more flexibility. It did not have the comprehensive framework to be agreed upon that Lieberthal's agreement did; instead, it separately inserted individual topics and was composed of many interim agreements. Summing up all the small agreements formed the main agreement. In brief, Roth's "interim agreement" was composed of multiple agreements.

Scholar Harry Harding also presented an "interim agreement." He proposed that if Taiwan did not seek independence, mainland China would not use force, and vice versa. His "interim agreement" would not freeze the status quo; instead, he wanted the situation to be stable and predictable by using a set of mutually guaranteed mechanisms to expand the cross-strait exchanges, raise Taiwan's international status, implement the three links, and increase dialogues via multiple channels. The U.S. AIT/Washington Chairman Richard Bush and AIT Taipei Director Darryl Norman Johnson also expressed similar viewpoints consecutively. Their key points were that the U.S. had no intention of acting as a mediator. Instead, both sides should resolve the problem in a peaceful manner and try to reach an "interim agreement" on their own.

The reason for the U.S. to propose an "interim agreement" was mainly due to the existence of too many unstable factors between the two sides after the 1995 Taiwan Strait crisis. The U.S. government was alarmed about the possibility of serious problems and was concerned about being dragged into it. The "interim agreement" proposal in one way reflected the U.S. evaluation of the cross-strait situation. It also showed that the U.S. was gradually losing patience. The U.S. hoped that the "interim agreement" would become part of the mechanism confidently established by both sides and would be used to keep the peace and safety of the Taiwan Strait.

The two sides had different responses to the "interim agreement" idea. Although the contents of the agreement did not particularly emphasize "one China" or the idea that China would eventually be reunified, it leaned in the direction of reunification. So, China still meant mainland China and Taiwan could not challenge this point. This was why Taiwan showed little interest in the "interim agreement." Taiwan's concern was that once within the framework of the "interim agreement," it would not be able to prevent reunification. Taiwan would prefer to have discussions on the establishment of mutual trust and insuring the safety and peace of the Taiwan Strait without reunification as the ultimate conclusion. For mainland China, the purpose of negotiation was to get Taiwan to promise to reunify, to put an end to the state of hostility between the two sides, and to sign peaceful agreements with the prerequisite of having a reunified future. An "interim agreement" without a reunification presumption would not be accepted by mainland China and an "interim agreement" with a reunification presumption would not be accepted by Taiwan. The positions of the two sides were so much at odds that the "interim agreement" proposed by the U.S. was stopped before it even started.

The U.S. Position on Cross-Strait Talks

After George W. Bush won the 2000 presidential election, the U.S. Committee on National Interests, the Rand Corporation, and the U.S. Senate Committee on Foreign Relations proposed suggestions about cross-strait relations. They agreed that the new administration should actively push for the two sides to restart the negotiations in order to help improve the status quo. However, Lee Teng-hui's "two-state theory" proposed in 1999 delayed the Koo-Wang meeting indefinitely. Later, Taiwan's political power changed hands and the DPP, which advocated Taiwan independence in its party charter, took power. This increased Beijing's worries and doubts, and the two sides still could not restart formal dialogues. This factor is one that makes Taiwan's future full of uncertainties.

On the surface, it seems that the U.S. has tried hard to push the two sides to engage in direct dialogue, as seen in its "interim agreement" proposal. As some Taiwan scholars have said, the two sides would enjoy benefits if they sign the "interim agreement," but the U.S. would enjoy even more benefits because it would no longer have to worry about being dragged into cross-strait clashes and it still could continue to play an important role between the two sides. Under the presumption of a stable development of cross-strait relations, the U.S. could simultaneously take care of its commercial, political, and security interests. Furthermore, if the "interim agreement" gives a hint of some later development, such as a metaphor that mainland China can tolerate Taiwan's not accepting the current reunification condition, then the U.S. will still have the right to question—and challenge—the mainland's position. (See *The Cross-Strait Order in the New Century* by Tsai Wei for more information.)

After the "interim agreement" was dropped, the U.S. tried many times to get the two sides to resume talks, but the Taiwan authorities did not respond at all. The U.S. told the outside world that it tried all it could, but the two sides insisted on their own ideas. Hence, they should not blame others. Was this the reality? Judging by the extent of the Taiwan leaders' dependence on and obedience to the U.S., if the U.S. really intended to push the two sides into negotiations, it only had to exert pressure on Taiwan or reduce the arms sale. Mainland China has repeatedly expressed that under the One-China Principle anything can be talked about (which completely conforms to the One-China Principle, by the way, and also is insisted on by the U.S.), so why did the U.S. let Taiwan refuse to negotiate? Wasn't this saying one thing and doing another thing?

Based on the above statements, although the U.S. repeatedly called for the two sides to begin negotiations as soon as possible, its real desire to see the two sides begin talks is doubtful. Perhaps what the U.S. wanted was to see a no independence, no use of force "interim agreement" that protected the safety of the Taiwan Strait and minimized U.S. involvement. As for the U.S. claim of not being the mediator, neither side believed that the U.S. would not pay any attention to the cross-strait negotiations. When the two sides resume talks, it is possible that Taiwan will seek to have the U.S. act as a middleman for consultations or to be a witness.

SECTION 4
DISCUSSIONS OF TAIWAN'S PRETEXTS FOR REFUSING CROSS-STRAIT NEGOTIATIONS

Lee Teng-hui and the DPP continuously told the Taiwanese people that as long as they faced a threat from mainland China, they had to be pro-U.S.

As long as it has U.S. protection, Taiwan can walk step by step; but negotiating directly with mainland China would only downgrade, localize, and marginalize Taiwan. This seemingly correct but erroneous logic was propagandized day and night through the mainstream media and has long become the public consensus in Taiwan. Anyone who wants to challenge this consensus will either be silenced or labeled. The fact of the matter is that anyone who has medium-level intelligence and is willing to think carefully will see through the absurdity of this set of logic. If Taiwan's greatest threat comes from mainland China, then shouldn't Taiwan directly face the mainland and seek ways of resolution instead of seeking the protection of a third party by paying any price—especially if this third party is the U.S., which has not always been pro-Taiwan? Furthermore, it would make sense for Taiwan to cling to the U.S. if the Chinese liberation army cries out for Taiwan's blood. But mainland China has proposed "peaceful reunification, one country, two systems" since early on. What is Taiwan still waiting for?

In order to deflect the responsibility for refusing to negotiate, Taiwan's government officials repeatedly emphasized that it was not that Taiwan did not want to negotiate, it was because mainland China has never given up the use of force. Hence, no talk could possibly be useful. To be fair, if mainland China really wants to play tough, judging from mainland China's military strength, it will be capable of achieving the purpose of liberating Taiwan. From the beginning mainland China did not want to use force because:

1. The use of force will affect the mainland's economic developments, the realization of a comprehensive modernization, and the progress of reaching a "well-to-do society."

2. Reunifying Taiwan by force violates the principle of "Chinese will not fight against Chinese" and will hurt Taiwan emotionally. It is not a good long-term policy for keeping order and stability.

3. Taiwan's economy depends increasingly on the mainland on a daily basis and cross-strait exchanges are more frequent. When conditions are ripe, the success of reunification will come naturally.

4. Using force will affect mainland China's international image. Since the establishment of the PRC, it has avoided wars of aggression.

5. The "one country, two systems" advocacy has gradually gained the Taiwan people's support. Jiang Zemin said during the 16th Communist Party Congress that "one country, two systems" should progress over time. After some time, the people in Taiwan should be willing to accept "one country, two systems" as the method for a peaceful reunification.

In order to express willingness to resolve the cross-strait problem peacefully, Jiang's Eight-Point Proposals pointed out, "Under the premise of 'one

China,' any problem can be talked about, including the various problems of the most interest to the Taiwan authorities." The "one China" idea also promised "consultations on equal footing." The 16th Communist Party Congress report introduced the "three things" that could be talked about. Taiwan's response to the above suggestions was that it did not believe mainland China's sincerity.

In order to push aside the responsibility of not being willing to negotiate, the government officials have told the Taiwanese people that it was not that Taiwan did not want to talk with the mainland but, at the negotiation table, the sovereignty problem would inevitably come up. By then, Taiwan definitely would be "minimized." First of all, the mentality of these officials was problematic. Taiwan does not think of itself as minimized by being regulated by U.S. domestic laws. It also does not think of itself as minimized when the obvious cross-strait matters depended on other people's view from tens of thousands of miles away. For the safety and benefit of the people of Taiwan, government officials should strive for the rights and benefits of the Taiwanese people. These officials should not ignore the people's needs and they should not blame mainland China every time Taiwan encounters problems on the international platform. Finally, anyone knows that negotiation means to vie with one another, to make progress or suffer setbacks, to have gains or losses. As long as there is patience and sincerity, there must be success. Shouldn't Taiwan at least find out what card mainland China is going to put on the table before deciding what card Taiwan will play? Why is Taiwan putting the cart before the horse? The former Prime Minister of South Korea, Kim Dazhong, advocated talking with North Korea and won the Nobel Peace Prize. However, people in Taiwan who advocated cross-strait talks were regarded as "traitors." Comparing the two cases would depress the people.

Another reason for the politicians' refusal of cross-strait talks is the mistrust of communists. "On the surface, they say anything can be talked about. Once put on the table, it is no longer the same matter." However, the PRC has never broken any agreements or treaties it agreed to since 1949. The PRC has even accepted contracts concerning China, signed by the KMT during the period when the KMT occupied the mainland. In addition, since Hong Kong and Macao implemented "one country, two systems," everything is adherent to the Basic Law of Hong Kong and Macao. Until the present time, nothing has been discovered to show that mainland China has crossed the boundary. What reason do Taiwan's politicians have to doubt mainland China's sincerity? Why would they rather believe the U.S., which has repeatedly broken its promises to Taiwan? Instead of holding on to

America's apron strings and being treated like a child, Taiwan should actively engage in talks with the mainland to resolve the disputes and create a new win-win situation.

SECTION 5
THE TWO SIDES SHOULD
START DIALOGUES AS SOON AS POSSIBLE

If the two sides agree to resume talks, then the selection of negotiation topics will lay the groundwork for successful negotiation. In the 1990s, the two sides engaged in many negotiations about practical matters. In the end, the political problem of "one China" was still non-negotiable. Hence, if the two sides resume negotiation and only discuss practical matters instead of political subjects, the results would be ineffective. According to the current cross-strait situation, if no political topic is discussed, the solution to practical subjects that have urgency and require extended consultation will not be solved. Concerning this point, the mainland scholar Chen Kongli suggested that the two sides begin the procedural consultations of the political negotiations and continue to develop discussions about practical matters. In this way, the topics on practical matters would not be intertwined with the political topics and could be solved more easily. (See "The Prospects of the Cross-Strait Negotiations" by Chen Kongli in the book of *The "One China" Principle from Every Aspect* for more information.) Whether his suggestions can be carried out remains to be seen.

The topics of the negotiations should be determined through consultations by both sides. The topics should touch upon the interests of the two sides and be of concern to both sides so that they would hope to strive for resolutions as quickly as possible. The topics should also be worthy of discussion. If negotiations are done in a timely and organized manner, solutions and/or partial resolutions would be possible.

Viewing the two sides, which topics will conform to the aforementioned criteria? One of Jiang's Eight-Point Proposals was that the two sides negotiate on the topic of "terminating the state of hostility," and this was of concern to Taiwan. In 1997, the MAC stated, "The priority of the cross-strait negotiations should be to end the state of hostility," and, "Top priority is the termination of the state of hostility and the signing of a peaceful agreement" (*China Times Daily News*, 08/09/1997). Later the MAC added, "We have already made preparations. As long as the other side is also ready, the two sides can begin an early-stage communication" (*China Times Daily News*,

09/04/1997). The first of the "three things" that could be discussed mentioned during mainland China's 16th Communist Party Congress was formally ending the state of hostility of the two sides. Clearly both sides agreed that this topic was urgent and worthy of discussion.

In addition, both sides mentioned negotiations on the three links. On the mainland side, the leaders in recent years and officials who have been responsible for cross-strait affairs always mentioned the three direct links whenever they spoke. Lien Chan expressed as early as July 1997 that "'one China,' three links, and ending the diplomatic wars . . . can all be the political topics of the cross-strait negotiations" (*United Daily News*, 07/31/1997). Then, DPP Chairman Hsu Hsing-liang made an even clearer statement, "Taiwan should immediately engage in negotiations with the mainland on the three links" (*The Central News Agency*, 01/15/1998). In 2003, Chen Shui-bian spoke often about negotiations on the three links. Although he always changed his mind, he continually maintained that the two sides must begin to negotiate on the three links. From this, we can surmise that the three links is a subject that both sides would be willing to discuss. Since it is an urgent matter and also easily classified as a practical matter, it can possibly become the first topic of negotiation.

The Three Links

At the present time, there are approximately three million round trips between the two sides of the strait per year. The Taiwanese people have to spend an extra US$0.6 billion every year to go through Hong Kong and Macao to enter the mainland. Goods from the two sides must pass through Japan or Hong Kong to reach their destinations. Every year this procedure incurs a US$1.0 billion additional cost. The total is US$1.6 billion plus wasted time. Taiwan would clearly benefit from the three links. The business circle in Taiwan finds the continuous government delay on the three links unbearable. The "Ten-Thousand-Word Letter," written by Chairman Wang Yung-ching of the Formosa Plastics Group, still echoes in our ears. The Pan-Green camp merchant, Chang Rong-fa, accused Lee Teng-hui and Chen Shui-bian of having no marine policies on November 5, 2003. If there was still no opening of the three links, his Evergreen Shipping Headquarters would consider moving to other countries (*United Daily News*, 11/06/2003). Some people say that after the opening of the three direct links, Taiwan's economy will further depend on the mainland. In fact, the trend cannot be reversed even without the three links. It is true that the mainland needs Taiwan's capital and technology, but if Taiwan's enterprises do not have low-cost labor, cheap land, and electricity from the mainland, they will not be able to compete internationally. Hence, the benefits due to the three links will be greater for Taiwanese people than for mainlanders.

During the 2000 presidential election, Chen Shui-bian promised direct transportation. After he was in power for three years, his attitude toward the three links changed four times. From the time he was elected until the beginning of May 2002, the attitude of Chen Shui-bian's administration toward the three links was to refuse "one China" but allow the push for the three links by trusted non-governmental representatives. In August 2002, Chen Shui-bian proposed "one country on each side" and the referendum, but he no longer mentioned the three links. In May 2003, after Taiwan's failure to enter the WHO, Chen Shui-bian again connected the One-China Principle with the three links. He clearly said that in the following ten months, it would be impossible for the two sides to have consultations on the three links. But, surprisingly, after just one month he proposed the "three stages of the three links." The preparation stage would continue until March 2004. The consultations stage would start three months after the preparation stage, and the realization stage would be at the end of the year. Chen Shui-bian's attitude toward the three links seemed to return to his initial point of refusing "one China" while agreeing to push for the three links again. This time he did not include the referendum, however.

The mainland defined direct transportation from the original "domestic transportation" route to the "cross-strait route." Mainland China considers this an economic and trade issue, not a political one. Since it does not involve the "one China" problem and could be negotiated by non-governmental representatives, the officials from both sides can conduct the negotiation in the name of experts. This was actually the model of negotiation for the establishment of the transportation center outside the mainland and the Taiwan-Hong Kong route. When Chen Shui-bian proposed the three-stage theory, he pointed out that direct transportation was not a purely economic issue and it could not exclude political considerations. MAC Chairperson Tsai Yin-wen further pointed out that direct transportation could have three impacts: political sovereignty, economic and trade, and safety. As a result of Tsai Yin-wen's statement, the Taiwanese people understood that the purpose of talking about the three links was just for the election. In reality, this subject could not be discussed at the negotiation table; or, if it was discussed, there would be no result.

To be fair, although the three links cannot solve all problems, it is the most important cross-strait topic at the current stage and it must be implemented. If the 2004 elected government does not realize this, people from all circles will not recpect this government anymore.

Termination of the State of Hostility

In 1995, Jiang Zemin proposed that reunification had two steps: The first step was to terminate the state of hostility under the One-China Principle and the second was reunification. For the mainland, the war with Taiwan was not yet over. After 1949, Chiang Kai-shek and Chiang Ching-kuo went to Taiwan and the two sides experienced military confrontations on a small scale. Only until 1979, the mainland promulgated peaceful reunification guidelines. The cross-strait military clashes no longer occurred, though the state of hostility continued. In order to end the state of hostility, the mainland required that Taiwan not declare independence or China would use force. The two sides could discuss reunification after signing an agreement to end the state of hostility.

Concerning this point, logically, Taiwan should have no reason to object. After all, if a war breaks out in the Taiwan Strait, the Taiwanese people will be the victims. In 2000, after Taiwan's political power changed hands, the DPP thought that the civil war problem between the KMT and the CPC was over and that the mainland should no longer be hostile to Taiwan. This, of course, was unrealistic. The Nationalist government's move to Taiwan was due to the defeat of the KMT by the CPC in the Civil War and up to the present day, the two sides still declare that there is only one China, but make different interpretations. The international community also recognizes that there is only one China. Hence, how is it possible to say that the Taiwan problem is not a problem left by the Chinese Civil War and that the two sides are not in a state of hostility? These statements are equivalent to saying, "Taiwan is already a sovereign country," and, "Mainland China is mainland China, Taiwan is Taiwan." These statements are unable to change the cross-strait reality or affect international public opinions. But they may make those pro-independence people take irrational actions to worsen the continued cross-strait state of hostility.

Because of the lack of mutual trust, getting the two sides to sit down and calmly negotiate how to terminate the state of hostility would be difficult. First of all, simply declaring, "Taiwan will not seek independence," and, "The mainland will not use force," would ignite both sides. Next, the real meaning of not seeking independence and not using force may not be accurately defined. Mainland China is worried about Taiwan's *de facto* independence.

Even if Taiwan does not declare *de jure* independence, but moves in the direction of independence, what can mainland China do? As for Taiwan, it is concerned with both the trust in mainland China's promise as well as its suppression. If China starts to use methods that are close to the use of true force, how will Taiwan respond?

Terminating the state of hostility is clearly not an easy task. But Taiwan may consider approaching it from another angle. From the time that Deng Xiaoping declared "one country, two systems," the mainland in fact was no longer hostile to Taiwan, especially to the Taiwan compatriots. Otherwise, why did mainland China give Taiwanese businessmen so much preferential treatment? Some people think that the mainland needs Taiwan's capital. In fact, until May 2003 the mainland was the largest creditor of the U.S., owning a US$290 billion government bond. As for the 1996 missile firing, China only intended to send a signal to the Taiwan independence supporters. Mainland China's missile bases are along the coast. This has been considered proof that mainland China intends to use force to invade Taiwan. But if missiles are not installed along the coast, where should they be installed? Mainland China has long maintained that it will not renounce the use of force, but that force will be used only to thwart Taiwan's independence or foreign intervention. Concerning foreign intervention, presently only the U.S. has such capabilities—but the U.S. has repeatedly announced that it will not interfere. Now even Chen Shui-bian's so-called protective angel— President George W. Bush—has changed from "not supporting Taiwan independence" to "opposing Taiwan independence" to even "against attempted Taiwan independence." It seems that the U.S. will not actively interfere. Even if Taiwan insists on independence, rejects the advice from the U.S., and provokes China's invasion by force, the U.S. may still not want to get involved. Taiwan should realize that when it really moves to independence, mainland China will not just sit and watch. But if China does use force, who should be blamed? In order to protect Taiwan's own safety and stability, the Taiwan authorities should really sit down and negotiate with mainland China. Taiwan does not have to worry about mainland China not keeping its promises because the safety of the Taiwan Strait matters to the whole of Asia as well as to the U.S. Whether mainland China will keep its promises is something that will be closely watched by the entire world.

The Contents of the "Two Systems"

Apart from the aforementioned topics, the two sides in fact can negotiate on some practical matters that concern Taiwan's realistic rights and benefits within the context of the "two systems." For example, cross-strait economics and trade can become an integral whole; the laborers and peasants of the two sides can have a planned division of work; both sides can have mutual recognition of educational backgrounds and share scientific and technological talents; and the mainland's navy and air force can protect Taiwan's fishermen.

The two sides can also negotiate on stopping the diplomatic wars. In Taiwan, political parties and scholars have proposed that the two sides stop the diplomatic wars as early as possible, but mainland China has not responded. That is because, internationally, China must adhere to the One-China Principle. But as long as the two sides are willing to sit down and negotiate, they must be able to find a compromise that satisfies both so that Taiwan no longer has to waste a huge amount of money every year for maintaining hypocritical international living space.

If discussing the above topics can produce results, Taiwan will reap the benefits of solving its current problems; namely, its economic depression, difficult government finance, and high unemployment rate. Most importantly, discussion will establish mutual trust and that will be beneficial when the two sides begin other cross-strait political topics.

Conclusion

Taking an objective view, reunification is the trend and it cannot be resisted by subjective determination. World politics and economics currently have been separated into the European Union, the Asia's 10+3 (the Association of Southeast Asian Nations has ten countries plus China, South Korea, and Japan) and the North America Free Trade Zone formed by the U.S., Canada, and Mexico in November 2003. In the future, the entire world will engage in group competitions through the various large regions. If Taiwan and mainland China are not reunified, where will Taiwan place itself? Both Hong Kong and Macao have signed the CEPA with the mainland, and this is equivalent to entering the 10+3. Who can Taiwan rely on in order to join any region?

If the Taiwan authorities and various political parties really love Taiwan and are truly thinking of the people, then they should face the international reality of Taiwan's present situation apart from the growth trend in the mainland and the decline in Taiwan. They should put their energy toward seeking the most favorable reunification conditions for the Taiwanese people. The Taiwanese people should also actively understand the contents of "one country, two systems" and fully express their opinions as they select the best way out for themselves.

CHAPTER 14

TAIWAN'S FUTURE
AND PEACEFUL REUNIFICATION

Chen Shui-bian won Taiwan's crooked presidential election and was inaugurated on May 20, 2004. Almost all of the people on both sides of the strait agree that, from then on, the road to peaceful cross-strait reunification would be more hectic. However, viewing the unprecedented new high of supporters for reunification and "one country, two systems" within the island during the year after Chen Shui-bian's victory in 2000, the DPP's continuing governance may not necessarily be proportional to the people's opposition on reunification.

The Taiwanese people have always been proud of their democratic system, and they use this to resist reunification with the mainland, which practices a different system. However, during the election in 2004, the candidates used the pretext of deepening the democratization to carry out a referendum and advocated writing a new Constitution, thereby creating an ethnic split and social turmoil. One day before the election, a suspicious shooting incident took place and following the election the scandalous ballot manipulations occurred. Taiwan's democratic system was certainly challenged. After the 2004 presidential election, Lien, Soong, and academic circles criticized Chen Shui-bian for playing populism and swore to recapture true democracy. It seems that, for the time being, Taiwan still is in its struggling war for democracy.

Following mainland China's rapid economic growth, its economic policies now determine the financial markets and the economic developments of Taiwan and Asia. Even the world economy cannot deny mainland China's influence. If Taiwan insists on not admitting "one China" or continues to use the shell of the ROC as a delay to change, then its survival will be difficult. The international living space issue that has been the biggest concern of the Taiwan leaders suffered an even stronger blockade before and after the May 20 inauguration. To make further diplomatic breakthroughs would almost be impossible, and it would be equally difficult to just keep the current small number of countries that have diplomatic relations with Taiwan.

SECTION 1
TAIWAN SHOULD ABANDON THE MYTH
OF A DISTORTED AMERICAN-STYLE DEMOCRACY

In Taiwan, democracy has always been publicized as a "universal value." As long as you hold the sign of democracy, you are progressive; otherwise, you are "anti-democracy." But, exactly what democracy *is* and whether it will bring about freedom, equality, and social justice have rarely been discussed.

Taiwan Is Only a "Country with Democratic Elections"

During the 2004 presidential election, the performances of the candidates, the use of the referendum to tie up the election, and the two bullets incident disgusted the people. The election events brought up questions within and outside the island as to whether Taiwan's democracy is actually democracy or just populism. Later, some people argued that the problem was not due to democracy itself; instead, there was not enough maturity in the implementation of democracy. In other words the Taiwanese people need more time before accepting the concept. For example, the well-known Taiwanese author, Lung Ying-tai, wrote an article in which she stated, "The U.S. democracy has had 200 years of implementing experience," whereas "Taiwan's democracy, from the time of abolishing martial law, is only a short 17 years old" (*China Times Daily News*, 04/15/2004). In political circles, not only did winner Chen Shui-bian declare that his reelection was a victory for democracy, but after the election the defeated James Soong also proposed the Alliance for a New Democratic Movement. On May 19, 2004, Lien Chan recommended during the KMT's Central Standing Committee to push for a new democraticism to ensure the value of democracy. Some scholars also initiated the "New May 4 Movement" before May 4 in an effort to "use the deepening of the democracy to confront the populist centralization." (On May 4, 1919, Chinese students in Beijing initiated a movement that served as a campaign to fight against feudalism and promote democracy and science.) Viewing these, we can see that in Taiwan democracy will continue to be the ideal for some time.

In fact, democracy is only a system design. Its main contents include elections, parliament, and the framework of three independent government powers. In order to inspect whether a country possesses all of the democratic systems, western political scholars separate democratic countries into two types: countries with democratic elections and countries with democratic constitutional governments. The former suggests that a "country's highest policymakers are produced from regular, free, and fair elections." The latter refers to a standardized value that uses the method of limiting the government power to achieve the purpose of protecting people's rights. In other words, if a country only has elections and does not limit its government powers to protect people's rights, then at most it is only counted as a country with democratic elections. According to the statistical estimates of the U.S. Freedom House, among 145 non-Muslim countries in the world in 2003, there were 112 countries with democratic elections, including most of Latin America, Asia, and the Eastern European countries. Most were newly developed democratic countries. The number of countries in the world that can be included as countries with democratic constitutional governments is very limited and most of them are concentrated in Western Europe and the North American regions. Japan is a special case in Asia.

Since all legislators of the Legislative Yuan were appointed by direct election in 1992 and the president was elected by universal suffrage in 1996, indeed it can be said that Taiwan has become a country with democratic elections. More than a decade of democratic development has not made Taiwan a country with a democratic constitutional government. However, some consider Taiwan only a semi-democratic country according to the categorization of western political science. The reasons are simple. Taiwan is just like other semi-democratic countries. Although its wielders of power are elected through votes, they often control the media, do not respect human rights, and suppress the opposition parties. They take advantage of the differences in ethnic groups and ideologies and of people's fear about political instability to consolidate their own power. Throughout the 2004 presidential election, Taiwan's intellectual and cultural circles generally felt disappointed about the democratic systems promoted by Chen Shui-bian and the DPP government. They have turned their hopes to the opposition parties and non-governmental forces, and hope that Taiwan will work unremittingly to become a complete democratic country and a country with a democratic constitutional government. This kind of self-examination no doubt is beneficial for the future development of Taiwan's democratic system. But regrettably, amidst the rhetoric of examining true versus false democracy, no one has pointed out that the democracy implemented in Taiwan is a distorted version of American democracy and Taiwan has suffered because of it.

The Distorted American-Style Democracy Does Not Work in Taiwan

In discussing democracy, no one will deny that Taiwan now is more democratic than it was when the Chiang families were presidents. Still, surveys reveal that Taiwan's most respected and supported leader is Chiang Ching-kuo. Why do people still cherish the memory of the period when Chiang Ching-kuo was in power?

Despite the fact that Taiwan was under martial law from 1949 to 1987, when the two Chiangs (father and son) were governing, the officials at least had a sense of integrity and did not dare link up with businessmen or financial groups. In addition, the government implemented the equitable agricultural land reforms so that the peasants could own the land they farmed. The government also had detailed plans for the establishment of industries in all aspects, such as the buildup of large steel factories and Taiwan's China Petroleum Corporation that led the oil chemical industries in Taiwan. Most importantly, the policies conformed to a fair and square principle. As a result, the large enterprises were willing to make investments, the medium-to small-sized enterprises could open their own businesses, and the industrial and agricultural businesses were well taken care of. Hence, most people felt satisfied with their lives and were hopeful about the future. This supported the "don't worry about not having enough, but do worry about no equalization" idea.

After Lee Teng-hui took power, he gradually abandoned the idealism of the Three Principles of the People and the principle of social fairness. Lee Teng-hui and the various levels of officials no longer drew a clear line of demarcation from financial groups, but on the contrary closely linked up with them. After 1996, Lee Teng-hui open-handedly helped, through various policies, the financial groups that supported him in the first presidential election and used government resources to nurture the financial groups so as to accumulate political capital for himself. The government's financial condition was getting worse with each passing year, the gap between the rich and the poor increased, ordinary people got poorer and poorer, and the unemployment rate jumped. Not until the problems got very serious and people were very angry did the government begin to distribute unemployment benefits and senior citizen and peasant annuities in an effort to buy votes. After the real estate industry's bubble burst, the government used public funds to supplement the interest payment of the property owners' loans. In the area of political systems, Lee Teng-hui copied the presidential system of the U.S. but without a system of checks and balances. All important positions were held by the people close to Lee Teng-hui. He also initiated amendments to the ROC Constitution six times and created a two-head system that gave even more power to the president than the presidential system did. From then on, the president had immense power but no responsibilities. He need not be questioned in the Legislative Yuan and he could appoint the president (or premier) of the Executive Yuan without the legislators' consent. Lee Teng-hui not only did whatever he wanted, but he also learned from some American politicians how to initiate populism to show that he represented the people's will. He linked up with financial groups to blow hot air and created an inflated economy in order to feign financial security—and, in reality, poison the voters.

After the DPP took power in 2000, it intensified the use of unreasonable policies to help the growth of financial groups. The DPP assisted large-scale enterprises and financial industries to merge, which made the rich richer. There was not enough talent within the DPP. Hence, after four years, Taiwan's economy had deteriorated and the social unfairness and injustice became more serious than they were during Lee Teng-hui's tenure. Politically, although Chen Shui-bian was elected by only 39.2 percent of the votes, he controlled all the power single-handedly. The result was chaos in the parliament and turmoil in the society. While the society demanded to be free from political corruption, Chen Shui-bian claimed that the Constitution had not been amended correctly to proceed with the work of writing a new Constitution that would project out sovereignty and independence. During the latter part of May 2004, former DPP Chairman Shih Ming-teh warned while he was in the U.S. that Taiwan's president enjoyed too many rights and benefits and too much power. Using the 2004 election as an example, though Chen Shui-bian won by a slim margin, he was able to take the power and reap the benefits. If the cabinet system were used instead, the confrontational situation of the blue and green camps would be changed to a better balance. In that case, the government could reflect the interests of all the ethnic groups like the Hoklo, the Hakka, the second generation of the mainlanders, and the Aborigines. The society would also be relatively stable (*China Times Daily News*, 05/28/2004). After viewing this, the heavyweight Taiwan independence supporters who originally hoped to implement the presidential system to promote Taiwan's sovereignty must have known that the presidential system was not suitable for Taiwan.

The people in Taiwan are all proud of Taiwan's gradual democratization. But they do not know that the economic slowdown, the increased rich-poor gap, and the overall sense of hopelessness about the future are related to Taiwan's implementation of a distorted American-style democracy. Of course, Taiwan is not the only country that has suffered after implementing American-style democracy. The Philippines and the Latin America countries have, too. After they implemented American-style democracy incorrectly, their economies inflated, their governments became more corrupt, and the wealth was unequally distributed. This is not because the people in Taiwan, the Philippines, and Latin America adhere less to their laws or because they have not implemented democracy long enough. It is mainly due to the wielders of power not implementing the checks and balances needed in their democratic political systems. The truth of democracy lies in limiting the government's power and protecting people's rights. In short, it is important for Taiwan to improve its democratic system, but it should not use democracy as an excuse to confront, or refuse to communicate with mainland China.

SECTION 2
DEFENDING THE REPUBLIC OF CHINA IS NO BETTER THAN ACCEPTING THE ONE-CHINA PRINCIPLE

Before and after the 2004 presidential election, Chen Shui-bian announced, "The Republic of China is Taiwan." During his inaugural speech on May 20, he repeatedly used the phrase "the Republic of China." But mainland China still criticized him because he did not abandon the Taiwan independence position or express goodwill and sincerity to improve cross-strait relations. This made political commentators sympathetic toward Chen Shui-bian. They thought that when Chen Shui-bian emphasized the ROC, he had actually responded to the One-China Principle. A *China Times Daily News* editorial criticized "Beijing's denial of the reality that 'the Republic of China' is still effectively exercising its sovereignty over Taiwan, Penghu, Kinmen, and Matsu, which not only distances the Taiwan people's hearts further away from Beijing, but also allows the Taiwan independence supporters inside Taiwan to find a way to get rid of the ROC. Beijing and the Taiwan independence organizations are in fact simultaneously extinguishing the Republic of China together!" The editorial also stated, "The Republic of China is already the highest common divisor that can be found," and, "If Beijing is not happy to see the Republic of China being erased by Taiwan's new Constitution or other methods, then please face the realistic existence of the Republic of China. Only by respecting this mainstream value, held by most people in Taiwan, will it be possible to have the likelihood of achieving true cross-strait reciprocity" (*China Times Daily News*, 05/28/2004).

The Republic of China Cannot Last Very Long

For more than a decade, Lee Teng-hui and Chen Shui-bian represented themselves as supporting the ROC, but in reality leaned towards Taiwan independence. Everyone in Taiwan knows this as a fact. Were people fooled by them just because they talked about the ROC and distributed a few thousand small national flags during the inauguration ceremony?

For more than 50 years, the Taiwanese have received an anti-Communist education. The ROC is indeed the memory shared by most of the Taiwanese people. It is inevitable to have emotional feelings toward the national flag and national anthem. But the reality indicates that the ROC is on the verge of collapse. First, let's talk about outside Taiwan. The people who have supported Taiwan independence for a long time have pushed for eliminating the ROC in the U.S. and Japan. Among them, FAPA, which devotes its efforts toward changing the ROC into the Republic of Taiwan, has been in existence for 20 years. Two of its main founders, Chen Tang-shan and Hsu Shih-kai, are currently the Minister of Foreign Affairs and ROC's Representative in Japan. Doesn't this mean that Chen Shui-bian's government primarily rewards their efforts to eliminate the ROC? Next, let's talk about inside Taiwan. After Lee Teng-hui finished his term, he threw away the ROC symbol like an old pair of shoes. In 2003, he not only announced that "the ROC is non-existent" and that "the ROC is not a country, it is only a name," but he also initiated a rally for Taiwan's rectification movement. Furthermore, no matter if it was "the Republic of China is Taiwan" invented by Chen Shui-bian at the latter part of his election campaign in 2004 or "Taiwan, the Republic of China," which slipped from Annette Lu's tongue in early June 2004 when she visited San Francisco, the fact of the matter is that even though the four words "the Republic of China" were still being used, the meaning had certainly changed.

Considering the above statements, only fools in Taiwan would truly believe that the ROC can exist on a long-term basis. Only those who are set in their ways might say, "The Republic of China is the highest common divisor," as long as it is kept, Taiwan will always be safe and sound. Facing this reality does not mean that the Taiwanese people have no other choice. The May 17 Statement clearly pointed out that the One-China Principle is that both Taiwan and mainland China belong to the same China. Isn't this the truth? Doesn't this conform to the regulation of the ROC Constitution and the goal sought by the NUG? The Taiwanese people should thoroughly think through whether they want to let the wielders of power use the people's will to keep a title that they no longer want for the sake of maintaining their political power, or whether they want to keep the country's integrity by continuing to be Chinese. Instead of waiting for the DPP to extinguish the ROC by making mainland China solve the Taiwan problem by force, why not accept a peaceful resolution now to accomplish China's reunification as early as possible? Besides, the present mainland China is already one of the very few strong and respected countries in the world. Why is it painful to be reunited with mainland China at the moment?

The mainland China authorities understand what the ROC means to the Taiwanese people. They have repeatedly promised to start reciprocal negotiations with Taiwan. Hence, as long as Taiwan authorities are willing to accept the One-China Principle and start negotiations with mainland China, the status of the ROC will definitely be dealt with reasonably. But if Taiwan's leaders still think about using the shell of the ROC continuously but play "one country on each side," then even if the ROC title is not changed, the two sides will make no progress.

No More New Names Should Be Created to Produce Confusion

In the middle of May 2004, Hsu Hsing-liang proposed that "one China can be a European Union" in Taiwan. On May 25, former DPP Chairman Shih Ming-teh, who was engaged in advanced studies in the U.S. at the time, also pointed out that in order to resolve the stagnated situation, One-China-European-Unionization could be a workable solution. He said that it was hard for the Taiwanese people to accept the One-China Principle proposed by Beijing. Hence, he suggested that the two sides use the One-China-European-Unionization model. He further said that if France and Germany, bitter rivals for generations, could become EU members together, then there is hope for Taiwan. Within the EU, large and small countries were all members of equal status. So, this deserves the consideration of the two sides of the Taiwan Strait (*China Times Daily News*, 05/27/2004).

The above statement is faulty. First of all, it was very courageous for Hsu Hsing-liang and Shih Ming-teh to openly criticize Chen Shui-bian before the presidential election. But from the talks they gave, we know that their Taiwan independence ideologies have not changed. People know that the countries that participate in the EU are all sovereign states and that after they join the EU they continue to operate according to their original political systems. What the so-called "one Europe" policy emphasizes is regional economic cooperation. So, if Hsu Hsing-liang and Shih Ming-teh call for all Asian countries to organize a "one Asia" economic entity, perhaps it would make some sense. If they describe the cross-strait reunification by using an EU model, then they are really making a laughingstock of themselves by copying others! If later the two are willing to call out the Chen Shui-bian administration for its improper acts or devote themselves to initiating ethnic blending movements, they should be able to make some contributions. But if they intend to work on cross-strait matters, they had better not create new terminology that seems novel but is really just a smoke screen. This would not be helpful in solving the cross-strait disputes.

From the previous confederation, federation, commonwealth, and "one China" roof to the present advocacy of the EU model, the Taiwan authorities and people in all circles can be said to have taken great pains. They have used all the names possible in their attempt to resist "one China" and "one country, two systems." This did not solve the problem. People from all circles, instead of creating unworkable situations and provoking nebulous terminology, should make the contents of "one China" and "one country, two systems" clearer. They should make sure that the Taiwanese people understand the merits and shortcomings of their policies and have the opportunity to express their opinions. Only by doing so can Chen Shui-bian's May 20 inaugural statement, "As long as it is the choice of the 23 million people in Taiwan, any model is workable," become a true pledge.

Section 3
Only Reunification Can Solve Taiwan's Problem

After May 20, 2004, Chen Shui-bian frequently stated that he would govern the country along a middle road and that his top priority would be to improve cross-strait relations and calm the public so that foreign investors would not take their capital away from Taiwan. Unfortunately, Chen Shui-bian did not keep his promise. Neither the Taiwanese nor the foreign investors believe that Chen Shui-bian has the ability and the determination to improve cross-strait relations or to fulfill his promise of direct transportation. In the area of international living space, despite the fact that Annette Lu made a tour through the U.S. at the end of May 2004, mainland China had already started to blockade the international living space of Taiwan. Exactly how far Taiwan will go before it begins to solve the difficult situation through cross-strait consultations is of great concern to the people.

The Economy

The statistical information of the past two years indicates that mainland China is the biggest factory, producer, and supplier in the world. It is also the most populated consumer market. On May 27, 2004, the *Washington Post* published an article entitled "The Unknown Great Wall," in which it pointed out that the economic development of mainland China would affect the entire globe. The report quoted the annual economic report of the Asian Bank, which listed mainland China as the world's largest consumer country of copper, tin, zinc, platinum, steel, and steel minerals. Its aluminum and lead demand is the second, and its nickel consumption is the third. The mainland is now the second largest petroleum consumer country. In 2003, its oil demand was 35 percent of the world's supply. Fifty percent of the world's cameras and 30 percent of its cooling systems and TVs are made in mainland China. The article reported that the economic expansion of mainland China did not necessarily damage other countries. In 2003, mainland China's imports increased by 40 percent and its neighboring countries in Asia became the biggest beneficiaries. The report expressed that no matter how mainland China's future economy changes, it will create an impact on other areas (*China Times Daily News*, 05/28/2004).

After March 20, the economic scholars in Taiwan predicted that mainland China could possibly use economic sanctions as an important balancing rod for its Taiwan policy. Then, the non-reciprocal cross-strait economic and trade exchanges would be revised. For example, Taiwan's need for the comprehensive three links is apparently larger than mainland China's need, hence the mainland no longer has to actively promote it. In addition, the mainland has always been dissatisfied with Taiwan businessmen who make money in the mainland but still support the DPP. Sooner or later the mainland will demand that Taiwan businessmen state their political positions. The unfortunate thing is that Taiwan still wants to rely on luck and assumes that politically it can follow a creative ambiguity policy to continue reaping benefits in economic matters. There are people in Taiwan who openly demand that the mainland separate business from politics, but the series of mainland policies that occurred since May 2004 finally caused the Taiwanese people to stop dreaming.

On May 7, 2004, Taiwan promulgated the cross-strait policy for Expeditious and Convenient Sea Transportation. The spokesman for mainland China's Taiwan Affairs Office, Li Weiyi, responded on May 12 that Taiwan's advocacy in adjusting cross-strait sea transportation violated the principle that domestic shipping could not be carried out by foreign ships. This action was another form of internationalizing the cross-strait shipping route and could not be accepted by the mainland. Li Weiyi further emphasized that mainland China's consistent position was to enhance the three links, but that it would not accept the position as being defined by "one country on each side" or the international three links (*China Times Daily News*, 05/13/2004). On June 1, Chen Shui-bian invited foreign investors for an afternoon tea since they had been selling off stock continuously for 19 days. He guaranteed that he would improve cross-strait relations. The American Chamber of Commerce published a white paper the next day which said directly that the Taiwan government did not pay attention to the developmental needs of its financial enterprises. As a result, Taiwan's economic development had suffered uncertainties and it had also lowered the enterprises' willingness to invest. The white paper called for the implementation of cross-strait direct transportation as soon as possible and suggested that the Taiwan government "strengthen the economic integration with mainland China." The U.S. Chamber of Commerce expressed that without direct transportation, Taiwan would gradually lose its competitiveness as a regional center. The high-level managers will be forced to move away from Taiwan, and Taiwan would then be classified as a local market instead of a regional center. According to the report, since 1996, the Taiwan white papers published by the U.S. Chamber of Commerce had already warned Taiwan of the possibility of being marginalized by itself. The 2004 white paper stated, "Now, this will quickly become a reality" (*China Times Daily News*, 06/02/2004).

On May 31, 2004, the editorial of the *People's Daily* overseas edition directly pointed a finger at the "green Taiwan businessman" Shu Wen-long, Chairman of the Chi-mei Corporation. On June 3, the Associate Researcher of the Taiwan Research Institute of the Chinese Academy of Social Sciences, Wang Jianmin, published an article on the Internet suggesting that in order to avoid Taiwan's independence, mainland China authorities should impose economic sanctions against Taiwan. His article caused the Taiwan stock market to drop significantly. The Executive Yuan subsequently announced that Taiwan businessmen should divert their investments to other countries. Shu

Wen-long pleaded with the mainland authorities to "separate politics from economics" and hoped that the Taiwan government would speed up its push for the three links to help bring about cross-strait exchanges (*Economic Daily News*, 06/02/2004). Quite a few presidents of various Taiwan Businessmen's Associations felt that Chi-mei should not be the only Taiwan enterprise that was "attacked in writing" by mainland China. It was altogether possible that there would be a second wave of attacks against the green Taiwan businessmen (*Commercial Times*, 06/02/2004). On June 5, the MAC notified mainland China that this matter should "stop here" (*Economic Daily News*, 06/06/2004).

During these years, Taiwan's policies toward mainland investments have been "no separation between politics and economics." What is the basis for demanding the mainland to separate politics and economy? If Taiwan businessmen really cannot invest elsewhere, even if the Taiwan government does not encourage or persuade them, probably they would still invest in the mainland. Similarly, if their investments in the mainland were tied up by certain conditions, most likely they would still happily accept some restrictions. Hasn't this already explained the present Taiwan economic situation and its future? In observing the speed of the mainland economic expansion, it is best to assume that if the Taiwan businessmen do not migrate there, others will. What could be the rationale for the mainland to allow Taiwan businessmen to make money and then return to Taiwan to support its independence? Observing this, we know that the tests for the Chen Shui-bian administration have just begun. If Taiwan's economy wants to survive, there is no choice but to have a comprehensive opening of the three links and to repair its relations with the mainland.

The International Living Space

Lee Teng-hui and Chen Shui-bian at various times have complained about mainland China's suppression of Taiwan's international living space. In fact, mainland China has repeatedly said that as long as Taiwan recognizes "one China" through consultations, Taipei will have more international living space. However, since Chen Shui-bian has not been willing to stop the Taiwan independence activities and refuses to negotiate, it is not possible for the mainland to loosen its grip on the international living space. After Chen Shui-bian's reelection, it seemed that mainland China decided to further suppress Taipei's international living space. Hence, Taiwan will face fiercer challenges when it tries to establish diplomatic relations with more countries or tries to enter international organizations.

Taiwan's Future and Peaceful Reunification

On March 30, 2004, soon after Chen Shui-bian was reelected, mainland China established a diplomatic relationship with Dominica in the Caribbean, which had a previous diplomatic relationship with Taiwan, and the cross-strait diplomatic war started again. On April 17, Taiwan hoped to use the status of observer to attend the WHO Assembly but suffered a set-back. People from Beijing's diplomatic circle stated that one of the impor-tant steps for Chen Shui-bian's gradual Taiwan independence was for Taiwan to obtain the status of a WHO observer. The purpose was to break through the mainland's blockade of the international community and to exhibit the reality of Taiwan being a sovereign state. In order to restrain Taiwan independence, it was quite obvious that the mainland would not let Chen Shui-bian achieve his purpose.

From the end of May to the beginning of June 2004, Vice President Annette Lu visited Central and South America, and made a transit stay in the U.S. At her first stop in Sarwado, she was met with an embarrassingly cold reception. Afterwards, she met with the protests of overseas Chinese at every stop. At the same time, President Nicanor Duarte of Paraguay announced that, due to an overall economic consideration of the South American Common Market, he would not exclude any possibilities of estab-lishing a diplomatic relationship with the PRC. Among the members of the South American Common Market, only Paraguay has a diplomatic relation-ship with Taiwan, making it the only obstacle for that common market to sign a free trade agreement with mainland China (*China Times Daily News,* 06/02/2004). It seems that Chen Shui-bian's beautiful dream of making a breakthrough in the international living space to project Taiwan's sover-eignty will yield nothing. Unless Taiwan recognizes the One-China Principle, it has no other outlet.

Of course, the U.S. is Taiwan's biggest supporter. Taiwan also believes that the U.S. hopes that through Taiwan becoming peacefully independent and the "no reunification, no independence, no war" situation, the U.S. will gain the biggest benefits. Chen Shui-bian thought that his inaugural speech satisfied the U.S. and that U.S.-Taiwan relations would gradually reach a better state as a result. Due to the constraints of rebuilding Iraq, Middle Eastern terrorism, and North Korea, it would be difficult for the U.S. not to coordinate with mainland China about the Taiwan issue. Even if mainland China and the U.S. have apparent differences concerning the basic premise of the Taiwan issue, the two countries have more cooperative efforts than disputes. In particular, the May 17 Statement shows that Beijing has res-olute determination and capability for reunification. In order to prevent a crisis in the Taiwan Strait, the U.S. will, at the very least, continue to send out clear warnings to Taiwan independence supporters. If Taiwan pays no attention to these warnings, it is very possible that the U.S. will offer no assistance to Taiwan.

Conclusion

Although the process of Taiwan's presidential election was brutal and the results were preposterous, Chen Shui-bian was still inaugurated. But the DPP's governance may not be enough to lead Taiwan in the direction of independence. The fight for true democracy between the Taiwan ruling party and the opposition parties may get a brief sounding, but very soon the Taiwanese people will discover that their only outlet is to properly deal with the cross-strait disputes. Considering that political and economic strengths show growth in mainland China and decline in Taiwan, and that mainland China has demonstrated real strength and determination about reunification, if Taiwan really wants to develop its economy and increase its international living space, it has no other choice but to accept "peaceful reunification, one country, two systems."

REFERENCES

CHINESE REFERENCES

Books and Articles

Central Communication Department of the Chinese Nationalist Party in China, *Taiwan's Future and "One Country, Two Systems,"* Beijing: United Publishing Company, 2002.

Chang, Ling-chen, *Taiwan on the Wrong Road,* Taipei: Strait Academic Publishing Company, 2000.

Chang, Ling-chen, *Taiwan's Distorted Mainland Policy,* Taipei: Strait Academic Publishing Company, 2002.

Chang, Wu-yueh, *Comparison and Research: The Interaction Models and Reunification Policies for Divided Countries,* Taipei: National Policy Research Center, 1992.

Chen, Chi-chee, *A Review of 30 Years' U.S.-China Policies,* the Expanded Edition, Taipei: Chong-hua Daily News Agency, 1991.

Chen, Chi-chee, *The Record of Cross-Strait Relations,* Taipei: The Research Center for the Cross-Strait Relations, the Cultural Foundation for the Nation's Development, 1998.

Chen, Daohua, *"One Country, Two Systems" and the Theory of Nation,* Beijing: The Publication of the Central Communist Party School, 2002.

Chen, Jie, ed., *A Hundred Questions and Answers for the Taiwan Compatriots,* Beijing: Huayip Publishing Company, 2001.

Cheng, Chu-yuan, *The Cross-Strait Economic Developments and Interactions,* Taipei: Linking Book Publication, 1994.

China Forum Editorial Committee, ed., *The Development of Cross-Strait Academic Research,* Taipei: China Forum Magazine, 1988.

China Tide Foundation, ed., *The Future Prospects of the Cross-Strait Relations in the 21st Century—Observation of the One-China Principle,* Taipei: Strait Academic Publishing Company, 1999.

Editorial Team of the One Hundred Tutorial Questionnaires for the Study of the 16th Communist Party Congress Report, ed., *The One Hundred Tutorial Questionnaires for the Study of the 16th Communist Party Congress Report,* Beijing: Publication Agency for the Party Making Reading Materials, People's Publishing Agency, 2002.

Feng, Chi-jen, *The U.S.-China Policy and the Taiwan Relations,* Taipei: Strait Academic Publishing Company, 2002.

Foundation on International & Cross-Strait Studies, *The National Security Provisions Protocol and Its Influence on the Contents of "One Country, Two Systems,"* Foundation on International & Cross-Strait Studies, August 2003.

Huang, Chien-zheng, "What We Should Know about the Characteristics of the American Policy Research Think Tanks," in *Review of National Policy Foundation,* p. 111–114, 12/05/2001.

Huang, Tien-chong & Chang Wu-yueh, ed., *The Cross-Strait Relations and the Mainland Policy*, Taipei: Wunan Book Publishing Company, 1993.

Institute of Taiwan Research of the Chinese Academy of Social Sciences, ed., *Taiwan's Politics and the Cross-Strait Relations during the Transition Period*, Beijing: Current Event Publication, 1991.

Li, Jiaquan, *Discussion on Taiwan's Mode of "One Country, Two Systems": a Win-Win Situation for Both Sides*, Beijing: Chinese Friendship Publishing Company, 2001.

Li, Zhefu, *Taiwan Strait: The 20-Year Swaying in the Storm*, Taipei: Strait Academic Publishing Company, 2001.

Liu, Kong-che, ed., *The Two-State Theory: A Comprehensive Observation*, Taipei: Strait Academic Publishing Company, 1999.

Lu, Xiaoheng, ed., *The Taiwan Issue in China's Foreign Relations*, Taipei: Strait Academic Publishing Company, 2003.

Mainland Committee of the Executive Yuan, ed., *A Collection of the Mainland Working Regulations*, edited by Taipei: the Mainland Committee of the Executive Yuan, revised 4th edition, 1999.

Mao, Zhu-lun, *Some Thoughts on the Corner of the Island*, Taipei: Strait Academic Publishing Company, 1998.

Mao, Zhu-lun, *Thinking and Interpretation*, Taipei: Strait Academic Publishing Company, 2000.

Shaw, Chong-hai, *The U.S. Role in the Nationalist and Communist Peace Talks*, Taipei: Wunan Publishing Company, Ltd., 1995.

Shaw, Chong-hai, *The Cross-Strait Relations and Strategies*, Taipei: Times Culture Publishing Company, 1996.

Shaw, Chong-hai, *The Mainland Policy and the Cross-Strait Relations*, Taipei: Huatai Bookstore, 2nd edition, 1996.

Shaw, Chong-hai, *The Current "Taiwan Research" in the Mainland*, Taipei: Huatai Bookstore, 1997.

Shaw, Chong-hai, *The Cross-Strait Relations: Consensus and Disparity*, Taipei: Wunan Publishing Company, Ltd., 1998.

Shaw, Chong-hai, *The Probe of 'One China' Principle in the Cross-Strait Negotiations*, Hong Kong: The Hong Kong Research Center for the Cross-Strait Relations, 1999.

Song, Xiaozhuang, *The Relationship between the Central Government and the Hong Kong Special Administrative Region under "One Country, Two Systems,"* Beijing: the Publication Agency for the Chinese People's University, 2003.

Strait Review Magazine, "The Strait Review Monthly," (Issues 1–155), Taipei: Strait Review Magazine.

Tsai, Wei, *The Cross-Strait Order in the New Century*, Taipei: Strait Academic Publishing Company, 2002.

Wang, Hsiao Po, *Essays on the Cross-Strait*, Taipei: Strait Academic Publishing Company, 1977.

Wang, Hsiao Po, *100 Essays on the Cross-Strait*, Taipei: Strait Academic Publishing Company, 1999.

Wang, Hsiao Po, *Discussion on the Chinese Nationalist Party: Criticism and Reconstruction*, Taipei: Strait Academic Publishing Company, 2003.

Wang, Jiaying & Zhen Chiyan, ed., *The Handover of Hong Kong and a Forward Looking of the Cross-Strait Relations*, Hong Kong: The Hong Kong Research Center for the Cross-Strait Relations, 1999.

References

Wang, Jing-ping, ed., *A Comprehensive Observation of the May 20 Inauguration*, Taipei: Strait Academic Publishing Company, 2000.

Wang, Jisi, ed., *Civilization and International Politics*, Shanghai: People's Publishing Company, 1995.

Xin, Qi, *Deliberation at the Cross-Century*, Beijing: Huayip Publishing Company, 2002.

Yan, Jiaqi, *The Conception of Confederated China*, Taipei: Linking Books Publishing Enterprise Company, 1992.

Yu, Ying-shi, *Democracy and the Cross-Strait Trend*, Taipei: SanMin Bookstore Co., Ltd., 1993.

Zhang, Lanchi, *Discussion on Reunification: Relations of Cross-Strait and China's Future*, Taipei: Strait Academic Publishing Company, 2003.

Zhang, Tongxin & Ho Zhongshan, *"One Country, Two Systems" and the Cross-Strait Relations*, edited by Beijing: the Publication Agency for the Chinese People's University, 1998.

Zhu, Weijiu & Wang Chongli, *The Policy and Legal Research on Cross-Strait Relations*, Taipei: Strait Academic Publishing Company, 2003.

Websites

www.5chinesenewsnet.com
www.advocates.org.tw
www.can.com.tw
www.chinatide.org.tw
www.chinatimes.com.tw
www.chinese.news.yahoo.com
www.dpp.org.tw
www.epochtimes.com
www.eurasian.org.tw
www.future-china.org.tw
www.hi-on.org.tw
www.huaxia.com
www.info.gov.hk
www.kmt.org.tw
www.libertytimes.com.tw
www.mac.gov.tw
www.macau.gov.cn
www.mofa.gov.tw
www.news.bbc.co.uk/hi/chinese/news
www.news.sina.com.tw
www.news.yam.com
www.newtaiwan.com.tw
www.np.org.tw
www.npf.org.tw
www.octs.org.hk
www.onechina.org.tw
www.people.com.cn
www.peopledaily.com.cn
www.pfp.org.tw
www.sef.org.tw
www.takungpao.com.hk

www.tsu.org.tw
www.udngroup.com.tw
www.whb.com.cn
www.xinhuanet.com
www.yzzk.com

ENGLISH REFERENCES

Books and Articles

Bernstein, Richard & Ross H. Munro, "China I: The Coming Conflict with America," *Foreign Affairs*, March/April, 1997.

Finkelstein, David M. & Maryanne Kivlehan, "China's Leadership in the 21st Century: The Rise of the Fourth Generation," Armonk: M. E. Sharpe, 2003.

Huntington, Samuel P., *The Clash of Civilizations and the Remaking of World Order*, New York: Simon & Schuster, 1996.

Shambaugh, David, "Facing Reality in China Policy," *Foreign Affairs*, January/February, 2001.

Terrill, Ross, *The New Chinese Empire: Beijing's Political Dilemma and What It Means for the United States*, New York: Basic Books, 2003.

Tucker, Nancy Bernkopf, "If Taiwan Chooses Unification, Should the United States Care?" *The Washington Quarterly*, March/April, 2002.

Websites

www.abanet.org
www.aclu.org
www.acus.org
www.aei.org
www.afit.org.tw
www.amnesty.org
www.asiasociety.org
www.brook.edu
www.cato.org
www.cceia.org
www.cfr.org
www.csis.org
www.foreignaffairs.org
www.fpa.org
www.fpri.org
www.heritage.org
www.hoover.stanford.edu
www.ifpa.org
www.ncafp.org
www.ncuscr.org
www.onr.navy.mil
www.rand.com

GLOSSARY

A/PRC: Asia/Pacific Research Center

ACUS: Atlantic Council of the United States

ADB: Asian Development Bank

AEI: American Enterprise Institute

AIT: American Institute in Taiwan

APEC: Asia-Pacific Economic Cooperation

ARATS: Association for Relations across the Taiwan Strait (of the PRC)

CAB: Constitutional Affairs Bureau (of Hong Kong)

CCD: Committee for the Constitutional Development (of Hong Kong)

CEPA: Closer Economic Partnership Arrangement

CPC: Communist Party of China

CSIS: Center for Strategic and International Studies

DPP: Democratic Progressive Party

EU: European Union

FAPA: Formosan Association for Public Affairs

GDP: Gross Domestic Product

HK SAR: Hong Kong Special Administrative Region

IMF: International Monetary Fund

ISA: Independent Solidarity Alliance

KMT: The Nationalist Party (or Kuomintang)

MAC: Mainland Affairs Council (of the ROC)

M SAR: Macao Special Administrative Region

NATO: North Atlantic Treaty Organization

NP: New Party

NPC: National People's Congress (of the PRC)

NUC: National Unification Council (of the ROC)

NUG: National Unification Guidelines (of the ROC)

Pan-Blue Coalition: A political coalition in Taiwan consisting of the KMT, the PFP, and the NP; supporters are called the Pan-Blue supporters

Pan-Green Coalition: An informal political alliance in early twenty-first century Taiwan consisting of the DPP, the TSU, and the minor Taiwan Independence Party; supporters are called the Pan-Green supporters

PFP: People First Party

PRC: People's Republic of China

ROC: Republic of China

SARS: Severe Acute Respiratory Syndrome

SCNPC: Standing Committee of the National People's Congress (of the PRC)

SEF: Strait Exchange Foundation (of the ROC)

TMD: Theater Missile Defense

TSU: Taiwan Solidarity Union

UK: United Kingdom

UN: United Nations

USSR: Union of Soviet Socialist Republics

VBA: Void Ballot Alliance

WHO: World Health Organization

WTO: World Trade Organization

YUAN: A branch of the ROC government (in Taipei)

ABOUT THE AUTHOR

Hsing Chi is a copartner of Hsieh, Chi & Hsieh Law Offices, an editor of the *Strait Review Monthly,* and vice president of the Alliance for the Reunification of China in Taiwan.

She was born and educated in Taiwan and earned a Juris Doctor in the United States. Not long after she became a member of the California Bar, she returned to Taiwan in 1989 to practice law. For the past 15 years, she has been associate professor of the School of Law at Soochow University, chairperson of the Taipei Awakening Association, and twice Member of the National Assembly of the Republic of China (the 3rd session from 1996–2000 and the *ad hoc* session in June 2005).

She is the author of several Chinese books, including *Women and Politics: The Women's Movement in Taiwan in the 1990s* (2000), *Women's Rights in Modern Society* (2001), *Family Law in the United States* (2002), *Life and Death: Discussion on the Legal Aspects of Euthanasia and Death Penalty* (2003), *"One Country, Two Systems" in Taiwan* (2003), *"One Country, Two Systems" in Taiwan, New Edition* (2004), *The Shock of the Enactment of the "Anti-Secession Law"* (2005), and *Analyzing "Ma Ying-jeou Phenomenon"* (2006).

ABOUT THE TRANSLATOR

Sheng-Wei Wang was born in Taiwan. She graduated from National Tsing Hua University with a B.S. degreee in Chemistry and earned a Ph.D. degree in Theorhetical Chemical Physics from the University of Southern California. She was a staff scientist at Lawrence Berkeley Laboratory after many years of scientific research at Caltech and Stanford Linear Accelerator Center. Prior to founding in 2006 the China-U.S. Friendship Exchange, Inc., she was also a self-made real estate developer for 15 years.

She considered herself nonpolitical until Taiwan's 2004 presidential election. She used her physics research skills to write a JFK-conspiracy-exposé arguing that President Chen Shui-bian's minor skin wound must have been staged. She briefed the U.S. State Department about her findings in May 2004 and was interviewed on TV. This investigation made her a well-known Chinese-American media figure.

In order to strive for peace across the Taiwan Strait, she is devoting her efforts to China's peaceful reunification. Her translated English book, *One Country, Two Systems in Taiwan* (a Chinese book by Taiwanese writer Hsing Chi), was published in the U.S. in 2006 by International Publishing House for China's Culture. Her earlier article, "The Answer My Friend Is Blowing in the Wind," was published in the *ELM* magazine on February 1, 2006. Her latest essays, "For Whom the Bell May Toll?" and "The Blue Danube on Gulangyu Islet," appeared on *American Chronicle's* May 1 and May 12, 2007, issues. Her forthcoming English-language book, *China's Ascendancy: "An Opportunity" or "A Threat?"–Facts and Fiction*, will be published in the U.S. in 2007.